DREADS AND DROLLS

Arthur Machen in 1927

DREADS AND DROLLS

by

Arthur Machen

Tartarus Press

Dreads and Drolls, by Machen
First published by Martin Secker (London), 1926
First complete edition published as a limited
edition of 350 copies in 2007 by Tartarus Press

This paperback edition published 2022 by Tartarus Press at
Coverley House, Carlton-in-Coverdale, Leyburn,
North Yorkshire, DL8 4AY, UK

ISBN 9781717969231

Please see rear of book for bibliographical information

CONTENTS

INTRODUCTION

ARTHUR MACHEN'S 'Dreads' and 'Drolls' first appeared in London's *The Graphic* between January and September 1925, and were collected for publication by Martin Secker on October 16th, 1926. On the day that the first trade and limited editions of *Dreads and Drolls* were presented to the public Machen published his last article in *The Graphic*. While the book had been going through the press he had written as many articles again in a similar vein, but these were not collected together as the earlier ones had been. Machen still had a good literary reputation, and was at the height of his popularity among collectors in America, but the demand for his contributions to newspapers and magazines was beginning to decline. His 'Queer Things' column in *The Observer* was to end in the new year, and though he would go on to write other pieces for *The Sunday Express* and *T.P.'s and Cassell's Weekly*, among others, times were about to be hard for Machen. Perhaps Secker could foresee no market for a second volume, but we now have the great pleasure of bringing together *all* of his contributions to *The Graphic* for the first time.

'Everything that is old is dear to me, but more especially the old which is ramshackle, disreputable, up a court or down an alley' writes Arthur Machen in 'The Mystery of Mr Haddock', and this sets the agenda for many of the tales that he relates. Among the curiosities of the past he finds 'Dreads'; murder, and punishment on the scaffold, along with terrible injustices and bizarre mysteries. Machen takes the word 'Dread' in the same way that it was used to describe cheap sensational story books of the mid-nineteenth century as 'Penny Dreadfuls'. He also tells stories which are amusing, curious and surprising; hence the term 'Drolls'. Many tales, of course, contain elements of both.

If Machen finds amusement, horror and wonder in the past, he also discovers it in his present day. He does not have an entirely reactionary reverence for times gone by; his fascination for characters, customs and institutions of previous centuries illuminates that which is of interest in his own time. To take 'Madame Rachel' as an example, Machen points out that the unscrupulous woman who tricked silly Mrs Borradaile out of a considerable sum in the 1860s has her successors in the Bond Street beauty parlours of the 1920s. He delights in presenting us with eccentric and colourful 'characters' from the past, but had the insight to affirm that they still existed in the 1920s (when newspapers are no longer interested in writers like him reporting them).

Today Machen's reverence for tradition and his complaints about modern standards might cause him to be described as a 'Grumpy Old Man.' It is not inappropriate to use this contemporary term to describe a commentator writing in the 1920s, for his grumbles are really no different to those writing newspaper columns today. He despairs of doctors advising him on exercise, diet, tobacco etc. He looks back at the gay Victorians and points out that they knew how to enjoy themselves. He claimed that the people of his own time are the most 'regulation-ridden' ever: 'If we want a box of chocolates or a packet of cigarettes after eight o'clock at night, we cannot get either without breaking the law'. Today, of course, he could buy cigarettes after eight o'clock, but how he would have complained that he couldn't smoke them in his local pub at any hour!

Machen draws many parallels between previous times and his own and he would not have been surprised, I am sure, to find that we can see further reflections in our own society almost another century on. Newspaper reports bring us stories today every bit as terrible, bizarre, wonderful and ludicrous as in previous centuries: crooks still come up with ingenious ways of fooling the gullible, curious crimes and terrible miscarriages of justice still occur, and those doctors still lecture us . . .

In the 'Note' that follows, Machen writes that 'most' of his 'Dreads' and 'Drolls' are 'strictly veridical', but admitted that 'here and there imagination plays a small part.' Noticing where Machen has embellished his picturesque explorations of history is a part of the charm of this collection. I take it that '7B Coney Court' has no basis in fact, and if it is a story that Machen has heard and re-told, then I have not come across it reported by any other source. Neglecting to admit when he was presenting fiction in a context where the reader might reasonably expect a factual account was something Machen made an occasional habit of, most famously in the instance of his 'Bowmen' story in the London *Evening News* of September 29th, 1914. 'The Man in the Blue Serge Suit' from the December of the previous year in the same news-paper inhabited similar territory, although that did not manage to excite the general public in quite the same way.

If '7B Coney Court' is an extreme example of where 'imagination plays a small part', here and there other inventions appear: his spoof sport of 'Dog and Duck' is reportedly played by the protagonists of 'The Highbury Mystery', and who knows how many other embellish-ments add colour to his histories? Grimaldi's *Memoirs* are acknow-ledged as giving him material for a couple of articles, a biography by A.E. Waite, and the *National Geographic* are mentioned, but other sources are given neither title or author. We know that there were many reports and accounts available to him when writing up the eighteenth-century case of 'Betty' Canning, but without his sources it is hard to know how 'veridical' tales such as that of Madame Rachel's Beauty Parlour really are. I assume that most have a basis in fact, perhaps in old newspaper and legal reports, but how often are such details as reported speech 'veridical'? However, these are minor concerns when Machen's intention is to point out how little human nature has changed through the centuries.

We can admire Machen, in the words he uses to commend Grimaldi, as a man with an 'admirable scent for mystery and capacity of creating it'.

R.B. Russell

NOTE

ALL THESE 'Dreads' and 'Drolls' appeared in *The Graphic*. They were gathered from all sorts of sources. Most of them are strictly veridical, but it may be confessed that here and there imagination plays a small part.

My favourite in the collection is, decidedly, the story of Grimaldi the Clown and his long-lost brother. It is an enigma of a tale. On the one hand, there is nothing improbable in the bare plot. Many lads, I have no doubt, went to sea in the adventurous times of the Napoleonic Wars, and were unheard of by their families for long years, often enough they were never heard of again. They were killed in one fight or another, they perished in African swamps, they became Archimandrites in Russia, or confidential advisers to the Dey of Algiers or to Prester John. And again there is nothing improbable in the adventurer's return with a heavy bag of gold, nothing improbable in the final disappearance of a young man who flourishes this bag of gold in the purlieus of Drury Lane as the chimes are ringing midnight.

That is the bare plot of the tale, and as I say, it is all probable enough; and yet I defy anybody to read Grimaldi's story without lifting an incredulous eyebrow. And I have come to the conclusion that this impression is due to Grimaldi's unconscious art. I have no doubt that the Clown spoke the truth; but he had within him that love of mystery and wonder which (as I have said till people are sick of hearing me say it) is the sure foundation, the only foundation of Art. Again and again in his odd book this note of mysteriousness occurs. Take, for example, the incident of the man with the silver staff. Grimaldi always declared that he never knew who this personage was. He didn't want to know. If he had made enquiries, I suppose he would have found that the mysterious stranger was Chief Bow Street Runner, or, as we should say, something big at Scotland Yard. And so, I daresay that the affair of Mr Mackintosh and his twelve friends—a tale absolutely Arabian, as Grimaldi tells it—would have seemed tiresome enough to a man without his admirable scent for mystery and capacity of creating it.

And thus in the business of the long-lost brother. It all happened, and there is nothing very remarkable in it—save for the wonderful though unconscious art which has made a plain tale of plain facts read like a subtle study in mysterious suggestion, a ghost story of the rarest kind.

This is a great gift: to be able so to tell the bare truth that it seems a magnificent lie. To many of us it is rather given to invent elaborate fictions which are plainer (and duller) than the plainest facts.

A.M.

THE MAN WITH THE SILVER STAFF

JOE GRIMALDI, the famous clown, whose life was edited by Dickens, had many strange adventures, and among them is the affair of the Man with the Silver Staff. This happened in the year 1798. Grimaldi had become engaged to his manager's daughter, and had settled in Penton Street, off Pentonville. He was employed at famous Sadler's Wells Theatre, and he was accustomed to pass from his house to the theatre by going across some pleasant pastures called Sadler's Wells Fields. These fields have long been covered by squares, the names of which are unfamiliar to most Londoners: Claremont, Myddleton, Lloyd, and Wilmington; and I will only say that he who is desirous of experiencing the sense of penetrating into outland and unknown territory cannot do better than explore this region, before the leases fall in and the great red flats go up.

One day, then, Grimaldi, on his peaceful way to rehearsal at the Wells, found the Fields occupied by a mob of about a thousand people, all of them scoundrels, engaged in a popular sport of the day. They were hunting an overdriven ox, and they were so densely packed and so extremely ruffianly that Grimaldi wondered whether he would not do better to turn back and go round by the Angel, Islington. Whereupon a young gentleman, looking at him attentively, came up to him and said.

'Is not your name Grimaldi, sir?'

'Yes, sir, it is,' replied Grimaldi. 'Pray may I enquire why you ask the question?'

'Because,' answered the stranger, pointing to a man who stood among a little group of people hard by, 'because I just now heard that gentleman mention it to a companion.'

Grimaldi looked round, saw 'the gentleman,' and was not at all flattered to hear that he was being noted by him. The gentleman was

'Old Lucas,' a 'desperate villain'—we should say, an infernal scoundrel—and Parish Constable of Clerkenwell. The fact is Mr Lucas was in the habit of taking advantage of his official position. He made a practice of accusing innocent people of this, that, or the other crime, of perjuring himself freely and of engaging other perjurers in the necessary quantities, and of pocketing certain small sums due to him on the conviction of the supposed guilty person. And so Grimaldi was not pleased to hear that Lucas had mentioned him, and still less pleased when he heard what came next. He asked the polite young gentleman if he were quite sure that Old Lucas had mentioned his name.

'Quite certain,' was the reply. 'I can't have made any mistake upon the subject, because he wrote it down in his book.'

'Wrote it down in his book?' exclaimed Grimaldi.

'Yes, he did, indeed,' replied the other, 'and more than that, I heard him say to another man beside him that "he could lay hold of you whenever he wanted you."'

Grimaldi was not at all pleased to hear this. However, he took the long way round to the Wells, avoiding the mad ox, and bad Lucas, and the worse mob, and forgot all about the matter in the business of rehearsal. In the evening, however, he recollected it and told the tale to his friends in the green-room, soon before the curtain went up. And Dubois, the comedian, and another actor named Davis, and Richer, the renowned rope-dancer, all roared with laughter, after the good custom of green-rooms everywhere. Dubois remarked that Old Lucas would stick at nothing, not even at Joe's life, to gain a few pounds, perhaps even a few shillings. Then they speculated as to whether the charge would be murder or only forgery, though, as one remarked, that made little difference, since it was a hanging matter either way. And poor Joe tried to laugh, too, but did not feel really happy; and then a theatre messenger came in and said that Mr Grimaldi was wanted directly at the stage-door.

'Who wants me?' enquired Grimaldi, turning rather pale.

'Old Lucas,' answered the messenger, with something between a smile and a gasp. Whereupon the green-room howled with laughter, the messenger joining in, till Mr Dubois perceived that Grimaldi looked very unhappy indeed. Whereupon Mr Dubois and the others said—again according to players' custom everywhere and always—that having had their laugh they would back up their friend to the uttermost of their power. The whole party trooped out to the stage-door and defied Lucas, who told Grimaldi that he must come with him directly to the police office in Hatton Garden; the actors asked for the constable's warrant, told him, one rather gathers, to go to hell, mentioning as, an alternative, a ducking in the adjacent waters of the New River. A joyous mob gathered at the sound of strife, and began to shout execrations against Lucas, who confessed at last that he had no warrant; 'because people generally knows that I'm in authority, and thinks that sufficient.' Whereupon the happy mob shouted again, derisively, and perhaps with a little threatening note, too. So Mr Lucas said that if Mr Grimaldi would promise to come to the police office in Hatton Garden the next morning, that would do; and Mr Lucas turned to go on his way. But the news became general that the villain of a constable was trying to arrest the great Grimaldi, the favourite of all London, and in a moment the whole quarter rang with whoops and yells. Here was better sport than ox-hunting. Mr Lucas ran for his life with a volley of rotten apples, mud, and so forth following after him— and the curtain went up at Sadler's Wells Theatre.

The next morning Grimaldi, accompanied by the famous ropedancer and the two comedians, attended before Mr Blamire, the magistrate of Hatton Garden. Old Lucas forthwith charged Grimaldi with hunting, and inciting and inducing other persons to hunt an overdriven ox in the fields of Pentonville, to the irritation of the ox and the hazard and danger of his Majesty's subjects. In confirmation of this, Lucas summoned a few friends, who confirmed him in every particular. On the other hand, Grimaldi told the truth, and called the young gentleman who had first given him warning of the threatening attitude of Lucas. The magistrate said, finally, that he was quite sure that Grimaldi's story was the true story and that Lucas and his friends were liars; still he was bound to act upon the deposition of the constable and his witnesses, and so he fined Grimaldi five shillings. As for Lucas, Mr Blamire told him to be careful. In great delight the actors bowed to the magistrate, paid the five shillings fine, with a mysterious

3

extra shilling 'for the discharge,' and, oddly enough, it was proposed and unanimously agreed that the party should adjourn to the King of Prussia (afterwards the Clown), a tavern opposite the Wells. Here they had a little lunch and made merry over the small profits accruing to Lucas on a five shilling fine. And in the middle of their mirth a man ran into the room and cried: 'Joe! Joe! here's Old Lucas again.' More roars of laughter. Grimaldi and his friends thought this was a capital joke—when in walked Old Lucas. He was, really, a surprising fellow, this Constable of Clerkenwell. He declared that Grimaldi had not paid the five shillings or the aforementioned one shilling, and that he must either pay or 'come along.'

'Not paid?' said the unfortunate clown. 'Why, I paid the six shillings before I left the office.'

Old Lucas only grinned, and said: 'Pay the money, or come on with me.'

Grimaldi swore he would not pay another farthing. The constable advanced to seize him and tore his shirt and waistcoat to ribbons. Whereupon, the mild Grimaldi was roused to anger and knocked Lucas down, causing the 'porochial' nose to bleed grievously. But he got up again and produced his staff, and the fight was just going to begin again when a Mysterious Stranger rose from his place in the tavern room. He rose and drew from his pocket a Silver Staff, which he shook at Lucas; and, at the sight of that Staff, Lucas withered and collapsed. At the command of him of the Staff, the whole party returned to the police office, where Mr Blamire remarked with amazement the change that had taken place in the shape of the constable's nose. And Mr Blamire seemed to know the Mysterious Stranger very well indeed, and greeted him cordially. The matter was heard, the Silver Staff corroborated Grimaldi's story, and Old Lucas was fined five pounds, the money to go to the poor of the parish. Whereupon Old Lucas foamed at the mouth, like the hunted ox, and swore with frightful oaths and 'great expressions of disrespect' that he would pay nothing. Then the worthy magistrate ordered Old Lucas to the cells, where he remained for five or six hours, devoting the whole time to howlings and imprecations, and at last paid up and wrote a penitent letter to Grimaldi.

And the Man with the Silver Staff? 'Who,' said Grimaldi, with profound respect and an air of great mystery: 'Who this gentleman was, I never could ascertain; but that he was a person possessing a somewhat high degree of authority was evident to me from the great respect paid to him at the police office.'

And here is another queer business in which Grimaldi was engaged, a few years later. He had a professional friend named Bologna, and Bologna knew a wealthy country gentleman, a Mr Mackintosh, who lived down in Kent. Now Mr Mackintosh had often pressed Bologna to come down to his place for the shooting and bring a friend; and so one October Grimaldi and Bologna hired a gig (the date is 1804) and drove in the direction of Bromley. Here they met a man in a fustian jacket, driving a lame horse in a taxed cart; and greatly to Grimaldi's amazement, this was Mr Mackintosh the wealthy. And the magnificent house was a small roadside tavern, kept by Mr Mackintosh's mother; and Bologna was mortified, and Grimaldi was inclined to laugh. However, the two actors had a good plain dinner, and in a day or two were taken out for the shooting.

'Now's your time,' said Mackintosh, pointing to a field where a great number of pigeons were feeding.

The actors were cross. They said they had come to shoot birds. Mr Mackintosh said that pigeons were birds, and the two comedians fired in a rage and slew twenty-five of them. 'And now,' said Mackintosh, 'if you will take my advice, you will cut away at once.'

They were the squire's pigeons. Grimaldi and Bologna were chased to the Lane by the squire's gamekeeper, on Mr Mackintosh's information, but that difficulty was surmounted by a moderate payment on account of the Pigeons, a rumpsteak dinner and a bottle of wine.

And so, you will say, the end of Mr Mackintosh and his odd sense of humour. Not at all. In three years' time a much smartened, spruced-up Mackintosh calls on Grimaldi, hopes his little joke has been forgiven, and trusts that Grimaldi and his wife will accept the hospitality offered by some friends in Charlotte Street, Fitzroy Square. Grimaldi drives round one night after the play, finds a splendid mansion, splendidly furnished, a blaze of light, luxurious furniture, and noble meats and nobler wines for supper. There were just twelve people present besides Mackintosh and Grimaldi: Mr and Mrs Farmer, host and hostess, and five other married couples, all exquisitely dressed. The jewellery of the ladies was superb, the liveries of the servants were gorgeous. Again and again the Grimaldis partook of this Arabian hospitality; and always the party was the same; the six ladies and six gentlemen, and Mr Mackintosh. Mr Grimaldi was a little perplexed; he thought that there was something peculiar about the manners of these people, but he could not quite say what it was. He puzzled his head, he felt that the Charlotte Street ways were different from the ways or the noblemen and gentlemen he met in the green-rooms of the Lane and the Wells; but he could not make out what the difference was.

And now for the solution of the puzzle. Alas! Mr Mackintosh and his friends were all 'desperate characters.' Mr Farmer had been reprieved while he stood on the drop under the gallows; they were a pack of burglars, forgers, passers of forged notes. And what did they want with Mr Grimaldi? Simply to be amused; that was all.

THE MYSTERY OF MR HADDOCK

EVERYTHING THAT is old is dear to me, but more especially the old which is ramshackle, disreputable, up a court or down an alley. Westminster Abbey is very fine, no doubt, but I feel, rightly or wrongly, that it has been furbished up, refaced, dusted and polished so that the real aspect of antiquity has departed from it. And, moreover, everybody knows all about it, and it rises clear and high from the turf, without the curious joy of obscurity, of the thing hidden away, that always seems a discovery, however often it may be found and re-found.

I cannot define this curious joy of the down-at-heel hidden in a dark place; but I know my heart still aches for Holywell Street and Wych Street and the purlieus of Clare Market and other ancient and decrepit quarters that have been taken from us. I am told that these places were hideously insanitary, reeking with evil odours, rats and smaller and yet more odious vermin. I daresay, and, indeed, I remember that the short cut to the Strand from Great Queen Street, which seemed to begin with an archway and a stable yard, was not exactly aromatic. But, together with flavours not pleasing, how these narrow and tortuous streets and nooks and corners were redolent of the eighteenth century. There were poky and obscure taverns, where highwaymen still seemed to hide, and windows at which Hogarthian faces gibbered: a brave quarter, I thought it.

It was something of all this that attracted me to a curious little book that came my way lately, *A Few Personal Recollections by an Old Printer*. The Old Printer wrote his memories thirty years ago, and he looked back over sixty years; so his story begins somewhere in the 'thirties of the last century. I knew I should like his book when I saw his description of the printing offices of his early days. None of them had been constructed for the purposes of printing; they were simply old houses, old corners of seventeenth-century galleried inns, in 'unsavoury thoroughfares,' 'disreputable districts'—I quote the Old Printer. The press, a wooden contraption much like the press of Caxton, was operated in the kitchen, and to the dingy caserooms upstairs came the Fleet Street authors, correcting their proofs and talking to the compositors. All this description appealed to me strongly, and so I read on, sure of finding more good things. And I found many good things, and, best of all, a Queer Story.

It begins well. Beside 'Mother Trimby's tavern' in Drury Lane was an inn yard, called George Yard, where some of the old galleries were still in place. Here was a printing office, and here the Old Printer met Laman Blanchard, 'an underpaid, struggling journalist, dramatist, and song-writer.' Blanchard had brought out a penny paper called *The Astrologer*, on which the printer was employed. He was a young man, but it struck him that astrology was nonsense, and he tried to find out whether Blanchard, 'a clear-headed, matter-of-fact man,' as he calls him, really believed in the science of the stars. Blanchard smiled and evaded the question, but he told the lad how *The Astrologer* came to be founded.

It all began in the green-room at Drury Lane. Here, beside the actors, their friends, playwrights and the rest of the company that were to be found in the green-rooms of those days, here used to sit a gloomy man named Haddock 'in some way connected with the theatre.' Haddock sat apart, spoke to no one, made friends with no one. One night while a certain actor was on the stage a messenger came with the news that a son had been born to him. Whereupon another actor, after the manner of actors—they use grease paint on the dressing-room walls now—wrote with chalk on the green-room wall:

Youngest child of James Blank, born Dec. 16, A.D. 1844.

And when this was done, the melancholy Haddock took the chalk, and, without a word, wrote underneath:

And died Jan. 21, 1845.

The company in the green-room were horrified. Thereupon, Blanchard, who was present, got a strip of paper and pasted it by the two ends over the gloomy one's inscription. Nothing more was said, and the matter was forgotten till January 21, 1845.

On that night Blanchard was again in Drury Lane green-room. Again Mr Blank was engaged on the stage. Again a messenger entered with news for him. 'What was the news?' asked Blanchard. 'His child is dead,' replied the messenger. Blanchard tore down the strip of paper that he had pasted over Haddock's inscription; and there was the event, predicted to the very day. And on that, the journalist began to think. Presumably—it is not exactly stated—he had some talks with Haddock; at all events, he was of the opinion that the gloomy man had the gift of prophecy. Whereupon Blanchard proposed that he and Haddock should go into partnership and start a paper to be called *The Astrologer*. Haddock agreed, and the paper duly appeared—twenty pounds was regarded in those days as ample capital for the projector of a new journal. And much to the astonishment of the projectors, who had thought that their customers and correspondents would be entirely of the uneducated class, letters of inquiry, requests for horoscopes, and so forth, poured in from the nobility and gentry—from people in society, as we should say.

One day, Haddock suggested a joint holiday. 'Very well,' said Blanchard, 'where shall we go?'

'What does it matter,' said the other. 'Let us go to the nearest railway, take the first train, and go to the end of the journey.'

This very spirited plan brought the two soothsayers to Dover one Saturday afternoon. The next day they climbed up Shakespeare's Cliff, and sat in silence, staring at the Channel below. Suddenly, Haddock got up and said:

'What a sensation it would make if I were to grasp you round the waist and jump with you off the cliff!'

It cannot be denied that Haddock had what the news-editors of today call 'a nose for news.' But Blanchard disliked the proposal, and said that they would go back to the town, if Mr Haddock pleased. Whereupon the prophet 'gave a hollow laugh,' and followed Blanchard back to Dover. The next morning Haddock took the first train back to London. Blanchard stayed till Tuesday, and on that day looked in at the *Astrologer* Office, 11 Wellington Street, North, Strand. Haddock's door was locked from the inside. Knocks obtained no answer. The door was burst open. On the table were the hat, coat and stick of Mr Haddock, but Mr Haddock was not there, 'nor' (says the Old Printer) 'according to Blanchard, whom I heard tell the story, was he ever known to have been seen afterwards. In reply to inquiries, Blanchard always confessed that he did not like to say where he thought Haddock had gone, although he had a shrewd suspicion.' And, soon after, *The Astrologer* ceased to appear.

Now the Old Printer says that Laman Blanchard was the most amiable of men, a man of the utmost kindness and benevolence. I quite believe it; but is it possible that he was also what, in our modern phrase, we call a leg-puller? I will not be absolute in the matter; but it suddenly struck me that the incident of the pasting of the piece of paper over Haddock's offensive inscription was not altogether convincing. When unpleasantness in chalk is to be obliterated in a hurry the natural man smears out the letters with his hand or the sleeve of his coat.

And so, I wonder. But it is an odd history, and Blanchard's unspoken conjecture as to Haddock's destination is a rare touch.

CEREMONY ON THE SCAFFOLD

ON THE TENTH of June, 1541, Sir Edmund Knevet was arraigned before the officers of the Green Cloth for striking one Master Cleer of Norfolk within the Tennis Court of the King's House. The sentence was that Sir Edmund Knevet must lose his right hand, and forfeit all his possessions.

Now supposing that the Board of Green Cloth existed still in all its vigour, with the old power of passing exemplary sentences, what would happen to plain Bill Smith of these days convicted of giving Tom Robinson one for himself within the verges of St James's Park? I can imagine the scene very well. Bill would be taken from his cell at eight o'clock one morning. He would be led to a dingy and despairing metal shed in the prison-yard by a couple of warders. Here there would await him the Governor of the Prison, the Medical Officer, perhaps the Chaplain, a skilled surgeon, an anaesthetist, a nurse (very bright and cheerful, with red cheeks), and an operating table. On this table Bill would be politely requested to place himself. He would inhale the very latest formula, the Medical Officer keeping in careful touch with his pulse. The distinguished surgeon would then amputate Bill's right hand, the dressings would be applied with the greatest care, and in due course the prisoner would be escorted to the hospital. Here he would remain for the next three weeks, being nurtured on a light but nourishing diet. On his release from prison he would be fitted with an artificial hand, of the newest pattern. Such would be the course of justice in 1926, if it had continued to order right hands to be cut off.

They did not do things in that shabby, hole-in-the-corner way four hundred years ago. The ancient chronicle from which I quote continues the story thus:

11

'Whereupon there was called to do execution, first the Serjeant Surgeon, with his Instruments pertaining to his office, then, the Serjeant of the Wood Yard, with a mallet and a block to lay the hand upon, then the King's Master Cook with a knife to cut off the hand, then the Serjeant of the Larder to set the knife right on the joint, then the Serjeant Ferrier with searing irons to sear the veins, then the Serjeant of the Poultry with a Cock, which Cock should have his head smitten off upon the same block and with the same knife; then the Yeoman of the Chandry with Sear-cloaths, then the Yeoman of the Scullery, with a pan of fire to heat the Irons, a chafer of water to cool the ends of the Irons, and two forms for all officers to set their stuff on, then the Serjeant of the Cellar with Wine, Ale and Beer; then the Serjeant of the Ewry with Bason, Ewre, and Towels.'

There! It must be confessed that there was nothing mean about the court of Henry VIII. If it was only a matter of cutting off a gentleman's hand, the thing was done magnificently; with—I think we may say—a sense of style. In this particular affair of Sir Edmund Knevet I am afraid that same of the company were disappointed; for when it came to the point of execution Sir Edmund confessed everything and submitted himself in every respect, only begging that the King's Majesty would take the left hand instead of the right, since with that hand, he said, he might live to do the King some service. Whereupon somebody ran to tell the King, and the King immediately forgave Sir Edmund, and left him both his hands and restored to him all his forfeited lands and goods. I am afraid, I say, that some of the company went away grumbling and asking (more or less) if they were going to have their money back; but I daresay there were others who were all for a happy ending. And I have no doubt that the seven Serjeants, the two Yeomen, and the King's Master Cook gave a good account of the Wine, Ale, and Beer. Things did not always end so pleasantly. When Nigel (he of 'The Fortunes') was in prison for drawing his sword on the villain, Dalgarno, in the precincts of the Court, Sir Mungo Malagrowther visited him, and, by way of consolation, gave a lively account of some proceedings under the Board of Green Cloth which he had once witnessed. The culprit, if I remember, bore the striking off of his hand bravely enough, but when it came to the application of those red-hot irons to the stump, he uttered an eldritch screech. The Palace Court, the body which once gave these savage sentences, lingered on far into the 'forties of the last century. Tip (otherwise Edward) Dorrit once occupied a stool in the office of an attorney 'in a great National Palladium called the Palace Court,' and indeed the Marshalsea, whence Tip came, was originally built as a prison for persons accused of offences committed within the verge of the Court. But I suppose that in its later years the tribunal bled its victims rather metaphorically than literally.

But as to the general question of the public ceremonial and elaborate execution of judgment upon criminals; how does it compare with our grim and secret way of carrying out the last doom of the law? So far as we are concerned, no doubt Charles Dickens, that determined and consistent denouncer of public executions, was perfectly right. Johnson was mistaken when he said that the pageant of Tyburn, with its long drive from Newgate, furnished an example to the populace. Dickens describes the execution of the Mannings and the demeanour of the crowd that waited all night to witness it; it is plain that the vilest degradation, not reformation, was the result of that hideous spectacle. But as for the criminal himself; there, perhaps, Johnson was right in thinking that he was fortified by the dismal pageantry, by the bell ringing at St Sepulchre's, by the flowers presented by lady admirers, by the last drink at St Giles's. Jonathan Wild is reported by Fielding to have picked the chaplain's pocket of a corkscrew going in the cart to Tyburn, and Sixteen Stringed Jack wore a bright pea-green coat as he went on his way to the Three Wooden Stilts. And, then, there was the admirable Colonel Turner, who was hanged in the seventeenth century for something like robbery with violence. He made what Leslie Stephen rightly called a superb dying speech. 'He spoke under the gallows as if he were the good apprentice just arrived at the mayoralty. . . .' He was brought up in an honest family in the good old times, he said, and lamented the bad times that had since come in. So the Colonel ran on happily, speaking of his loyalty to the King, his firm piety, his detestation of profane swearing and drunkenness; in a word of his well-nigh saintly character. At last the hangman put the rope round his neck.

13

'Dost thou mean to choke me, fellow?' asked the Colonel. 'What a simple fellow is this! How long have you been executioner that you know not how to put the knot?' Then, as he was putting on the white cap, he saw a lady at a window. He kissed his hand to her, said, 'Your servant, Mistress,' and pulled down the cap, undaunted to the last, as an eye-witness of the scene reports.

It is clear that Colonel Turner would not have liked our modern ways of doing things.

MR LUTTERLOH

ON A FAMOUS evening Mr Boffin called on his literary man in ordinary, Mr Silas Wegg. He was in a cab, blocked up with books, and he called excitedly:

'Here! lend a hand, Wegg, I can't get out till the way is cleared for me. This is the *Annual Register*, Wegg, in a cabful of wollumes. Do you know him?'

'Know the Animal Register, sir,' said the Impostor, who had caught the name imperfectly. 'For a trifling wager, I think I could find any Animal in him, blindfold, Mr Boffin.'

I shall never pretend to the minute knowledge affected by Mr Wegg; but I have been glancing through an odd volume of the *Register*, and have certainly come across some very queer animals.

And the first of them is a literal animal, the swallow. The account quoted in the *Register* is from *Barrington's Miscellanies*. It seems that during the winter the swallow hides itself under water. This is a well-known fact, and Linnaeus is quoted in support of it, with many other witnesses. For example, Mr Stephens, A.S.S.—there seems to me something ominous about these letters—used to pick up bunches of swallows or martins from a pond at Shrivenham, where his father was vicar. 'The birds were carried into the kitchen, on which they soon afterwards flew about the room, in the presence of his father, mother, and others, particularly the Rev. Dr Pye.'

I find it very hard to resist the Rev. Dr Pye. There is something orthodox, comfortable and full-bodied in his style. I wish I could have seen him as he walked abroad, in wig, cassock, gown and bands, round of speech, I am sure.

But, indeed, a host of witnesses to the submersive habit of the swallow are cited, including a Brentford man and Sigismond, King of

Poland. The Brentford man said he had caught specimens in the eyt opposite the town, and the King affirmed on his oath to Cardinal Commendon that he had frequently seen swallows which were found at the bottom of lakes.

And before we laugh, let us remember how many of us saw Russians, thousands of them, in England, in the year 1914. The *Annual Register* from which I am quoting is dated 1781.

And then there are the other Animals, the featherless bipeds. There is a full account of the trial of Lord George Gordon for High Treason on February 5, 1781, with a very vivid description of the scene at the doors of the House of Commons (see *Barnaby Rudge*, Chapter XLIX). And here I came across a very odd animal. There is a well-known passage in Boswell's *Johnson* in which Johnson and Boswell decide that Fleet Street (or the town) is better than Greenwich Park (that is, the country). Boswell fortifies himself in this opinion 'by the authority of a very fashionable baronet in the brilliant world, who, on his attention being called to the fragrance of a May evening in the country, observed, "This may be very well; but for my part, I prefer the smell of a flambeau at the playhouse." ' A footnote informs us that Mr Boswell's smart friend was Sir Michael le Fleming. I have never heard more of him, and never expected to hear more of him. A learned Boswellian surmises that, on the evidence given, Sir Michael was probably an unprofitable friend for Boswell, and so the matter ended, as I thought. And here, to my amazement, the fashionable, brilliant and—may one surmise?—somewhat sophisticated baronet, makes his appearance in the Gordon trial. The Rev. Thomas Bowen was offici-ating as Chaplain to the House of Commons on June 2, 1780. Giving evidence, he says that, prayers ended, he sat under the gallery, near the door. In and out of the House comes Lord George, telling his support-ers in the lobby what was going on within. This intelligence comes in gusts to the Chaplain, thus:

Lord George: 'Mr Burke, member for Bristol [*the* Burke] has said— ' and then the door was shut, and no more was heard.

Again: 'Lord North calls you a mob': 'Mr Rous has just moved that the civil power be sent for, but don't you mind; keep yourselves cool; be steady—' and so on, and so on. And then the Chaplain saw a gentleman go up to Lord George and speak to him, and as soon as Lord George saw who it was, he called to the people, 'This is Sir Michael le Fleming; he has just been speaking for you.' He seemed to be remarkably pleased with Sir Michael, the witness testified: 'patted or stroked, his shoulder, and exhibited a kind of joy, which the witness knew not how to describe.'

Dear me! Who would have thought that Boswell's brilliant, fashionable, playhouse-flambeau loving baronet was a stout Protestant after all?

But the most awe-inspiring of all the Animals in this *Register* of 1781 is a certain Mr Lutterloh. He and his strange name and his strange career are to be found in the account of the arrest, trial, conviction and condemnation of Henry Francis de la Motte for treasonable practices. De la Motte was a French nobleman, with the queer title of Baron Deckham. He had been colonel of the regiment of Soubise in the last war, and had shown gallantry. He had lived beyond his income, and taken refuge in England, and had then, so said the prosecution, engaged in the treasonable practice of furnishing the French Government with information as to his Majesty King George's forces and plans. He had resided in Bond Street, at a Mr Otley's, a woollen-draper, for some time. The story begins with Mr De la Motte visiting the Secretary of State—of his free will or in response to a hint does not appear. On his way upstairs he dropped several papers full of guilty matters, which were picked up by the messengers and carried with him to the Secretary, Lord Hillsborough. Thereupon, De la Motte was immediately committed a close prisoner to the Tower on the charge of high treason. And here is the first shock: Would a man guilty of such practices fortify himself for a visit to the Secretary of State by stuffing his pockets with treasonable documents, and then carelessly strew the Secretary's stairs with them, as if they were roses? But I lack space in which to tell the whole story of poor De la Motte—the evident source and prototype of Darnay in 'The Tale of Two Cities.' I do not know whether he were guilty; but the case against him has an ill look—for the Government and its agents. The dignity and nobility of his demeanour during the trial were remarked by all, and after the dreadful sentence had been passed, Mr Akerman, the gaoler, said that he never in his life saw a man in De la Motte's position with more becoming firmness and fortitude. But the mysterious Mr Lutterloh? After the examination of the papers which Mr De la Motte had so thoughtfully dropped on the Secretary's stairs, orders were issued for the apprehension of Henry Lutterloh, Esq., of Wickham, near Portsmouth. The messengers found Mr Lutterloh ready booted to go a-hunting, but when he was told of the messengers' business 'he did not discover the least embarrassment.' His keys, his papers were all at their service. He was a German, who had lately taken a house near Portsmouth. He kept a pack of hounds, and was very popular with the neighbouring gentry.

And yet, as it turned out at the trial, Mr Lutterloh had been a servant (discharged on suspicion of thieving), a chandler in Great Wild Street, Drury Lane, a bankrupt and a fugitive, and a book-keeper at the George Inn, Portsmouth. He confessed in the witness-box that the prisoner, De la Motte, had raised him from beggary to comfort by his generosity. But a powerful feeling came upon Mr Lutterloh, urging him to make some restitution to the country he had injured. Also, he said, he felt a desire to enrich himself. And so he swore the generous French gentleman's life away.

I am sure that Mr Dunning and Mr Peckham did their best for the defence. But I wish the prisoner's solicitor could have briefed Mr Stryver and Mr Sydney Carton.

A LAMENT FOR LONDON'S LOST INNS

AMONGST THE pleasant recollections of old, vanished London that I possess, none is more agreeable than my memories of the old inns. I do not mean the inns which would now be called hostels—in an attempt to be older than the old—that is, the various Inns of Chancery, though of these I could tell a long tale. I remember well the joy of turning aside from the gaiety of the Strand when the Strand was the cheerfullest, most delightful street in all London, and, as I believe, in the world, and going up a little quiet way and so into Clement's Inn, with its fine Hall, its lawns, its peace and quiet, and its Garden House, a red brick, mid-Georgian house in the middle of a green garden. Once when I turned thus aside, the Garden House was empty, and I asked the rent. It was only £120 a year; but it was slightly beyond my means. And then there was New Inn, as peaceful as Clement's, which it adjoined, but not so green. There were some sad, broken fragments of it surviving off Aldwych up to two or three years ago, but I am afraid these are now gone. The main entrance to New Inn was in Wych Street.

'The gentleman next in esteem and authority among us is another Bachelor who is a member of the Inner Temple. He is an excellent Critic and the time of the Play is his hour of business; exactly at five he passes through New Inn, crosses through Russell Court, and takes a turn at Will's till the play begins.'

Thus the Spectator, and thus, I think, we see one of the sources of the younger Dickens. Lyons' Inn, where the old Globe Theatre stood, was gone long before my day. Barnard's, which Pip in *Great Expectations* disliked so thoroughly, has been converted into the Mercer's School, its hall happily intact; Clifford's (one of the choicest specimens of the Inns of Chancery) survives in a fragmentary state, but, I am afraid, will not last much longer. Thavie's Inn, the residence of Mr

19

Jellaby, still exists by Holborn, but looks exactly like a street. I suppose it was rebuilt soon after the Society of Lincoln's Inn sold it in 1771. It was named after John Thavie, an armourer, who lived in the reign of Edward III. Thus do old, old names, even the names of lesser men, cling to our London byways.

But it is not of the inns of this sort that I am thinking, but rather of those inns of common, not of legal, entertainment. It is odd to note that the word is fast becoming—if it has not become—obsolete, together with tavern; the reason being, as I suppose, that the things themselves are gone, or almost gone. We have hotels and we have 'pubs'; scarcely inns or taverns. One of the noblest of the old inns that I remember was the Bell, in Holborn, to which the Amersham coach used to run up to 1880, or thereabouts. Facing the street, it was seen to be a late seventeenth-century building of dim and yet warm old brick, with a fine coat of arms in terra-cotta set into it. But within, under the archway, it was, in my recollection, almost a replica of the White Hart Yard, as shown in the *Pickwick* plate, depicting the first appearance of Mr Samuel Weller. There were two tiers of galleries leading to the bedrooms, running round three sides of the court. In a word, you turned from Holborn into the seventeenth century, as, by the way, you may still turn if you will take the trouble to walk under Gray's Inn archway through South Square into Gray's Inn Square. Then, near at hand, was Ridley's Family Hotel, with bow windows bulging over the Holborn pavement; a sound, comfortable, snug-looking place, where I can see archdeacons reading the *Times* after breakfast. Of the taverns of former years my chief recollections cluster round the Cock, standing where a branch of the Bank of England now stands, near the corner of Chancery Lane. I had several chops in that old coffee-room of the Cock, where Tennyson called for his pint of port, of which he wrote one of the finest things in the lighter vein that have been written in English or in any other language.

Thus to the head-waiter :

> Live long, ere from thy topmost head
>   The thick-set hazel dies;
> Long, ere the hateful crow shall tread
>   The corners of thine eyes ;

20

A LAMENT FOR LONDON'S LOST INNS

Live long, nor feel in head or chest
  Our changeful equinoxes,
Till mellow Death, like some late guest,
  Shall call thee from the boxes.

My occasional visits to the old vanished tavern were paid in its last days, in '82 or '83. I do not know what I could have been reading, what eighteenth-century stuff was in my head—I was twenty at the time—but I had a vague idea that I should meet 'the wits' at the Cock, otherwise, 'the most respectable authors of the day.' I should think I was about a hundred years too late. I met no wits at the Cock, and I found that the coffee-room began to empty soon after nine, when, according to my out-dated fancies, it should have begun to be brilliant. But the odd thing is that once upon a time the sort of thing that I expected to happen did really happen.

'I was about seventeen when I first came up to town, an odd-look-ing boy, with short rough hair, and that sort of awkwardness which one always brings up at first out of the country. However, in spite of my bashfulness and appearance, I used now and then to thrust myself into Will's to have the pleasure of seeing the most celebrated wits of that time, who then resorted thither. The second time that ever I was there, Mr Dryden was speaking of his own things, as he frequently did, especially of such as had been lately published. "If anything of mine is good," said he, " 'tis *MacFlecknoe*; and I value myself the more upon it, because it is the first piece of ridicule written in Heroics!" On hearing this, I plucked up my spirit so far as to say, in a voice just loud enough to be heard, "that *MacFlecknoe* was a very fine poem, but that I had not imagined it to be the first that ever was writ that way." On this, Dryden turned short upon me, as surprised at my interposing; asked me how long I had been a dealer in poetry; and added, with a smile, "Pray, sir, what is it that you *did* imagine to have been writ so before?" I named Boileau's *Lutrin*, and Tassoni's *Secchia Rapita*, which I had read, and knew Dryden had borrowed some strokes from each. " 'Tis true," said Dryden, "I had forgot them." A little after Dryden went out, and in going spoke to me again, and desired me to come and see him next day. I was delighted with the invitation; went to see him accordingly and was well acquainted with him after, as long as he lived.'

Thus it was at Will's, the Great Coffee House in Covent Garden, as Pepys called it. It was No, 1, Bow Street, on the west side at the corner of Russell Street, and was perhaps the most illustrious of London taverns, from the Restoration to early Hanoverian days. It was here that 'old Swinney' described Dryden as holding court. He told Dr Johnson that 'at Will's Coffee House Dryden had a particular chair for himself, which was set by the fire in winter, and was then called his winter-chair; and that it was carried out for him to the balcony in summer, and was then called his summer-chair.'

Decidedly, I was a little late in searching for the wits at the Cock.

MADAME RACHEL

THE OTHER DAY, reading the paper, I came upon a half-column that interested me. It was headed: 'Slimness-While-You-Wait,' and a sub-heading ran: 'The "Boiled Cyclist" Treatment.' Who could resist such invitations as these? Not I.

I found that the article concerned a new 'Beauty Parlour' in the Bond Street quarter. And how pleasant it is, by the way, to note the manner in which America is restoring to us the good old English word, 'parlour,' which we had lost awhile. Well, in this Beauty Parlour, the lady who would achieve perfection of form must undergo many severe trials; and, indeed, this is the way of perfection of every kind, and there is no escape from it. And the trials of Bond Street are hard to bear; they almost recall the terrors which, in popular tradition, are supposed to await him who would pass through the Third Degree of a venerable secret order. Thus I read:

'First she (the person to be initiated in these mysteries) has to strip herself of her clothing and sit for twenty minutes in the 'reducycle bath.' The bath is surrounded by canvas which is fastened round her neck. In its interior a bicycle is fitted, and the client sits on the bicycle saddle and works the pedals as though she were actually riding quickly along a road.'

Then follows the Shower. To it succeeds the Roller, painted a pale mauve, 'with kinks in it.' Then the Candidate is vested in a bathing costume, and there ensues the Ceremony of the Exercises on Coloured Mats to the music of the gramophone. Altogether, it strikes me as a strange but gorgeous rite; and I trust and believe that She renews her youth, in the fashion of that other She of Sir Rider Haggard's invention.

23

In the bad old days, there were beauty parlours in Bond Street, though they did not call them then by that name. But there was no science then; only a great deal of wickedness. Listen, therefore, to the story of Sarah Rachel Leverson, called Madame Rachel, who lived at the corner of New Bond Street and Maddox Street, and said that she could make ladies beautiful for ever. Madame Rachel drove, on the face of it, much the same trade as that plied by Dickens's famous Miss Mowcher. She sold all sorts of cosmetics, enamels, paints, powders, rouges, unguents. She constantly proclaimed that she could make women beautiful for ever, and she came at last to Marlborough Street police station and to the Court of the Recorder of London, in the year 1868. The complainant was a Mrs Borradaile, widow of a Colonel, who said that Madame Rachel had swindled her, one way and another, of £3,000.

'On my first visit'—testifies Mrs Borradaile—'I spent £10, and in the course of two or three days I had invested £170 with her. I paid her various sums of money for cosmetics, and so forth, during the latter part of 1864 and the commencement of 1865. Before purchasing these articles I asked her to do something for my skin, and she promised that if I would follow out her course of treatment in every particular she would succeed in making me beautiful for ever.'

Poor Mrs Borradaile! Serjeant Ballantine was retained for the prosecution—with him Mr Straight and Mr Montague Williams and the last testifies that Mrs Borradaile was 'a sparse, thin, scraggy-looking woman, wholly devoid of figure; her hair was dyed a bright yellow; her face was raddled with paint.' The matter went far beyond selling creams and powders, and Arabian herbs and nonsense of every sort in boxes and bottles and baths.

'On one occasion,' said the witness, 'I called on Madame Rachel, who told me that she had had an interview with the gentleman who had fallen in love with me. On asking his name; I was informed that it was Lord Ranelagh. I asked when he had met me, and the reply was, both before and after my marriage. . . . Madame Rachel said that she would introduce me to him the next day. . . . I called at Maddox Street, where the prisoner lived. Madame Rachel opened the door and said, 'I will now introduce you to the man who loves you.' She then introduced me to a man whom I believed, and still believe to be Lord Ranelagh. I said to him, 'Are you Lord Ranelagh?' and he answered, 'Yes; here is my card.' He then handed me a card, which I returned to him. The gentleman who gave me the card is the gentleman I now see in Court.' This gentleman in Court, thus identified, was undoubtedly Lord Ranelagh. He gave evidence. He said he had often been in Madame Rachel's shop. He thought he had seen Mrs Borradaile once at the shop, but he had no recollection of being introduced to her. He was asked, it would appear, what business he had in Madame Rachel's shop at all. He answered, 'You don't suppose I went there to be enam-elled.'

Which reminds me of 'Charley Pyegrave, the duke's son.'

'He goes into a perfumer's shop, and wants to buy a bottle of the Madagascar Liquid.'

'Charley does?' said Steerforth.

'Charley does. But they haven't got any of the Madagascar Liquid.'

'What is it? Something to drink?' asked Steerforth.

'To drink?' returned Miss Mowcher, stopping to slap his cheek. 'To doctor his own mustachios with, you know.'

Well, the elderly woman in the shop said to Charley:

'Begging pardon, sir, it's not—not—not ROUGE, is it?'

'Rouge,' said Charley. 'What the unmentionable to ears polite do you think I want with rouge?'

But what was Lord Ranelagh doing at Madame Rachel's? Well, the curious are advised to consult the rumours of the time.

Madame Rachel, then, quite persuaded Mrs Borradaile that Lord Ranelagh was desirous of marrying her. And, at Lord Ranelagh's express desire, Mrs Borradaile was to go through an extra process of being made beautiful for ever. The poor, silly woman accordingly sold out securities and paid Madame Rachel £800 on account of £1000 'for bath preparations, spices, powders, sponges, perfumes, and attendance, to be continued till I (Mrs Borradaile) am finished by the process.' And from this moment the story surpasses the very bounds of extravagance. Madame Rachel said she was going to marry this happy couple 'by proxy,' otherwise 'by letter writings.' There were plenty of letter-writings handed over by Madame Rachel to Mrs Borradaile. Sometimes they were signed 'William,' sometimes 'Edward,' Lord Rane-lagh's name being Thomas; but, as Madame sagely observed, this was a wise precaution since letters are apt to be left about. They were odd letters. They all dwelt on the importance of keeping 'Granny' (Madame Rachel) in good temper. They warned 'Darling love, Mary, my sweet one,' not to hold any communication with her family or with Lewis and Lewis—suspicious and untrustful tribes, both of them. The letters were in different handwritings, but, as 'Granny' explained, Lord Ranelagh had hurt his arm, and sometimes made his servant write for him. Affectionate letters these: 'I shall be at your feet—those pretty feet that I love—and you may kick your ugly old donkey'; 'I would rather be shot like a dog than leave England without you'; 'I heard you were insulted by a cabman in Oxford Street, yesterday. I wish I had been there'; 'Mary, my heart's love, is it your wish to drive me mad? Granny has my instructions. Do as she tells you. . . . What is the meaning of the delay, at the eleventh hour? Granny lent me the money. You shall pay her, my own sweet one. Get the lace today and fear nothing. It will be £35.' Clothes and lace and jewellery were necessary for the wedding, said Granny, and Mrs Borradaile bought them—and Granny took care of them. Presumably, suspicion began to rise in the foolish woman's heart; she said she could not get any of these articles back. 'You must ask the man who loves you for them back,' said Madame, and she brought her victim a lighted cigar, 'saying that Lord Ranelagh's love for me was as warm as that.' That must have reassured Mrs Borradaile, since soon after she executed a bond for £1,600. This was for Lord Ranelagh, but Granny took care of it, and I suppose Granny also took care of a carriage which Mrs Borradaile bought for her wedding.

And the end of the story? Five years' penal servitude for Granny.

SIR BENJAMIN THE 'BARON'

IT WAS WITH considerable delight that I read the other day an article 'sticking up' very bravely for Harrison Ainsworth, and Dick Turpin, and the Ride to York, and the *Tower of London*, and all that world of brave things. I was pleased, because a man likes to have his opinions confirmed by high authority; and I have always had a very tender feeling for Harrison Ainsworth, recollecting how he made my ten-years'-old blood run cold by his description of the Subterranean Temple of the Demon in the *Lancashire Witches*. And it was of Harrison Ainsworth that I was chiefly thinking when I once observed that, though the Victorians did not always write well, they always wrote with a relish.

Things happened in those old Victorian storybooks. There were lonely inns in which travellers were apt to be murdered. And these travellers were not always what they seemed. The names they gave were not always their own names. The apparent merchant sometimes turned out to be something very different. Sometimes they shuddered as they dismounted from their coaches. Sometimes they wrote vehemently as soon as they entered; sometimes they consigned papers to the fire and watched these papers burn to the last ember. Now and then the (apparently) faithful attendant of the Mysterious Stranger was not what *he* seemed. There were cases in which the traveller was seen one moment in the inn yard, and then had vanished in the twinkling of an eye, and had vanished for ever. Perhaps years afterwards a skeleton was discovered, buried deeply not far from the inn yard; and wife or sister, grown old and sick with vain waiting, came and gazed doubtfully with dim eyes upon the relics—and wondered.

There! Can you imagine what would happen if one submitted the above as an outline or sketch of a possible plot to our really modern writers, the veritable Georgians? I don't think that they would be cross, or snap your head off, or wonder audibly what theatre put on transpontine melodrama in these days, or say it was interesting to find that Sue still found readers. There would be nothing violent of this kind; only the slight movement of a weary brow, before the conversation flowed back to its proper channel of 'complexes' and skin disease. Because you see, the Georgian novelist knows that the stuff of which we have been talking is not Life, has no relation to Life, and in a word, doesn't happen. Exactly. And it all happened on the twenty-fifth of November, 1809, at Perleberg, a small Prussian town between Berlin and Hamburg. A coach and four drew up at the White Swan, and a tall, handsomely dressed man, wrapped up in a fur cloak lined with purple velvet, got down. He said he was in a hurry and wanted his lunch at once, and so, accompanied by his secretary and his servant, he entered the White Swan. It was noon when he arrived, and when he had finished his lunch he began to ask questions. Were there many soldiers stationed at Perleberg; who was in command? Captain Klitzing, of the Brandenburg Cuirassiers. Very good; where did he live? The stranger got the captain's address, and ordered his horses to be put in at once. He did not seem to notice two Jew dealers who came into the inn as he was lunching. He went to Captain Klitzing's house and found the captain with so bad a cold that he could hardly speak. The stranger said that he was Baron de Koch, that he was a merchant, and that he was now on a business journey to Hamburg. But, he added, trembling, he had seen something at the White Swan that frightened him, something that made him fear for his life; finally, that he would be grateful if Captain Klitzing would give him a guard during the few hours that he was at Perleberg. Captain Klitzing laughed at the request for a guard, whereon the stranger's nerves got worse and worse. So the Captain said he should have two of his cuirassiers, and as the Baron trembled with cold—or terror—he was given a cup of hot tea, and he drank it gratefully, his hands shaking so that some of the tea was spilt, Then he put on the fur cloak with the velvet lining and went back to the White Swan. He ordered the horses to be taken out of the carriage, and sat down with a pile of papers about him, and began to write at top speed.

Seven o'clock in the evening. The Baron finished writing, burnt some documents, and once more ordered the horses to be put in. The soldiers were told that they could go, and as some of the witnesses declared, the Baron strolled into the inn kitchen and hung about there among the stablemen and postboys. It was said that some of these fellows must have seen him drawing out a full, fat purse and dangling a handsome watch in an absentminded sort of way. In the street a dim oil lamp hung up high in the air, and a stableman with a horn lantern was helping the postboy to harness the horses. The Baron stood there in the street, watching the horses being put in. On the steps of the inn, the Baron's secretary, having paid the bill, was talking to the landlord. Everything was ready. The postillion was standing with his hand on the saddle, waiting for the word to mount and away . . . when it suddenly became evident that the Baron had vanished.

And the mystery was never solved; it remains a mystery to this day. No time was lost on that dark and bitter night of November 25, 1809. The White Swan was searched, the posting-house was searched in vain; there was no trace of the traveller in the stables, in the outhouses, or in the street. The secretary sent a messenger to Captain Klitzing; no news of the Baron there, since his afternoon call. Then more ransacking of all the houses of the quarter, everybody joining in—except the two Jew tradesmen, who got into their carriage and resumed their journey. People remarked that they were the only persons present who took no interest in the quest for the lost Baron. Captain Klitzing remembered that his visitor appeared to be in mortal terror, to anticipate some dreadful fate. The Captain had laughed at the time; but now he began to wonder. He sent some of his men to seize the vanished stranger's travelling carriage; he gave orders that the Baron's secretary and his servant should be detained at an inn at the other end of the town; soldiers are posted at the White Swan; the civil magistracy is dragged out of bed to lend its aid, and the civil magistracy beats up Perleberg all through the night; and finds nothing. Meanwhile, the active Klitzing examines the Baron's secretary, and makes some strange discoveries. To begin with; the secretary confessed that though he had been known as Fisher, he was really Krouse. And as for the 'Baron de Koch, merchant,' he wasn't a baron, and he wasn't a merchant. He was Sir

Benjamin Bathurst, late English Ambassador Extraordinary to Vienna. His mission to Vienna had failed, and he was making his way to England, via Hamburg. He had with him papers supposed to be of the highest importance. His false name, his lack of ambassadorial state were due to his desire to avoid the attentions of the French soldiers, who were then patrolling all Germany. Fisher, or Krouse, had been for some time a courier at the British Embassy at Vienna. The servant's name was Nicolaus Hilbert. Captain Klitzing left Perleberg, as he said, for a short journey of the utmost consequence. In reality, he consulted his military superior, who told him all about Sir Benjamin, the enormous importance of his mission, and the fury of Napoleon over the part which England had tried to play. But it was not known till later that before Sir Benjamin Bathurst left Vienna the Prussian Government had warned him to keep a sharp look-out on Krouse.

And after? Very little of consequence. The two Jew dealers were tracked to their abode. They were well-known people with the best of characters. The dubious Krouse and the servant pass out of the story. A week after the disappearance of Bathurst, his trousers were found in a thicket by two poor women gathering sticks. That thicket had been searched before without result. There were two bullet holes in one leg; but experts declared that the trousers had been held up, empty, to be fired at. In one pocket there was a letter, written, no doubt, at the White Swan. It was from Sir Benjamin to his wife. He told her of his fears. He was afraid, he said, that he would never see her or England any more. He added that if he were murdered it would be the doing of d'Entraigues, then the agent of Russia; a secret man, d'Entraigues, who had served all nations, and betrayed them all. And nothing more was ever known certainly. It was rumoured that Sir Benjamin was alive and a prisoner at Magdeburg, in French hands. Mrs Bathurst—perhaps a wife, perhaps a widow—resolved to follow up this clue. Nothing came of her journey, save this: that she found that her intention of making it was known in Paris before it was suspected in London. She returned to London, and there the secret man, d'Entraigues, called on her. He said that her husband was dead, that the Governor of Magdeburg had been his gaoler till, on the order of Napoleon, the prisoner had been 'put out of the Emperor's way.' And d'Entraigues promised to tell Mrs

Bathurst the whole story. But soon afterwards he was assassinated by a dismissed servant, who immediately committed suicide. People said that at last the secret man had paid the penalty of knowing too much.

Years later, in 1852, Mrs Thistlethwayte, Sir Benjamin Bathurst's sister, was told that a skeleton had been found buried under a stable in Perleberg. The skull had been fractured by a blow of a hatchet; there were circumstances which linked the former owner of the house with Sir Benjamin's visit to Perleberg; this man, named Mertens, had been a servant at the White Swan. But Mrs Thistlethwayte looked closely at the skull, and said that she was sure, from the shape, that it could not be her brother's.

But she may have been mistaken.

OUR BETTY'S DAY OUT

ON MONDAY, the first of January 1753, Mr Edward Lyon, of Aldermanbury, a London tradesman, gave his servant girl, Elizabeth Canning, a day out. She was to pay a visit to her uncle, Mr Thomas Colley, of Saltpetre Bank, spend the whole day with the family, and come back in the evening. And so Elizabeth duly turned up at the Colleys at twelve o'clock in the morning, and stayed till about nine in the evening. According to her uncle, Mr Colley the glassblower, the girl was looking very well indeed; 'I never saw her better, as I know of,' were his very words. For dinner there were potatoes and cold mutton, cooked on Sunday—England was always England! In the afternoon Mr Colley went to his work in the glasshouse, and Elizabeth and Mrs Colley, her aunt, had tea. Elizabeth did fairly well at dinner, not so well at tea, and not much with the roast sirloin of beef for supper. The party drank 'ten shilling beer,' but apparently in the strictest moderation. Then the evening wearing on, it was time for Elizabeth to get back to her place, and uncle and aunt saw her to the end of Houndsditch and left her there. This was some time after nine o'clock at night; and so the Colleys went home to Saltpetre Bank, and went to bed.

Apparently, Betty, as her friends called her, had stayed a little late at Saltpetre Bank, for Mr Lyon, her master, came to her mother, Mrs Canning, soon after nine, in some perturbation. He wondered, he said, that Elizabeth had stayed so long, and as she said, Mrs Canning was frightened out of her wits. She sent her three other children to beat about in the fields for their missing sister, and then she sent the apprentice to the Colleys. The Colleys, roused from their bed at midnight, could only say that they had seen Betty well on her way down Houndsditch. Very definitely, Betty was not to be found anywhere.

The poor mother did all she could. She advertised for her daughter two or three times; but heard nothing of her. She went to all the people and places she could think of, enquiring for Elizabeth; no result. She tried the Wood Street Compter, where drunks and disorderlies and waifs and strays, and all the flotsam and jetsam of midnight London were apt to be carried in those days; and if you want to know what the Wood Street Compter, with its inhabitants, two-legged and six-legged, was like, you had better read Ned Ward's *London Spy*. But the Compter knew nothing of Miss Canning. Then, the Church was called in. Bills entreating the prayers of the congregation for Elizabeth's return were given in at the Aldermanbury Church and at the Cripplegate Church, and at the meetings, and at Mr Wesley's. Nothing happened! Then Mrs Canning seems to have murmured to herself some equivalent of the classic tag: if the heights do nothing, I will even move the depths. She consulted a person variously known as 'the conjurer,' 'the astrologer,' and 'the cunning man'; and he seemed to know something, though Mrs Canning was vague as to the exact nature of the interview.

The cunning man lived in the Old Bailey. He had a black wig over his face, and his fee was a shilling. He was on the whole consoling: he said, 'Make yourself easy, she'll come home again.' His method of divination is to me obscure. 'He only asked me two or three questions,' said Mrs Canning, 'and wrote scribble, scribble, scribble along.' But when the lady was asked whether the cunning man had mentioned an old woman in connection with her daughter, then her story becomes confused. At first she denied that the astrologer had said anything about an old woman, and then again that he might have done so; 'for what I know.'

'Whether he did not tell you that she was in the hands of an old black woman?' was the next question.

'The word 'black' I don't remember,' replied Mrs Canning. 'I know he frighted me. When he shut the door, and lighted the candles up, he looked so frightful, I was glad to get out at the door again.'

Somehow I am reminded of a certain story of the inimitable W.W. Jacobs, a story about Mr and Mrs Boxer, and a mother-in-law, and a cunning man named Silver. Mr Boxer said, after the consultation, that he thought somebody had been talking; and I wonder whether some-body had been talking to the conjuror of the Old Bailey.

But the days went by; and still there was no trace or sign of the missing Elizabeth. There was some indistinct story told by 'a gentle-woman at an oil-shop, the sign of the Two Jars, through Bishopsgate, towards Cornhill.' She said she had heard a 'young voice' scream out in a coach on the night of Elizabeth's disappearance, but nothing came of this. But at last, on the night of January 29th, at about quarter after ten o'clock, Elizabeth returned to her mother's house.

Thus James Lord, the apprentice: 'I have been apprentice to Elizabeth Canning's mother between six and seven years. . . . On the 29th of January, the night before King Charles's Martyrdom, I was just going to make fast the door, going to bed; somebody lifted up the latch; it goes with a bit of string; mistress was down upon her knees a-praying to see her apparition, before she came in.' This, the apprentice explained, he had seen Mrs Canning doing several times, since her daughter's disappearance, 'praying to God to hear somewhat of her . . .'

'I had the candle in my hand, and was going to make fast the door, and she came in: mistress was praying; mistress asked who was there? I then looked her up in the face, and thought it was somebody else come to enquire tidings after her; I did not know her at first: after I had looked her in the face again, she frightened me because she looked in such a deplorable condition.'

The 'prentice cried out it was 'Our Betty,' and Mrs Canning fell down in a fit.

There seems no doubt that our Betty was in a most deplorable condition. She was e'en almost spent, said James Lord; 'she was e'en almost dead, as black as the chimney-stock, black and blue.' She was scarcely clad in miserable clouts and an old dirty ragged bed-gown—a dressing-gown is, I think, indicated—and a petticoat that looked as if it had been draggled in country dirt. Different people had different theories about the 'black and blue' appearance of the unfortunate girl's face and arms and hands. The apprentice thought that she looked as if she had been beaten, a family friend took it to be numbness, occasioned by cold, and it was, indeed, very cold weather. And Mr Bakler, the apothecary, who was called in on January 30th, said that he found Elizabeth in a very low and weak condition, 'very much emaciated and wasted,' 'half-starved,' 'with cold clammy sweats upon her,' 'her arms were black and livid,' and her nails 'of a sort of bluish cast.' And the physician, Dr Eaton, confirmed the apothecary. Elizabeth Canning, he declared, was in a very weak state; her symptoms corresponded with those of a person 'that had suffered hunger, thirst, and cold, and great hardship.'

Mrs Canning, in her vivid manner, described her daughter's entrance. 'When she came up so,' said the mother, 'I took her to be an apparition'; and she proceeded to exhibit to the Court, before which she was giving evidence, the strange manner of this coming up. 'She came in this posture,' bending double and walking sideways, holding her hands before her. And the news of this marvellous return went like fire about the dark street, and neighbours came pouring in from all sides, tumbling out of their beds, no doubt, in their eagerness to hear the story. But, oddly enough, when we try to discover what story they did hear, we find ourselves entangled in doubts and difficulties. According to Mrs Canning, Elizabeth said that she had been set on by two men soon after her uncle Colley left her in Houndsditch; that these two men had first robbed her of her money—about twelve shillings—had then given her a violent blow and pulled her along in an unconscious or semi-unconscious state, till coming to herself, she found that she was on a large road, where there was water. Then the two men took her to a house, and she was shut up in a room with hay in it. There was an old woman in that house and two young women; and peering out through some chink or crevice of her prison, she saw the Hertford coach going along the large road. And she spoke of some Mother Wells or Wills in connection with the house where she had been kept a prisoner.

Now there are difficulties here. When Elizabeth swore her information before the Alderman, she said nothing about the hay in the room, though she gave a close description of the room. And—more important, Mr Scarrat, a neighbour, a strong believer in Miss Canning's story, declared that he had said on the night of the return: 'I'll lay a guinea to a farthing she has been at Mother Wells's, for that is as noted a house as any is: she said, her name is Mother Wills or

Wells.' And it seems pretty clear that it was Mr Scarrat who suggested the name Wells; and, pleased with his success, Mr Scarrat proceeded to suggest a great deal more, and Elizabeth agreed with everything; and they got on very comfortably indeed in this fashion, till a most remarkable story shaped itself, which led to three criminal trials, one sentence of death, and one of seven year's transportation to New England. A remarkable story indeed; since there is no reason to suppose that there was a word of truth in it from beginning to end.

℘

Last week it was told how Elizabeth Canning, a London servant girl, given a day out on January 1, 1753, disappeared, but turned up on January 29, with the story that she had been set upon, beaten, kidnapped and robbed.

But where had Elizabeth Canning been from January 1 to January 29, 1753? That question must wait a little. We must deal first of all with the story she told when she crawled into her mother's house.

Now, as I said last week, there are great difficulties in getting at the exact truth here. Here was this girl, in miserable condition, with suggestions and leading questions pouring in upon her on every hand; what did she say at the moment? Probably the first outline was that she was set upon by two men Houndsditch way, hit hard by one of them, robbed, dragged, half-senseless, past Bedlam to some house on the Hertford road, where she had been shut up till her escape on January 29. But this simple tale was elaborated. A couple of days after the return of Elizabeth she and her friends went before Mr Alderman Chitty and applied for a warrant gainst Susannah Wells, of Enfield Wash, on a suspicion of having robbed Elizabeth Canning of a pair of stays of the value of ten shillings—a hanging matter in these days. Susannah, it may be stated, from the beginning was by no means a lady of high virtue, and her house in Enfield Wash was, in the delicate phrase of Smollett, a house of no very extraordinary fame. Alderman Chitty was dubious. Could Elizabeth describe the room where she had been shut up? Certainly: it was a little, square, dark room, in which was an old stool or two, an old table, and an old picture above the chimney. Here was Elizabeth imprisoned, and here she slept, as she said, on the bare boards. Whereupon the Alderman issued his warrant, and the next day Elizabeth and her friend went down to Enfield Wash, carrying the officer and his warrant with them.

The officious Mr Scarrat was one of the party. He, it will be remembered, was one of the swarm of neighbours who poured into Mrs Canning's house on the night of Elizabeth's return; it was he who, hearing some broken phrase about the Hertford road, immediately said the house where Elizabeth had been shut up must be Mother Wells's. And, by the way, it turned out that Mr Scarrat knew Mrs Wells's house quite well. But Mr Scarrat, for one reason or another, had become an enthusiastic champion of Elizabeth's story, and he and his friend, Adamson, went on in advance of the rest of the party, and secured all the people they found in Mrs Wells's house. These were Mrs Wells, a girl named Virtue Hall, a very hideous old gipsy, Mary Squires, her son and her daughters, a man with the old name of Fortune Natus, and Judith, his wife.

Now when Scarrat and Adamson made this sudden raid of theirs, they immediately went all over the house to find the room in which the girl had been shut up. She had given her description to the Alderman, and, no doubt, their task would be easy. But it was nothing of the kind. There was no room which answered in the least to Elizabeth's description. But the two zealous men were not to be outdone, and settled on a sort of loft, or lumber-room, which was approached from the kitchen by a door and a short flight of stairs. And in this loft there was a great deal of hay, and as it turned out, the labourer, Fortune Natus, and his wife, Judith, slept on a hay-bed there. Now Elizabeth had said nothing about hay; she said she had slept on the bare boards. And, worse still, she had described the room as square, dark, and little. But it wasn't square, and it wasn't little. It was thirty-five feet long by nine feet eight inches broad. And, far from being dark, it was singularly light. Moreover, the things which the girl had said were in the room, were not in the room. So Adamson rode back and met Elizabeth's coach, and asked her if there was any hay in her prison. Whereupon Elizabeth said, 'Oh, yes'; and the case became clear.

The girl was brought to the house and taken into the kitchen. The door to the loft was left open, but she did not say: 'That's the place where they shut me up.' She took no notice of it, and said nothing. Then she was brought into the room where all the people of the house had been enclosed, and arranged in a certain order. Mother Wells sat on the right side of the chimney, the hideous old gipsy woman, Mary Squires, on the left. And, let it be noted, that the ugliness of old Mary was something far beyond the measure of common ugliness; as the poor creature said of her face, 'God never made such another.' And yet, Elizabeth Canning had said nothing of this. We may conjecture, if we will, that Susannah Wells, whom Mr Scarrat knew quite well, was an ordinary-looking old woman.

And now an odd thing happened. Between the arrival of Elizabeth at the house, and her being taken into the parlour where Mother Wells and the other people of the house were detained there was an interval of five minutes. In that interval, the old women changed places; we are not told why. And so, when Elizabeth came into the parlour, she at once identified Mary Squires as the woman who had robbed her of her stays. In vain the gipsy protested that she was in Abbotsbury, in Dorsetshire, on the first of January, and for several days after; in vain her son said the same. Mary Squires was arrested, tried for her life, found guilty and sentenced to death. Three good men of Abbotsbury, in Dorset, swore that Mary Squires, her son and her daughter were down in their country from the 1st of January to the 10th. But the jury took no notice of what was said by John Williams, or William Clarke, or Thomas Greville.

And here it may be explained that all London had gone mad over the case. Everybody was quite sure that Elizabeth Canning was a heroine, and that anybody who was not quite sure of this was a scoundrel. I don't know in the least how this happened; there never was, and there never has been, a popular delusion—say, rather, mania—in any way comparable with it. The Russians and the Angels of 1914 were popular delusions, but they were at least comfortable lies at a time when comfort was badly needed. But what comfort could there be in believing that a humble servant-girl had been robbed of her stays and shut up in a hay-loft and kept there on bread and water? I do not know; but, nevertheless, all London foamed at the mouth as it contemplated the virtue of Elizabeth Canning. As for the few who doubted Elizabeth, they declared that the Methodists had something to do with it, thereby showing that there were fools outside the Canning party as well as in it. So far as I can see, the only circumstance that can be pleaded in justification of the Canning maniacs is the fact that Elizabeth said the old gipsy told her that if she would go their way— not the way of virtue, but the way of Virtue Hall—she should be richly dressed.

Well, the time drew near for the gipsy's execution. Luckily for her, the Lord Mayor of London, Sir Crisp Gascoyne, presiding judge at the Old Bailey trial, made up his mind that it wouldn't do. He, therefore, held an inquiry and laid a memorial before the King, who in his turn laid the case before his attorney-general and solicitor-general. Mary Squires was first respited and then received a free pardon, and one feels sure that poor old Mary never lacked a subject of conversation for the rest of her days.

And then came the great case. On the 29th April, 1754, Elizabeth Canning was set to the bar at the Old Bailey and charged with wilful and corrupt perjury, with 'taking her corporal oath and swearing upon the holy gospel of God'—to a mass of lies, specified at some little length in the indictment, which runs to five thousand words, and must have taken an hour to read. The whole matter was resifted with the utmost thoroughness. Witnesses for Mary Squires who had been terrorised by threats of violence, so that they were afraid to give evidence at the first trial, now appeared; and the County of Dorset, one might almost say, trooped up to town to confirm the report of John Williams, William Clarke and Thomas Greville, valiant men of Abbotsbury. Thirty-two of them, farmers, ale-house keepers, school-masters, excisemen, carters, servants, maltsters, threshers, weavers, carpenters, blacksmiths: all the life and state of the Dorset countryside took their corporal oaths on the holy gospel of God that Mary Squires could not be at Enfield Wash in the beginning of January, for the sound and sufficient reason that they had seen her, bought goods of her, drunk with her in Abbotsbury and round and about Abbotsbury on the various dates from January 1 onwards of the year 1753.

DREADS AND DROLLS

Thus Melchisidech Arnold, Blacksmith and violinist: 'I am a blacksmith and live at Abottsbury; I know the old woman perfectly well, and the girl on the left hand, and the man behind her; they are her son and daughter; the last time I saw them all three was in January last twelvemonth . . . the young man and young woman danced and I played on the violin.' And all the rest of the Dorset chorus to much the same effect, giving us, by the way, a wonderfully vivid picture of life in the West Country 172 years ago. And at the end the jury, still firmly believing in their hearts in the virtue of Elizabeth Canning, strange as it may appear, were induced by the court to find Elizabeth Canning guilty of wilful and corrupt perjury, and she was transported to New England for seven years.

But where had she been and what was she doing or suffering from the night of January 1, 1753, to the night of January 29? Nobody knows, and I suppose that nobody ever will know. The Crown suggested, feebly enough, that there might have been a baby in the case; but brought not a jot of evidence in support of this suggestion. Then the Crown, more feebly still, hinted that Elizabeth might have been undergoing a certain specified medical treatment; but the physician who was called in on Elizabeth's return, declared that this was quite out of the question. The Crown hinted again that Mr Scarrat, the officious, knew a great deal about the case that he had not divulged; but nothing came of that.

The problem of Elizabeth Canning is one of those puzzles which will never be solved.

HOW THE RICH LIVE

THIS IS TO BE a talk about some wealthy men that I have known and heard of. I was once a wealthy man myself; a friend of mine confessed to me quite lately that he had been a capitalist in his day; and then there is a great figure in musical history, known well enough for his work, but not generally recognised as being amongst the very rich. To begin with my friend. This is Mr Lenville, the well-known actor. We were talking the other day as we often do talk about the old times of the stage, of which I know a very little, and he a great deal; the old times being understood to be somewhere between thirty and forty years ago. There is no doubt that they were bad old times. Now a bright young gentleman 'walks on' for six months or so. He has little paragraphs in the papers about the amazingly brilliant way in which he walks on, and how interesting it is that he should walk on at all. Then he has a small part; and there are portraits and clever caricatures as well as paragraphs. Then he models in clay a little, and the public interest, as the paragraphists declare, is enormous, so that he gets quite a large part and delivers it so naturally that very few people beyond the front row of the stalls hear a word he says. The bright young man's fortune is then made. Things were very different in the time of which Mr Lenville was talking. In those days people had to learn how to act before they were heard of in the western theatres of London. They learned how to act by playing dozens, hundreds of parts in all sorts of obscure playhouses in the country and in the unknown suburbs. They laboured in stock companies in northern towns, at the Britannia, Hoxton; they went on tour in repertory. They were hungry for experience—and for bread and cheese and beer. They tried the booths for a while, some of them, and learned what 'nunty munjare' means, and how to put the 'portable' together, take it to pieces, and get the snow off the roof; also to paint scenery and manufacture dress shirts and shoes and mediaeval armour out of white paper, American cloth, and sheet tin, and, by the way, to learn the text of any part ever written in rather less than no time. I remember one of the old stock managers saying to me:

'So I made up my mind to put up "Venice Preserved," and gave the company three days for study. The Heavy Man said to me: "Look here, I can't study the Cardinal in three days." I talked to him. "You play the Heavy Lead, don't you?" "Yes," he said, "but I can't study 500 lengths in three days." "Well, the Cardinal is the heavy part, isn't it?" "I know." "Then," said I, "you'd better go"; and one of the Responsibles took it on, and was perfect on the night.'

Well, it was of such times as those that Mr Lenville was telling me. He and his friend, Mr Folair, were in a very bad way. There was nothing doing, and very little to eat. So the two of them walked up one fine morning to the Grand, Islington, where a stock company was running, in the hopes of getting an engagement. But there was no vacancy. They came out into the sunlight, with twopence between them, and walked over to the Angel, and, boldly entering the public bar, ordered a pint of four ale, which they drank slowly, in alternate sips, out of the pewter pot. And as they drank, they discussed the best way to walk home. This was an easy problem for Lenville, who lived in Marylebone, but a formidable business for Folair, an inhabitant of uttermost Hammersmith. And so Lenville gave his views on the subject of the shortest cut to Hammersmith, illustrating his remarks by drawing a kind of diagram, or map, with his stick on the sawdust of the floor.

'Here you see,' said Lenville, 'you get up by Portobello Road,' and drew the stick firmly along in the direction of Notting Hill Gate. *Something glittered in the disturbed sawdust.* The two men hardly dared to believe in that which they saw. It was a half-sovereign—otherwise wealth beyond the dreams of avarice. 'Do we hand it over to the barman?' whispered Folair. Lenville replied in words which signified that they emphatically didn't, and as he spoke his pipe dropped from his hand on to the floor. He picked it up, and soon after the pair of players were having some more beer and sharing the change.

'And I never felt so well off before or since.' So Mr Lenville ended his tale.

And I, too, I have known wealth in my day. I was living in Queer Street at the time, a quiet place enough to look at, but not really so quiet as it seemed, being close to a certain Grove, where there are streets even queerer. Well, in those days, I went out regularly to get the supper beer. Not in the honest, manly way of the Briton, who carries the jug in his hand and boldly enters the jug and bottle department, rejoicing in the brown foam that crowns the vessel. This was too high for me; so I used to go to the saloon bar and buy a quart bottle of beer and smuggle it back in a bag or great coat pocket, the whole being done in a very careless, easy manner. But one night there was only fivepence-halfpenny in the house. It is true the bottle of beer cost only fourpence; but it was my custom every evening to have a small glass of something with bitters in it. This cost threepence; and I was ashamed to go to the public-house and omit this decorative part of the cere-mony—and yet there was only fivepence-halfpenny in the house. And then, as I fumbled aimlessly, desperately, about in odd corners and disused places, there appeared and was manifested in a dusty drawer, a shabby little old purse, with a broken fastening. I opened the purse, and at the bottom of it was a sixpence and a shilling, both black from lying by. How rich, how glorious a superfluity! I tasted in their acutest savours the delights of wealth!

The last story of the wealthy was told of himself by the mighty John Sebastian Bach. When he was a lad—it was soon after his voice had broken—he had a great desire to hear an illustrious organist of Ham-burg, one Reinken. Bach was very poor, and the long journey had to be done on foot, and coming back, he found himself a far way from his home, with hardly any money left in his pockets. He sat down on a bench outside an inn, very hungry, very weary. Suddenly, a window was opened, and two herring heads fell at Bach's feet. He picked them up; there might be a scrap or two of herring left that he might eat. And behold! he found on examination that in each head was a piece of gold. He never found out how it had happened, but, refreshed, he went back and heard the great Reinken once more, and was able to go on his way home at ease and rejoicing.

So much of wealthy men. I once knew a poor man. He was a country squire with an income of ten thousand a year, in the time when ten thousand bought twice as much as it will buy today. This squire wished very violently to set up a coach and four, and to possess a steam yacht; but found that he could hardly afford the upkeep of both. In the end, he fixed on the coach, and drove it about bravely enough and tried to smile. But he longed all the while, very bitterly and grievously, for the steam yacht.

I was sorry for him.

THE HIGHBURY MYSTERY

WHEN THOMAS PINCH and his sister Ruth, having accomplished their unpleasant discussion with the brass-and-copper founder of Camberwell, went into the wild of London to look for lodgings, Tom suggested Islington as a promising quarter for their search. It is needless to say that Tom knew nothing whatever about Islington—or any other part of London. But an old phrase was in his mind, and it tempted him.

'It used to be called Merry Islington, once upon a time,' said Tom. 'Perhaps it's merry now; if so, it's all the better. Eh?'

'If it's not too dear,' said Tom's sister.

'Of course, if it's not too dear,' assented Tom. 'Well, where is Islington? We can't do better than go there, I should think. Let's go.'

So far as I remember they did not find much mirth in Islington, though they did find two bedrooms and a triangular parlour which suited them very well. But the fact is that Tom Pinch went to Islington a little too late; just as I went to the old Fleet Street tavern in 1881, hoping to meet there the Principal Wits of the Town: a little too late. Islington was once a noted place for its houses of entertainment, for its bottled ale and skittles, its cakes, custard, stewed prunes, and so forth; and thus merry to seventeenth and eighteenth-century London. And in an Islington tavern just 160 years ago there was a meeting not devoid of mirth, or at least of cheerfulness, which yet linked itself on to a mysterious and terrible crime; the murder of Thomas Jenkyns, a retired merchant, of Enfield Wash. The body of this Thomas Jenkyns was found on the night of September 23, 1765. It was lying in a pool of blood in a field near Highbury. The poor man's throat had been cut from ear to ear, as the two men who found the corpse declared. And as for these two men, Thomas Brown and Richard Staple, inhabitants of

45

some festering maze of alleys between Holborn and Clerkenwell, I am afraid they did not bear the best of characters. Bow Street knew them, and they were known also at the taproom of the Bell, where they met friends of the same way of thinking as themselves. There had been a little highway robbery and a little burglary in their stories, and they had just missed the gallows more than once. So it may be as well not to consider too curiously what the two were doing in Highbury Fields at ten o'clock of this dark September night. Mr Thomas Brown told of the horror of his friend and himself when they stumbled on the murdered man.

'We were hard put to it to know what to do,' he declared. 'It seemed as if the poor man's head was almost cut away from his body, and I said to my friend, Richard Staple, who was with me, 'Why, Dick,' said I, 'this is a villainous to do. For if we shift to raise the body, 'tis a great chance that the man's head will fall apart, and I cannot abide the thought of it.' 'Why, Tom,' said he, 'I am much of your mind in the business. What if we leave ill work as it lies, and go home peaceably by another way.' But I would not have that neither, lest, as I said, we should both be nabbed for the fact and come to Tyburn at last. And so we made shift to raise the dead man tenderly, I holding his head to his shoulders and trembling a great deal, and in this way bore him as far as Islington, without any misadventure, it being late of a dark night, with a cold wind rising, and very black clouds, and scarce anyone abroad.'

This is, certainly, not a very merry opening, and, indeed, mirth is only a brief interlude in the tale. The cheerful relief is afforded by the evidence of Simon Murchison, who kept a snuff-shop in Norton Folgate, of William Frost, a brass-founder, of Clerkenwell, and of Abraham Lewis, clockmaker, of Devizes. It was largely on their evidence that Anthony Mullins, citizen and haberdasher, was arrested and charged with the murder, a week after the discovery of the crime by the dubious Brown and Staple. The three elderly tradesmen had met by chance—they had not known each other before—at the Bowl and Sword tavern at Islington on the afternoon of September 23, and had got into conversation, all agreeing that things were not as they were in the reign of King George II.

'We all grew to be pretty dismal over the bad times,' said Abraham Lewis, ' 'till at last I said, "Why, this will never end it or mend it. Come! let us go and bump it at Dog and Duck, and I will be surety for the first bowl of punch, the lowest notch of the three to be debtor for the second." '

The three went out into the alley behind the tavern, and it is interesting to note that Mr Murchison ordered pipes and a plate of tobacco, and that Mr Frost paid for a bottle of brandy 'to hearten the bowl,' and so they went to their match, which Mr Frost won.

'And while we were in the garden-house at the side of the alley, drinking our punch, and smoking tobacco, and talking of the game, two men came out from the tavern and sat on a bench by the wall, speaking together very seriously, but not as we could hear what they said. They called for liquor and drank two glasses apiece and went out, and we saw no more of them.' The three identified the murderer and the murdered.

'I know him,' said Lewis, pointing to Mullins, 'by his great beaked nose, and the dead man I could swear to any day, for as he lifted his glass I saw that his little finger was crooked back as if it had been broken, and I saw the body, and the little finger was crooked as I saw it on the live man.' Then Frost had seen the prisoner read a paper which Jenkyns had given to him, and Mullins had drawn out a tortoiseshell and gold spectacle-case of curious workmanship, and just such a spectacle-case was found on Mullins when he was taken. There were other witnesses who had seen Mullins and Jenkyns walking on the way to Highbury Fields a little later in the afternoon: there seemed no doubt as to the verdict which the jury would bring in.

Then came the surprise of the case. The prisoner's two clerks, Mr Osborne and Mr Nichols, swore that their master had not stirred out of his counting-house from dinner time till eight o'clock in the evening. Osborne sat at a high desk facing Mr Mullins's private counting-house, which was separated from the rest of the room by a glass partition. Nichols's stool was under a window and commanded a view of the door.

'I was busy with a great account,' said Osborne, 'but ever and again I looked up from my book, and there sat my master, as he was always accustomed, but very still.'

Counsel: 'Was he not used, then, to sit still in, his counting-house?'

Osborne: 'Why, not so. He would rise now and again commonly, and walk a little to and fro, and so sit down again. And twice or thrice in an hour he would come out and speak with us about the occasions of the day.'

Counsel: 'And did he not stir at all on this afternoon?'

Osborne: 'He sat still at his desk and never moved till it was past eight in the evening.'

And then a very curious point arose. Nichols, the other clerk, had been strangely overcome towards the end of the afternoon. He had come up to Osborne, looking very ill and pale, as Osborne said, and complaining that his heart was heavy, and that 'he was sadly oppressed.' Osborne, belonging to a pre-scientific age, advised his fellow-clerk to go to the Mitre and drink a little ale, and Nichols did so, 'looking fearfully to the place where Mr Mullins sat, with no candle by him.' A moment later, Mr Mullins rose and came down to the general counting-house and asked Osborne where his fellow was. On hearing of his occupation, Mullins said, 'Ah, poor child! He might do worse than drink a cup of ale.' Then Nichols returned, and soon after the two clerks went on their way, one to his lodgings by Pedlar's Acre, the other to see the fireworks, at Marylebone Gardens. But when counsel for the Crown cross-examined Nichols as to the nature and cause of his seizure, the witness said:

'There came a great trembling upon me, and a dread on my heart and a sickness in my stomach . . . and I feared very much. And so I looked round on my stool to see if my fellow Osborne was in his place, and looking down on the floor of the counting-house I could have sworn that there was a great pool of blood there, with bubbles of blood in it, and I had almost swooned away.'

Naturally, Mullins was acquitted on the evidence of his two clerks. But what is the solution of the puzzle? When I treated this curious case some time ago, I mentioned the theory that has been advanced by some occultists of our day. These persons hold that while the natural body of Anthony Mullins was committing murder at Highbury, his 'astral' body appeared all the while in the counting-house in the City. I was unable to accept this tempting solution, and declared my opinion that the two clerks perjured themselves to save their master from the gallows. But there is this difficulty: Why should the clerk Nichols have invented the outrageous tale of the visionary pool of blood?

DEADLY NEVERGREEN

THERE IS A great talk of ghosts just now. They call them spirits, but ghosts is the good and ancient word of England. These ghosts come when the lights are out, and utter nothing or very little of consequence; and sometimes their remarks are 'evidential' and sometimes they are not 'evidential,' and on the whole nothing much happens. But how is it—if ghosts are, in fact, accustomed to revisit the lands beneath the moon—that anyone dares to pass the intersection of the Edgware Road with the Oxford Road after night has fallen? For it is stated that the ghosts of men who have died violently are given to revisit the scenes of their taking off. The murdered haunt the places of their dreadful endings; how is it, then, that the site of Tyburn Tree is not dense with the spirits of the great multitude of men and women who perished awfully there during the space of three hundred years or more? One would have said that the very ground would cry out with the agony of all these unhappy souls, that perished there by the old torturous method of execution: the cart driven on, the poor wretch left dangling in the air, to strangle by slow and excruciating degrees. But there are no reports of ghosts by the place of Deadly Nevergreen, Tyburn Tree.

One of the strangest of the ends made at Tyburn was that of Lord Ferrers, who was executed on May 5, 1760, for the murder of his steward, John Johnson. It is probable that Lord Ferrers was, in fact, a homicidal maniac, but, being tried by his peers, he was found guilty of murder and condemned to death, and accordingly was hanged with infinite pomp and ceremony. Every courtesy was shown this unhappy nobleman. He was allowed to drive from the Tower to Tyburn in his own landau, drawn by six horses, instead of in the mourning coach which had been provided by some friends. Mr Sheriff Vaillant attended him, and observed 'that it gave him the highest concern to wait upon him upon so melancholy an occasion, but that he would do everything in his power to render his situation as easy as possible.' Earl Ferrers replied politely, and, being dressed in light clothes, embroidered with silver, remarked that his dress might seem strange, but that he had a reason for wearing it. It is said that this gay and rich habit was his lordship's wedding suit, and that he remarked that the latter occasion was as good a one for wearing it as the former. And so the procession set forth: a large number of the constables of Middlesex, a party of horse-grenadiers, and a party of foot, Mr Sheriff Errington's coach, the famous landau and six, Mr Sheriff Vaillant's chariot, a mourning coach and six, and lastly a hearse and six. This horrid pageantry set out from the Tower soon after nine, but moved so slowly that Tyburn was not reached till a quarter to twelve. The condemned man behaved with the greatest calmness, hinted very politely to the chaplain that he was a Deist, censured the late Lord Bolingbroke for suffering his religious sentiments to be given to the world, and as to the late Mr Johnson, whom he had shot dead, protested that he had not the slightest malice against him, but 'he had met with so many crosses and vexations he scarce knew what he did'—he had been a good deal worried, as we should put it.

At last the procession got as far as Drury Lane, and here Lord Ferrers said that he was thirsty and would like a glass of wine and water. But Mr Sheriff Valliant pointed out that the dense crowd would become still denser if a halt were made, and that his lordship might be disturbed thereby, whereupon the Earl answered: 'That's true, I say no more, let us by no means stop.' They drew near to Tyburn, and Earl Ferrers said that there was a person waiting in a coach, for whom he had a very sincere regard, and of whom he would be glad to take leave before he died. Again the Sheriff was polite, but firm. He said that if his lordship insisted it should be so, 'but that he wished his lordship, for his own sake, would decline it, lest the sight of a person, for whom he had such regard, should unman him, and disarm him of the fortitude he possessed.' Again my lord gave way, and now the landau was over against the place of death.

And here it is to be noted that there were two instruments of execution at Tyburn. One was the permanent three-legged structure, the true Tyburn Tree which stood where the two roads meet. The other was a temporary scaffold sometimes erected in the Oxford road, by the park railings. It was on this scaffold that Lord Ferrers suffered. It was covered with black baize, and on two black cushions the condemned man and the chaplain knelt and repeated the Lord's Prayer together. Lord Ferrers took leave of the chaplain and the two sheriffs with many polite expressions, desiring Mr Sheriff Vaillant to be so good as to accept his watch. Then he called for the executioner, who desired his forgiveness, and his lordship, intending to give the man five guineas, gave it to the assistant hangman by mistake. Hence an 'unseasonable dispute between these unthinking wretches.' But Mr Sheriff Vaillant instantly ended that. And then:

'His neckcloth being taken off, a white cap, which his lordship had brought in his pocket, being put upon his head, his arms secured by a black sash from incommoding himself, and the cord put round his neck, he advanced by three steps upon an elevation in the middle of the scaffold, where part of the floor had been raised about eighteen inches higher than the rest, and standing under the cross-beam which went over it, covered with black baize, he asked the executioner, 'Am I right?' Then the cap was drawn over his face; and then, upon a signal given by the sheriff (for his lordship, upon being asked, declined to give one himself), that part upon which he stood instantly sunk down from beneath his feet, and left him entirely suspended; but not having sunk down so low as was designed, it was immediately pressed down, and levelled with the rest of the floor. For a few seconds his lordship made some struggles against the attacks of death, but was soon eased of all pain by the pressure of the executioner.'

It was his lordship's misfortune that he made the experiment of the New Drop in a very early and ineffective stage of that invention.

It was one of the ugly features of the eighteenth century that it was by no means the rough mob of London that alone took pleasure in these hideous scenes. Boswell was an amateur of executions, and there were many elegant gentlemen who made a point of being present and write to each other, in unspeakably loathsome terms, on the matter. Thus Gilly Williams writes to George Selwyn :

'Harrington's porter was condemned yesterday. Cadogan and I have already bespoke places at the Brazier's. I presume we shall have your honour's company, if your stomach is not too squeamish for a single swing.'

And so again, the Earl of Carlisle, another of Selwyn's correspondents, writes of Hackman, the murderer of Miss Reay:

'He was long at his prayers; and when he flung down his handkerchief for the signal for the cart to move on, Jack Ketch, instead of instantly whipping on the horse, jumped on the other side of him to snatch up the handkerchief, lest he should lose his rights. He then returned, to the head of the cart, and jehu'd him out of the world.'

Dickens has been accused of grossly libelling the famous Lord Chesterfield by his character of Sir John Chester in *Barnaby Rudge*. All good friends of Dr Johnson will agree that it is impossible to speak too harshly of the detestable Chesterfield. But, that apart, it is doubtful whether a more odious type has ever existed than the bad Whig noble of the eighteenth century.

POLITE CORRESPONDENCE

THEY TALK MUCH of Dr Johnson's Letter to Lord Chesterfield. Certainly, it is an amazing, a triumphant epistle. It is, perhaps, the palmary example of how agony long endured, shame, misery and humiliation can at last turn to flame and a sword, and rend and devour and hew asunder the wretched tormentor who is found at last to be but a Wig and buckram and a grin and a black heart.

Listen to the phrases. They are well known, and yet I think that they cannot be too well known.

'When upon some slight encouragement I first visited your Lordship, I was overpowered, like the rest of mankind, by the enchantment of your address; and could not forbear to wish that I might boast myself *Le vainqueur du vainqueur de la terre*—that I might obtain that regard for which I saw the world contending; but I found myself so little encouraged that neither pride nor modesty would suffer me to continue it. When I had once addressed your Lordship in publick, I had exhausted all the art of pleasing which a retired and uncourtly scholar can possess. I had done all that I could, and no man is well pleased to have his all neglected, be it ever so little.

'Seven years, my Lord, have now passed since I waited in your outward rooms, or was repulsed from your door; during which time I have been pushing on my work through difficulties of which it is useless to complain, and have brought it at last, to the verge of publication, without one act of assistance, one word of encouragement, or one smile of favour. Such treatment I did not expect, for I never had a Patron before . . . the notice which you have been pleased to take of my labours, had it been early, had been kind; but it has been delayed till I am indifferent, and cannot enjoy it; till I am solitary, and cannot impart it; till I am known and do not want it.'

'Till I am solitary and cannot impart it.' Johnson's wife had died in the interval between the beginning and the end of the Dictionary. An absurd woman, they say, many years older than Johnson, given to 'cordials' somewhat too freely, given also to the extravagant use of paint as applied to the face; but yet the Doctor loved her dearly. It would have been an exquisite joy to tell his 'Tetty' how the great Lord Chesterfield was the fervent friend of the poor, ragged, starving scholar, the approver of his work and his helper in it. But Tetty was dead, and it had never been possible to utter that comfortable word; and so, I say, agony turns to flaming fire, to this great letter of denunciation.

There is no letter that I know of worthy of being compared with it. But Johnson's letter is tragedy; the spectacle of a soul on fire, while yet the tears rain down from the man's eyes. There is no spectacle, I think, that can be paralleled with this. But if I were compiling an anthology of letters, I believe that I could find something on the comic side, worthy at least of being in the same volume.

A little way off the white limestone road that winds by the river from Newport to Caerleon-on-Usk, in Monmouthshire, there is, or was, an ancient dwelling called St Julians. In this place lived, in the time of Queen Elizabeth, a certain Sir William Herbert, third son of the first Earl of Pembroke. This gentleman was once annoyed by a Mr Morgan, who is only known as the object of Sir William's fury. And thus we begin:

'Sir—Peruse this letter in God's name. Be not disquieted. I reverence your hoary hair. Although in your son I find too much folly and lewdness, yet in you I expect gravity and wisdom. It hath pleased your son, late of Bristol, to deliver a challenge to a man of mine, on the behalf of a gentleman (as he said) "as good as myself"—who he was, he named not, neither do I know; but if he be as good as myself, it must be either for virtue, for birth, for ability, or for calling and dignity: for virtue, I think he meant not, for it is a thing which exceeds his judgment; if for birth, he must be the heir male of an Earl, the heir in blood of ten Earls, for in testimony thereof I bear their several coats. Besides, he must be of the blood royal, for by my grandmother Devereux, I am lineally and legitimately descended out of the body of

Edward IV. If for ability, he must have a thousand pounds a year in possession, a thousand pounds more in expectation, and must have some thousands in substance besides. If for calling and dignity, he must be knight, or lord of several seignories, in several kingdoms; a lieutenant of his county; and a counsellor of a province.

'Now, to lay all circumstances aside, be it known to your son, or to any man else, that if there be anyone who beareth the name of gentleman, and whose words are of reputation in his county, that doth say, or dare say, that I have done unjustly, spoken an untruth, stained my credit and reputation in this matter, or in any matter else, wherein your son is exasperated, I say he lieth in his throat, and my sword shall maintain my word upon him, in any place or province, wheresoever he dare, and where I stand not sworn to observe the peace. But if they be such as are within my governance, and over whom I have authority, I will, for their reformation, chastise them with justice, and for their malapert misdemeanour bind them to their good behaviour. Of this sort I account your son, and his like; against whom I will shortly issue my warrant, if this my warning doth not reform them. And so I thought fit to advertise you hereof, and leave you to God.'

How magnificent is 'my grandmother Devereux!' The race of such grandmother's is, I am sure, extinct. No man can write such a letter now. No man dares in these days to think so nobly of himself and his ancestors. Sir Leicester Dedlock, even, would not have addressed Mr Lawrence Boythorn in this superb and exalted manner. He would have instructed Mr Tulkinghorn to take some kind of proceedings, and though Mr Tulkinghorn was a great man in his way, after all he was but an attorney. And recourse to an attorney is but a shabby substitute for the resounding boasts and the terrific threats of 'old Sir William Herbert of St Gillyans,' as his age called him.

And now for an example of a very different school of letter-writing. We are to fall a little in the world. Our polite correspondent is neither a Georgian saint and sage, nor a high Elizabethan gentleman. He is Mr Percy Mapleton, generally known as Lefroy, who is in Maidstone Gaol, awaiting his trial for the murder of Frederick Isaac Gold upon the 27th of June, 1881. He is addressing a lady who, I believe, was a relation of his:

'MY DARLING ANNIE,

'I am getting this posted secretly by a true and kind friend, and I trust you implicitly to do as I ask you. Dearest, should God permit a verdict of 'Guilty' to be returned, you know what my fate must be unless you prevent it, which you can do by assisting me in this way. Send me (concealed in a common meat pie, made in an oblong tin cheap dish) saw file, six inches or so long, without a handle; place this at bottom of pie, embedded in under crust and gravy. And now, dearest, for the greater favour of the two. Send me, in centre of a small cake, like your *half-crown* one, a tiny bottle of prussic acid, the smaller the better; this last you could, I believe, obtain from either Drs Green or Cressy for *destroying a favourite cat*. My darling, believe me when I say, as *I hope for salvation,* that this last should only be used the last night allowed me by the law *to live,* if it comes to that last extremity. Never while a *chance of life remained* would I use it, but only as a *last resource. . . . By* packing these, as I say, carefully, sending with them a tin of milk, etc., no risk will be incurred as my things are, comparatively speaking, never examined. Get them yourself soon, and direct them in a feigned hand, without any accompanying note. If you receive this safely, and will aid me, by return send a postcard, saying: "*Dear P, Captain Lefroy has returned.*" '

It has been remarked, I believe, that the profuse use of the italic character is often a sign of a weak and confused mind. It is certainly evidence of such a state in this extraordinary letter of Lefroy's. It will be noted that he italicises phrases which need no italics. 'As I hope for salvation,' is quite clear in Roman type; 'a chance of life,' 'a favourite cat' are phrases which involve no obscurity. There are, indeed, phrases which the commentator might write in italics or mark with bracketed notes of exclamation, and chief of these is Lefroy's remark that his things were, 'comparatively speaking, never examined.' How do you 'comparatively speaking,' never examine anything? Clearly, the man's mind was a heap of foolishness and confusion; he doesn't even understand how a meat pie is made, as appears by his idle talk about 'under crust.' He has been reading silly fictions about prisoners escaping by means of hidden files, the kind of fiction with which Tom Sawyer embittered the life of the unfortunate Jim, who 'mashed his teeth' by biting on a brass candlestick concealed by Tom in the negro's prison fare. And the 'feigned hand' of Lefroy is much on the level of the 'nonnamous letters' which Tom insisted on writing to Jim's gaolers. And it must be said that the poor woman to whom this extraordinary letter was addressed seems to have belonged to the crazy world which Lefroy himself inhabited. She replied. She did not say, as kindly as might be, 'don't talk nonsense.' She did not perceive that the file business was sheer idiocy, but:

'First I must tell you that the delay about what you mentioned has happened through our being told that only two shops in London make them, but trust before you have this it will have arrived safely; if so, say in your next: "The little basket with butter, etc., came safely." '

And her letter, too, is full of italics, and many phrases are in 'small caps.' Lefroy, clearly, was a man of confusion, and lived in a world of confusion. If he had avoided italics, he might have avoided Maidstone Gaol, the hangman and the rope.

HOW CLUBS BEGAN

ONE OR TWO shop fronts of our old Regent Street still survive amongst the ruins and the new buildings which are more depressing than any ruins. But the goodly street is ended, and it seems fitting that Mr Jaschke, the Barber of Kings, did not long survive the destruction of his famous shop. There was a picture in his window that was one of the features of London, like the Filter in Fleet Street and—in the same thoroughfare—the Meerschaum Pipe, with the carving of the Battle of Leipsic on the bowl, priced at one hundred guineas. Mr Jaschke's picture represented a personage in the costume of a hundred years ago. Long, dark locks flowed luxuriant and profuse over his shoulders, and the inscription was, 'The Secret of Beau Brummel.' It advertised some cunning preparation which would make baldness impossible; and it is gone, like many another London landmark. Too many, indeed, of these landmarks have departed from us, and the men who come back to us after their years of service in the Malay States and China and Persia will look round vainly, seeking for things that are to be seen no more. It was not so formerly. Twenty years ago a friend of mine who had been in China for some time came back and found London the same as ever. 'Nothing has changed,' he said. 'The chickens are still feeding in the window of the incubator shop at the top of Regent Street.' The chickens have long flown away.

But about Mr Jaschke and his shop. We have all heard how King Edward pronounced him to be the perfect barber; the man who knew not only the art of beard-trimming in perfection, but also that more difficult art of hearing everything and saying nothing. Royalty was the province of Jaschke's razor and scissors; his back shop was called the House of Lords, so noble was the custom of the place. And, considering these things, the awful question has just struck me: What would have happened to me if I had strolled into Jaschke's and asked for a shave or a hair cut? This is a very deep and perplexing question, but the situation is not without precedent. Newman Noggs, it may be remembered, once escorted Miss Morleena Kenwigs to a highly genteel establishment in Soho, where they not only cut and curled ladies elegantly and children carefully, but shaved gentlemen easily. And while Morleena's pigtails were being attended to there presented himself for shaving a big, burly, good-humoured coal-heaver, with a pipe in his mouth, who, drawing his hand across his chin, requested to know when a shaver would be disengaged.

The journeyman, to whom this question was put, looked doubtfully at the young proprietor, and the young proprietor looked scornfully at the coal-heaver, observing at the same time:

'You won't get shaved here, my man.'

'Why not?' said the coal-heaver.

'We don't shave gentlemen in your line,' remarked the young proprietor.

'Why, I see you a-shaving of a baker, when I was a-looking through the winder, last week,' said the coal-heaver.

'It's necessary to draw the line somewheres, my fine fellow,' replied the principal. 'We draw the line there. We can't go beyond bakers. If we was to get any lower than bakers, our customers would desert us, and we might shut up shop.' The situations seem to me fairly analogous. But what would I have said, if I had ventured into the 'House of Lords' at Jaschke's, asked for a shave, and been told that Jaschke didn't shave gentlemen in my line? Should I have observed, 'I see you a-shaving of a temporary major,' and would Jaschke have replied that he drew the line at temporary majors? It is a curious and a doubtful point.

And that consideration led me to another curious point, how, formerly at all events, things that were nominally public were, in fact, private. In the mythical days before the War you might find yourself in an old-fashioned country town and wander into the bar-parlour of an old-fashioned inn. There would be half a dozen comfortable-looking men, substantial farmers and tradesmen, talking together over their reasonable potations, and by the fire an inviting and an empty chair. In it you would sit down, and as you did so a round man would beg your pardon 'but that's Mr Apple's chair.' 'He's sat in that chair every night for thirty years, has Mr Apple,' another round man would say to his neighbour, and there would be nothing for it but to get up as quickly as possible and leave Mr Apple his place by the hearth. And in some such fashion, I suppose, certain of the old coffee-houses and chocolate-houses were converted from a public to a private use, sometimes by way of business, sometimes by way of pleasure.

Lloyd's was once Lloyd's Coffee House, and White's was White's Chocolate House in the year 1700, and for some time after. Indeed, as late as 1733, the proprietor, Mr Arthur, 'having had the misfortune to be burnt out of White's Chocolate House, is removed to Gaunt's Coffee House, next the St James's Coffee House in St James's Street, where he humbly begs they'—'all noblemen and gentlemen'—will favour him with their company as usual.' Evidently, it was still an open house, in name at all events; and it would probably be a difficult matter to trace the successive steps by which White's became a club in the modern sense, open to its members, but strictly private as far as all others were concerned. Possibly a room was at first appropriated to the use of a few constant and privileged customers, who constituted the club and eventually took possession of all the rooms in the Choco-late House. There was, no doubt, a transitional period, as Davies, writing of Colley Cibber, remarks:

'But Colley, we are told, had the honour to be a member of the great club at White's and so, I suppose, might any man who wore good clothes and paid his money when he lost it.'

Indeed, it is certain that Colley Cibber was a member, since a book of rules and list of members dated 1736 contains his name, with those of the Duke of Devonshire, the Earls of Cholmondeley, Chesterfield and Rockingham, Sir John Cope, and Major-General Churchill. It seems likely, then, that Davies—he was the Tom Davies who kept the bookseller's shop in Russell Street, Covent Garden, where Boswell first met Johnson—was wrong in thinking that any well-dressed man who paid his gaming debts could be a member of 'the great club at White's.' There might have been a public room into which the well-dressed man might stroll; but I do not think he would stay very long in the room occupied by the Duke and the Earls.

The first traces of a club subscription are to be found in the 1736 rules. It is directed that 'every member is to pay one guinea a year towards having a good Cook,' and it was not till 1775 that this guinea became ten and of general application. A few years later an order was made that dinner should be served daily while Parliament was sitting, the reckoning to be twelve shillings a head: in our money, at least two guineas, and probably more. The old Chocolate House, as it existed in the days of the *Tatler* and *Spectator* had been distinguished for 'gallantry and intrigue, pleasure and entertainment,' the later club had become the headquarters of high play. Walpole writes in 1750:

'They have put in the papers a good story made on White's. A man dropped down dead at the door was carried in; the club immediately made bets whether he was dead or not, and when they were going to bleed him the wagerers for his death interposed, and said it would affect the fairness of the bet.'

And so Lord Lyttleton says that he trembles to think that 'the rattling of a dice-box at White's may one day or other (if my son should be a member of that noble academy) shake down all our fine oaks.'

Indeed, the rules deal more and more with the apparatus of gambling. A rule of 1736 directs that 'every member who is in the room after 7 o'clock and plays is to pay Half a Crown.' Note, by the way, that the phrase 'in the room' goes to confirm my conjecture that the original club occupied one room in the Chocolate House; there being other rooms open to Davies' man in good clothes, who was not a member. Then, the 'Picket Cards' are to be charged to the Dinner or Supper Bill, and the Quinze players are to pay for their own cards, the Dice used at Hazard are to be paid for by Boxes, and it is ordained that each member who plays at Chess, Draughts, or Backgammon 'do pay One Shilling each time of playing by daylight and half a crown Each by candlelight.'

But White's, like the barber in *Nicholas Nickleby*, did draw the line somewhere. There was a Rule that 'No Member of the Club shall hold a Faro Bank.'

THE INGENIOUS MR BLEE

'STEPHEN M'DANIEL, John Berry, James Egan (otherwise Gahagan) and James Salmon were indicted, for that, at the gaol delivery for our sovereign lord the King at the county gaol at Maidstone for the county of Kent, on Tuesday, the 13th of August, in the twenty-eighth year of our said sovereign lord the King, Peter Kelly and John Ellis were, in due form of law, indicted for a robbery on the King's highway on James Salmon, by putting him in corporal fear and danger of his life, in the parish of St Paul, Deptford, in the county of Kent, and taking from him one linen handkerchief, value 4d., two pair of leather breeches, one clasp knife, one iron tobacco box, one silver pocket-piece, one guinea, and one half-crown; and that the said Peter Kelly and John Ellis were tried and convicted for that robbery; and that the said M'Daniel, Berry, Egan, and Salmon, on the 23rd of July, 1754, in the City of London, were accessories before this felony was committed; and feloniously and maliciously did aid, abet, assist, counsel, hire and command the said Ellis and Kelly to commit this robbery, against the peace of his majesty, his crown and dignity.'

Thus in these words were the Right Honourable Theodore Janssen, Esq., Lord Mayor of the City of London, and his Majesty's Justices of Oyer and Terminer introduced to what Mr Sampson Brass would have called a pretty little conspiracy. And the person who unveiled it all, for good reasons, no doubt, pertaining to his comfort and peace of mind and of body was a Mr Thomas Blee, who lodged at John Berry's house and did odd jobs, very odd jobs indeed, for him. It seemed that there was what we should call a Little Syndicate, consisting of Berry and his fellows at the bar of the Old Bailey. They all lived round and about Hatton Garden and the backways of Holborn, and they had quiet little drinks together over business in the taproom of the Bell and in other vanished taverns. The syndicate was in low water in July, 1754, and Berry sent his man Blee—how did Stevenson miss so wonderful a name while he was thinking of his pirates and villains at large?—to M'Daniel, and a sort of unofficial committee meeting was held. At the end of it they both said to Blee: 'Tom, money grows scarce, you must give a sharp look out for a couple to go upon the scamp now, and if you cannot get two, you must get one.' The 'scamp,' Thomas Blee explained, meant the highway. But Thomas was troubled with scruples. He told Berry and M'Daniel, as he swore, that Kidden's was so bad an affair that he did not choose to be concerned more. Kidden had been tried, condemned and executed a year before; and since secrecy is now valueless it may be mentioned that the business of Berry and his syndicate was to lure poor runagates into the commission of felony, to get them condemned and executed, and then to pocket the reward. It was Fagin, and perhaps rather worse than Fagin, long before Fagin's day; but it will be noted that Mr Berry's beat was not very remote from that of Dickens's Jew.

Well, Thomas Blee, remembering poor Kidden's end, had scruples, but they were overcome. The next day Berry, M'Daniel and Blee went into Spa Fields—all grey squares and grey streets now between Sadler's Wells and Islington—and looked for idle fellows, at first without success. Then there was another and a fuller committee meeting at the sign of Sir John Oldcastle; in this Salmon, the breeches maker, was included. There was a good deal of discussion as to where the robbery should be committed, and it was pointed out that there were peculiar advantages attached to the road between New Cross turnpike and Deptford, since the inhabitants of East Greenwich offered a special reward of twenty pounds for the apprehension of highwaymen and footpads. And it was settled that Mr Salmon should be the gentleman to be robbed, and that a Mr Egan should act as 'fence,' to buy the stolen goods, and the happy party calculated that what with the official reward and the unofficial reward they would make twenty pounds apiece—about £100 of our money, I suppose. And a day or two later, the friends met together at the Bell, in Holborn, and made the most minute arrangements as to the various identifiable properties that Salmon was to carry; in order that he might be robbed of them. So everything was settled very comfortably, and it only remained to find a couple of young fellows to play the part of the thieves; and that was the business of good Thomas Blee. Accordingly, Mr Blee went to work. He found two likely young fellows, known pickpockets, down in Fleet Market, Farringdon Street. These were Kelly and Ellis, and Blee told them, according to his instructions, that he knew where to get 'a brave parcel of lullies'—otherwise, a parcel of linen. And then followed the most elaborate proceedings. Blee had to show his two prospective highwaymen to Berry and the other members of the syndicate that their skilled eyes might see whether the two young men were suitable for the purpose; and there were meetings at the Plumb Tree ale-house in Plumb Tree Court, Shoe Lane, and occasions when Blee stood by Ellis and Kelly in the Artillery Ground—where the White Regiment was marching. Everything was satisfactory.

'Mr Berry,' said Thomas Blee, 'do you think they will do?' And Mr Berry said, in his hearty way:

'Do! Damme, I have done less than they over, for March and Newman were less.'

I am not quite clear as to the precise sense of this remark. It may mean that Mr Berry was quite satisfied that Ellis and Kelly were not too young to be hanged. At any rate, he was pleased, since he gave Blee sixpence, double his usual gratuity. The affair seemed very promising, and the day for the robbery had been settled, when the plan was a little disarranged by some trouble in the Artillery Ground, where Kelly and Ellis usually 'worked'—in the sense that the Artful Dodger and Charley Bates worked.

'About half-an-hour after that,' says Thomas Blee, 'there was hue-and-cry after a pickpocket. M'Daniel came to me, and said, 'The chief person is a-ducking in the Pyed-Horse Yard; follow him, and give him some gin, for they have almost killed him.'

Blee found Ellis and gave him a penny or two and went back and reassured M'Daniel: 'then he and I came out of the Artillery ground together; as we were coming out of the ground, we met one they call Plump (his name Brebrook) and another fellow they call Doctor, that was turnkey at Clerkenwell Bridewell. Plump, seeing M'Daniel and I together, said to me, "You rascal, you deserve to be hanged for that affair of Kidden." '

The day was finally settled. Berry gave Blee the extraordinary sum of five shillings 'to flash to the boys,' to dazzle them, that is, with the sight of so much money, for Blee usually gave them gin by ha'porths. So the party set out on the way to Deptford, calling by arrangement with the syndicate at certain taverns on the way. At one of these taverns there was almost a misadventure. Kelly caught a glimpse of Berry, lurking in obscurity, and on coming out observed with an oath to Blee: 'There is that old thief-catching son of a bitch, your old master.' But Blee soothed his fears, and a breast of lamb was bought in the Borough Market, and fried for dinner at the Black Spread Eagle in Kent Street. The three drank together, and slept in the fields, Salmon and Berry always, as it were, round the corner, slinking on the track of Blee and his victims, communicating with Blee under the very noses of Kelly and Ellis. Salmon came into a tavern where Blee and his young friends were sitting, and, taking a place near them, began to speak of walking to London. Then Berry passes the tavern window and beckons to Blee with an evil crook of his finger, and so Blee gets his last instructions, and the three steal out on the track of Salmon. Up to this time, be it remembered, the two dupes thought they were to steal 'lullies,' or linen. But the sight of Salmon walking before them on the dark, lonely road had the desired effect. Kelly observed: 'There is that old blood of a bitch, the breeches-maker in Shoe Lane . . . let's scamp him.' Accordingly, Salmon was set upon by all three and robbed according to plan. The next day, Egan, the receiver, or fence, of the comedy, was 'discovered' in the Black Spread Eagle by Blee, and over a breakfast of lamb's liver and bacon, washed down by a pot of 'twopenny'—the eighteenth-century equivalent of the 'four ale' of pre-War days—the stolen goods, all carefully marked for identification, were handed over to the fence. Kelly and Ellis were arrested, tried, and condemned to death in due course; and everything seemed to point to a large reward and a happy ending for everybody concerned—save Kelly and Ellis.

But something went wrong. The constables arrested not only Kelly and Ellis but also Thomas Blee. This may have been a blunder, a pure accident, or Kelly and Ellis may have given Blee away, or Mr Berry may have considered in his wisdom that Blee's time was come, and that he was ripe for the journey in the Tyburn cart. But Thomas did exactly as might have been expected. He turned King's Evidence at the first possible moment; and the little syndicate found themselves in the dock at the Old Bailey pleading not guilty to the indictment quoted at the head of this article. They called divers friends to give evidence as to character, and the said friends declared in cheerful unison that Berry and the rest of them bore the worst characters possible. The verdict was Guilty, and sentence seven years' imprisonment, two turns in the pillory, and a fine of one mark each. The sting of the sentence was in the pillory. M'Daniel and Berry, pilloried near Hatton Garden, were with difficulty rescued by the sheriff from the fury of the mob. Then Egan and Salmon stood in the pillory at Smithfield. At the end of half an hour's hail of oyster-shells and stones, Egan was struck dead, and Salmon dangerously wounded. In the end, Salmon and Berry died in Newgate, and M'Daniel 'procured himself to be sent abroad for life to the Indies as a soldier.'

OLD DR MOUNSEY

SOMETIME IN the summer of 1768, Dr Samuel Johnson supped at the Crown and Anchor, in the Strand, with a little company that Mr Boswell had collected to meet him. The company consisted of Dr Percy, afterwards Bishop of Dromore (Percy's 'Reliques'), Dr Douglas, Mr Langton ('Lanky'), Dr Robertson, the historian, Dr Blair (Blair's 'Rhetoric') and Mr Thomas Davies, the bookseller of Russell Street, Covent Garden. The Scots were all prudent and silent, but Johnson was 'in remarkable vigour of mind and eager to exert himself in conversation.' He did exert himself in conversation: to the following effect:

'He was vehement against old Dr Mounsey, of Chelsea College, as "a fellow who swore and talked bawdy." "I have been often in his company (said Dr Percy), and never heard him swear or talk bawdy." Mr Davies, who sat next to Dr Percy, having after this had some conversation aside with him, made a discovery which, in his zeal to pay court to Dr Johnson, he eagerly proclaimed aloud from the foot of the table: "O, Sir, I have found out a very good reason why Dr Percy never heard Mounsey swear or talk bawdy; for he tells me he never saw him but at the Duke of Northumberland's table!" "And so, Sir (said Johnson loudly to Dr Percy), you would shield this man from the charge of swearing and talking bawdy because he did not do so at the Duke of Northumberland's table. Sir, you might as well tell us that you had seen him hold up his hand at the Old Bailey, and he neither swore nor talked bawdy; or that you had seen him in the cart at Tyburn, and he neither swore nor talked bawdy. And is it thus, Sir, that you presume to controvert what I have related?" ' Whereupon Dr Percy left the room in a huff, and next morning Dr Johnson observed complacently that there had been 'good talk.'

Of course, the passage had been long familiar to me, but not reading Boswell in the luxury of an annotated edition, I had always speculated vainly as to this 'old Dr Mounsey,' who appears on the great
lantern show for a moment, sets Johnson and Percy by the ears, and
then vanishes. It was only the other day that I found in an odd old
book (published, strangely enough, at Louisville, Kentucky) the true
history of Dr Messenger Mounsey (or Monsey), Physician to Chelsea
Hospital.

He was the son of a country parson, who refused in 1689 to take
the oath of allegiance to the Usurpers, William and Mary. He was
educated at Cambridge and settled down as a physician in Bury St
Edmunds, where he married a widow with a handsome jointure. He
made an income of £300 a year, and grumbled because he had to work
too hard for it. Fortunately for him, Lord Godolphin was seized with
apoplexy on a journey to his country seat, and Bury was the nearest
point where medical help was to be had. Dr Mounsey was called in,
Lord Godolphin got better, liked his physician's talk, and made Dr
Messenger for life. He had an apartment at Lord Godolphin's town
house, was made Physician to Chelsea Hospital and saw all the best
company of the age, from King George II downwards. For a time he
was a great friend of Garrick's; but Garrick had a sly tongue, and the
Doctor had a rough tongue, and the friendship ended in offence and
epigrams. Garrick used to make comic business out of Mounsey's
oddities for the entertainment of his friends; Mounsey said that
Garrick would never leave the stage 'so long as he knows a guinea is
cross on one side and pile on the other'—so long as guineas have heads
and tails—and the two became sworn enemies. The fact is that Dr
Mounsey was an intensely rude old man, or, in the elegant phrase of
my authority, 'it became the fashion for the young, the delicate, and
the gay to exclaim against him as an interrupter of established forms,
and as a violator of those minute rules of good breeding which, however trifling they may appear to the sage and the philosopher, contrib-
ute essentially to the ease and comfort of modern life.' Yet the queer
old man had, like the greater Doctor of his age, an interior benevolence. Once, going along Oxford Market, he observed a poor woman
asking the price of a fine piece of beef.

'The brute answered the woman, "One penny a pound," thinking, no doubt, it was too good for her. "Weigh that piece of beef," said the Doctor.

' "Ten pounds and a half," said Mr Butcher.

' "Here, good woman," cried the Doctor, "hold up your apron and take that beef home to your family."

' "God bless your honour!"

' "Go off, directly, home; no compliments! Here, Mr Butcher," continued the Doctor, "give me change out of this shilling for that poor woman's beef."

' "What do you mean, Sir?" replied the Butcher.

' "Mean, Sir! why to pay for the poor woman's beef, what you asked her; a penny a pound. Come, make haste and give me three halfpence; I am in a hurry."

' "Why, Sir . . ." said the Butcher.

' "No why sirs with me," answered the Doctor, "give me my change instantly, or I will break your head." The Butcher again began to expostulate, and the Doctor struck him with all his force with his cane.'

But the principal adventure of his life seems to have been the affair of the bank-notes. Dr Mounsey, who was born in 1693, not long after the foundation of the Bank of England, had an old-fashioned distrust of 'securities' of all sorts, and so, being bound on a summer holiday, he hid his notes and gold in his fireplace, putting them under the 'cinders and shavings' of the laid fire. A month later Dr Mounsey returned and found his housekeeper entertaining a few friends to tea in his sitting-room. The fire had just been lighted; the kettle was on the hob. 'He ran across the room like a madman, swearing his housekeeper had ruined him for ever, and had burned all his bank-notes. First went the contents of the slop-basin, then the teapot, and then he rushed to the pump in the kitchen, and brought a pail of water, which he threw partly over the fire and partly over the company, who in the utmost consternation retreated as speedily as possible. His housekeeper cried out: "For God's sake, Sir, forbear, you will spoil the steel stove and fire-irons." "Damn the stove, irons, you, your company, and all!" replied the Doctor, "you have ruined and undone me for *ever*; you

have burned my bank-notes." "Lord, Sir,' said the half-drowned
woman, "who'd think of putting bank-notes in a Bath stove, where the
fire is ready laid?" "Fire," said he, "who'd think of making a fire in
summer-time, where there has not been one for months?" ' The notes
were recovered in a damaged and dubious condition. But Dr Mounsey's patron, Lord Godolphin, said that he would go with him the next
day to the Bank of England, and everything would be quite all right.
But Godolphin had told the King, and the King said that he must hear
Mounsey tell the tale of the burning notes and the drenched tea-party.
And so, when the Doctor came, King George II was hidden in a
cupboard, and was so much amused that he kicked the cupboard door
open. 'God!' said the Doctor in a rage, and then saw who had been
listening, and with considerable tact ran on his sentence, 'bless your
majesty; this may be a joke with you and his lordship, but to me a loss
of near £400.' But Lord Godolphin assured him that he should have
his money, and made an appointment to meet him at the Bank a little
later. Dr Mounsey, in the interval, transacted some business at the
Horse Guards, and took water at Whitehall for the Bank. In going
down the river he felt that he must have a look at the bank-notes, to
make quite sure that they were safe. So he pulled out his pocket-book;
and a gust of wind blew the notes out of the book and into the river.
'The Doctor, with a volley of oaths—the other Doctor was right on
one point, at all events—desired the waterman to put back, for that his
bank-notes were overboard. He was instantly obeyed; and when he
reached them he took the hat from his head, and, dipping it in the
river, took up his notes, together with half a hatful of water. With his
hat, the notes, and the water under his arm he was landed at the
famous stairs called the Three Cranes in the Vintry, and walked
straight to the Bank.

'What have you under your arm?' asked Lord Godolphin. 'The
damned notes,' replied the Doctor, throwing the hat on the table with
such violence that the water spurted into the faces of the City Kings
who sat about the board. 'There,' said the Doctor, 'take the remains of
your damned notes, for neither fire nor water will consume them.' He
got his money in full, but he did not go away in peace. He had forgotten all about the watermen and the fare from Whitehall. They were

waiting outside the Bank, howling for their money, and swearing that the Doctor was a madman. When he came out, one of the watermen laid hold of him—and was instantly knocked down for his pains. However, a crown for the little mistake, with half a crown for the fare, adjusted this little difficulty, and Dr Messenger Mounsey resolved to invest his money in the Funds for the future.

This remarkable character outlived Dr Johnson by five years, dying in 1789, at the age of ninety-six. Naturally, he made an eccentric will. He left the bulk of his money to his daughter, tying it up by a complicated system of entail to her female descendants. He mentioned in his will a young lady on whose wit, taste and elegance be 'lavished encomiums'—leaving her an old battered snuff-box, worth about sixpence. He mentioned also another young lady to whom he had intended to bequeath a legacy. But she turned out 'a pert, conceited minx,' so she got nothing. Then came annuities to two clergymen, who had turned Unitarian.

And I am wondering whether Dr Johnson knew all that there was to be known about Dr Messenger Mounsey. He abominated foul and blasphemous language, no doubt; he would have detested a man who abused the Church of England and comforted heretics. But if he had known of the principal clause in old Dr Mounsey's will, by which large property was not only left to a woman but entailed in the female line, then he would have dismissed Dr Mounsey as a wild and irresponsible madman, fit for Bedlam and nothing else.

CASANOVA IN LONDON

THE EIGHTEENTH CENTURY, that extraordinary, admirable, and detestable age, gave us all manner of wonderful things and men, but was, above all, rich in adventurers, in the species which was rightly named *chevaliers d'industrie*. Rightly, because there was always something of polish, of singularity, of distinction about the eighteenth-century rogue. The species, I think, is extinct. We have swindlers now in plenty, confidence men in abundance. There were some highly ingenious artists in knavery engaged in the case of 'Mr A.' And we have occultists, and occult cranks, and founders of new religions, and initiators in secret rites, enough and more than enough. And again, we have dons, learned men, in profusion. But the type that combined all these types in one has ceased to exist. There is no modern translation of Casanova; swindler, cardsharper, occult quack, profligate, dealer in all the mysteries, man of the world—and LL.D. of the University of Padua at the age of fifteen. There were, as I say, some very clever people who interested themselves in the unfortunate Indian Rajah's banking account; but not one of them, I feel sure, could have written as a degree thesis; *Utrum judaei possint construere novas synagogas:* 'Should the Jews be allowed to build new synagogues?' Then, on the other hand: Madame Blavatsky told some amazing tales about Mahatmas, and deceived many persons in high official places. But I never understood that she made much money by it, 'it' being taken to mean Theosophy, the 'ancient wisdom religion'. Casanova, on the other hand, was accused by the nephew of Madame la Duchesse d'Urfê of having swindled his aunt of a million francs, forty thousand pounds or more. The nephew may have exaggerated, for he was in a rage. But it is certain that Venetian Casanova did very handsomely out of Madame d'Urfê's Rosicrucian delusions.

73

This ingenious gentleman, Giovanni Giacomo Casanova, visited our shores in the early 'sixties of the eighteenth century, soon after the accession of King George III. He had hired a packet at Calais, and was delighted to accommodate the Duke of Bedford on board. The passage took two and a half hours, and at Dover 'the custom-house officials made a minute, offensive, and even an impertinent perquisition.' Still:

'England is different in every respect from the rest of Europe; even the country has a different aspect, and the water of the Thames has a taste peculiar to itself. Everything has its own characteristics, and the fish, cattle, horses, men and women are of a type not found in any other land. Their manner of living is totally different from that of other countries, especially their cookery. The most striking feature in their character is their national pride; they exalt themselves above all other nations.'

Casanova had business in London. He had to call on the famous Madame Cornely, Cornelis, or Cornelys. This lady, an old Venetian friend of our adventurer, had used in her time many names, but had finally and for English use coined a new one out of the name of a Dutch lover, Cornelius Rigerboos. She had settled down in Carlisle House, Soho Square—afterwards in the occupation of Crosse and Blackwell—just opposite to the Venetian Embassy, and here she gave balls, concerts and masquerades to the nobility and gentry on the most splendid scale. But, somehow, she displeased the Grand Jury of the County of Middlesex, who presented her as a public nuisance. Madame was ruined. She became a vendor of asses' milk at Knights-bridge, and died at last in 1797, a prisoner in the Fleet.

But when Casanova called on her in the early sixties, she was in all the splendour of success. In her own words:

'I give twelve balls and twelve suppers to the nobility, and the same number to the middle-classes in the year. I have often as many as six hundred guests at two guineas a head.'

She had two secretaries, over thirty servants, and her gross receipts were £24,000 per annum. And she felt able to be insolent to her old friend Casanova, who resented her behaviour, and took a furnished house in Pall Mall, china, linen and plate included, for twenty guineas a week. He was in disgrace with his own government, since he had broken prison in a spectacular and amazing manner, and so he was presented at Court by the French ambassador, the Comte de Guerchi. King George III spoke in a low voice, but his Queen seems to have been lively. She spoke of the Venetian Ambassador Extraordinary:

'M. Querini amused me extremely, he called me a little devil.'

'He meant to say,' replied Casanova, 'that your highness is as witty as an angel.'

And one seems to hear the voice of a later member of the Royal house remarking severely: 'We are not amused.'

Casanova had managed to get introductions to fine company in England. He called on Lady Harrington and played whist for small stakes, losing fifteen guineas. He was given a lesson in English manners.

'You paid in gold,' said Lady Harrington. 'I suppose you had no bank-notes about you?'

'Yes, my lady, I have notes for fifty and a hundred pounds.'

'Then you must change one of them or wait till another time to pay, for, in England, to pay in gold is a solecism only pardonable in a stranger. Perhaps you noticed that the lady smiled.'

Many things struck Casanova as strange. He was invited by a younger son of the Duke of Bedford to oysters and champagne at a tavern. They drank two bottles of champagne, and the Duke's son made Casanova pay half the cost of the second bottle. And the tavern cooking: they laughed at Casanova when he said that he did not care to dine at taverns, because he could not get soup.

'Are you ill?' said the Englishmen. 'Soup is only fit for invalids.'

The English of the day, says Casanova, were wholly carnivorous; they ate neither soup nor dessert: 'which circumstance made me remark that an English dinner is like eternity; it has no beginning and no end. Soup is considered very extravagant, as the very servants refuse to eat the meat from which it has been made. They say it is only fit to give to dogs. The salt beef which they use is certainly excellent. I cannot say the same for their beer, which was so bitter that I could not drink it.'

Casanova went to Drury Lane. By some accident the company could not give the piece that had been announced. The house was in an uproar. 'Garrick, the celebrated actor, came forward and tried in vain to restore order. He was obliged to retire behind the curtain. Then the King, the Queen, and all the fashionables left the theatre, and in less than an hour the house was gutted, till nothing but the bare walls were left. After this destruction, which went on without any authority interposing, the mad populace rushed to the taverns to consume gin and beer. . . Such are the English and above all the Londoners. They hoot the King and the royal family when they appear in public, and the consequence is that they are never seen, save on great occasions, when order is kept by hundreds of constables.' Casanova went everywhere; he was to be seen alike in high company and in low. He went to Ranelagh and to Vauxhall, preferring the latter. He strolled into coffeehouses, and now and then caught odd scraps of conversation—when the language used was French or Italian. Thus:

'Tommy has committed suicide, and he was right, for he was in such a state that he could only expect unhappiness for the rest of his life.'

'You are quite mistaken,' said the other, with the greatest composure. 'I was one of his creditors myself, and on making an inventory of his effects I feel satisfied that he has done a very foolish and a very childish thing; he might have lived on comfortably, and not killed himself for fully six months.'

And, then, Casanova met Miss Charpillon, of Denmark Street, Soho, and this turned out to be the most unfortunate meeting of his life. Miss Charpillon robbed, swindled, humbugged the experienced old profligate to her heart's content. She drove him to the point of suicide. She belonged to a Swiss family of hereditary bad character, and a few years later she triumphed almost as completely over another wily old practitioner of bad morals, the famous Jack Wilkes. Jack recovered; but Casanova was never quite the triumphant rascal again. One of the consequences of his entanglement with the terrible Charpillon was an appearance before Sir John Fielding at Bow Street. The woman had sworn an information against him. He was arrested and taken before the magistrate, whom he confused with the illustrious novelist, dead in Lisbon many years before.

'At the end of the room I saw a gentleman sitting in an armchair, and concluded him to be my judge. I was right, and the judge was blind. He wore a broad band round his head, passing over his eyes. A man beside me, guessing I was a foreigner, said in French:

' "Be of good courage, Mr Fielding is a just and equitable magistrate."

'I thanked the kindly unknown, and was delighted to see before me this famous and estimable writer, whose works are an honour to the English nation. . . .

' "Signor Casanova," said he in excellent Italian, "be kind enough to step forward. I wish to speak to you."

'I was delighted to hear the accents of my native tongue, and making my way through the press, I came up to the bar of the court, and said:

' "Eccomi, Signore."

'He continued to speak Italian, and said: "Signor de Casanova, citizen of Venice, you are condemned to perpetual confinement in the prisons of his Majesty the King of Great Britain." '

This was Sir John's little joke. He explained to Casanova that an information, supported by witnesses, charged him with 'intending to do grievous bodily harm to the person of a pretty girl,' and that, in consequence, he must be kept in prison for the rest of his days. Casanova declared that he had no intention of doing harm to the pretty girl, who was, of course, Miss Charpillon, of Denmark Street. Then two householders were summoned, and Casanova was bailed out, after a brief visit to Newgate, which struck him as 'a hell such as Dante might have conceived.'

He left London and England in a hurry. There was a forged bill of exchange and a talk of hanging, and Casanova wisely posted away with all speed on the Dover Road.

'DOUBLES' IN CRIME

THERE ARE CASES, in life and at law, which must ever remain mysteries. We may be assured, as reasonable beings, that the verdict was truly given, that the truth of the matter was reached, and yet at the unreasonable back of our heads there will be that little jot of hesitation, that unjustifiable 'and yet,' which refuses to be quashed or put out of court.

There is such a case as this in Montagu Williams's wonderful volume of reminiscences. The affair happened somewhere in the mid-'eighties, and in its day was known as 'The Brighton Bigamy.' One Miss Emma Dash met a gentleman on the Parade at Brighton, shortly before Eastertide. He introduced himself. He said he had met Miss Dash at a dance in London, and he was allowed to join the young lady, who was promenading with her brother. Captain McDonald—that was the name he gave—told the story of his heart. He was a sea captain, and four years before he had been engaged to a lady, who, her mother said, was over young to marry yet. So the Captain waited; but when he returned from his last voyage he found his sweetheart married to another. And he drew a moral: if he ever did get married, he avowed, he would take his wife aboard with him. Captain McDonald, it appeared, was every inch a sailor. One might almost venture to call him a Jack Tar. There were no cautious delays, no slow deliberations for him. He was full of the rush, the fine impulsiveness of the deep blue mariner—of fiction. That very afternoon, on permission given, he called on the young lady and her mother, and drove Miss Dash to Lewes. They dined at the White Hart and drove back to Brighton. At the station, the Captain took train to London, promising to send a wire to Miss Dash. The wire was duly received; it requested Miss Dash to meet the 12.34 train, and, if possible, secure the man who had driven them to Lewes. The two met, drove to Worthing, dined there, and returned to Brighton. The Captain saw Miss Dash home, and asked the mother for the daughter's hand. Mrs Dash said that really they had known him for a very short time; still, she gave her consent. Captain McDonald thereupon said that he would get the licence directly. In the course of conversation he happened to mention the name of his ship: it was the *Kaikoura*. Next day came the Captain with the licence, and the two went to a clergyman. The Captain, evidently unprejudiced by any ecclesiastical bias, said he would like to be married on Good Friday. But the clergyman declined, and it was arranged that the wedding should take place the day after, Easter Eve. They were duly married at St James's Church, among those present being Mrs Dash, a Miss Lewis, and a Mr May. After the breakfast Captain and Mrs McDonald went away to Chichester. They came back to Brighton on Easter Monday, and the Captain departed, to go to his ship, as he said, there to make arrangements for the due reception and entertainment of his bride. But he never came back.

Some months afterwards, a Mr Osborne, who had been one of the wedding guests, was at a garden-party at Fulham, given by the Butchers' Company. There he saw a gentleman dressed as a Highlander, and he thought he recognised him as that missing Highlander, Captain McDonald. Osborne thereupon tapped his man on the shoulder, and accused him of being Miss Dash's recreant husband. The Highlander denied it, and said his name was Malcolm. He was detained, and poor Miss Dash—or Mrs Captain McDonald—was brought up from Brighton, and promptly identified the man as her husband. Mr Malcolm denied everything. He said he had never been to Brighton in his life, and that he was married to another lady. When it came to the trial, the bride, the priest, and all the wedding guests swore without hesitation that Malcolm and McDonald were the same. On the other hand, Montagu Williams, defending, called, as he says, a host of witnesses who swore, also without hesitation, that the prisoner was in London on the days when, according to the prosecution, he was courting Miss Dash and getting married at Brighton. Mr Malcolm, who was a meat-salesman at Newgate Market, received a most excellent character; he was, they said, the strictest of teetotallers. And Mr Williams, his counsel, was able to produce a better piece of evidence even than this. He called the manageress of the hotel at Brighton where Captain McDonald told Miss Dash that he was staying, just before the wedding. The manageress swore that on the night before Good Friday a Captain McDonald was undoubtedly staying at her hotel, and also that the prisoner was, most certainly, not the Captain McDonald whom she had entertained. But then, again, all the wedding guest witnesses recognised on Malcolm's face a scar which, they said, they had seen on the face of McDonald. The signature on the marriage register was produced, and the master-butcher, Malcolm's employer, admitted, against his will, that, in his opinion, the name McDonald was in the handwriting of his man, Malcolm. And then, a very odd circumstance: McDonald had told Miss Dash that his ship was called the *Kaikoura*. And this was the name of a ship which had brought over a consignment of meat from Australia to Malcolm's master—a short while before McDonald went courting at Brighton.

The general defence was that Malcolm must have a double, a man exactly like him, who could honestly be mistaken for him. And this strange thing happened, in fact, which happened in fancy in the 'Tale of Two Cities.' 'While I was addressing the jury,' says Montagu Williams, 'and dwelling upon the probability that there were two men concerned who closely resembled one another, an individual, either by accident or design, wandered into the Court and took up his place underneath the dock, when it was immediately perceived that he bore a striking resemblance to the prisoner. It was, of course, not for one moment suggested that he was the mysterious bridegroom.'

The jury disagreed. The case was tried again in the following sessions, but by that time Montagu Williams was too ill to undertake the defence. 'O Jaggerth, Jaggerth, Jaggerth! all otherth ith Cag-Maggerth, give me Jaggerth.' Malcolm was defended by another counsel, found guilty, and sentenced to five years' penal servitude. And, apparently, the verdict was a just one, since Montagu Williams adds: 'It subsequently transpired that Miss Dash was not the only woman with whom he had committed bigamy.' And yet, what about that 'host of witnesses' (say half a dozen) who swore that Malcolm was in London, not at Brighton, on the critical dates? Professional perjurers, hired on the Jaggers system? Possibly. And the hotel manageress, with her evidence as to a Captain McDonald, who was not the prisoner, Malcolm, staying at her hotel? Here it would be interesting to consult the full report of the case. In the summary before me, it does not appear whether the manageress were asked if this guest of hers were like the prisoner, though she was sure he was, in fact, not the prisoner. There, evidently, is the real point. McDonald is not a very rare name. It might easily happen that a veritable McDonald and a man who had falsely taken the name might be in Brighton at the same time.

'CHARACTERS'

I AM WONDERING as I look through my book of 'Characters' whether the number of queer people in the world has actually diminished in the last hundred years, or whether they are simply neglected, suffered to go about dressing oddly, behaving oddly, talking oddly, and dying oddly, without the tribute of more than a brief paragraph in the newspapers. On the whole, I am inclined to think this latter the true explanation of the case. For, as I remember, I once tried to draw a pale outline of a truly remarkable character who lived in our day; say some fourteen or fifteen years ago. In those days I was connected with a daily paper, and in the routine of the office I was sent down one fine day to Reigate, to make enquiries about a certain Mr Campo Tosto, who had lived near that town, and had left his wealth—wealth of a curious kind—in a somewhat curious manner. At Reigate, I found that Mr Campo Tosto's house was about four miles away, and that it was situated in a hamlet called Burnt Green. I began to be entertained. Decidedly, there was to be something odd about this tale. Here was the late Campo Tosto living at Burnt Green; which was to all intents and purposes a translation of his name into English. Very good; elated, I hired a trap at Reigate, and we drove on our way. I asked the driver if he knew anything about Campo Tosto, deceased. Not much; he was a queer old gentleman; he didn't like people about his grounds, and sometimes he would shoot at trespassers.

'Shoot!' said I. 'Shoot at them with a gun?'

'Yes, with a gun now and then; but mostly with a bow and arrows!'

Now there were two oddities mentioned in the paragraph on which my enquiries were based. The wealth of Campo Tosto consisted almost wholly in antiquities and objects of art. The late fifteenth century had been the queer old gentleman's favourite period; and his collection

82

contained all sorts of pieces of that age: pictures, chests, spike candle-sticks, statues; valued, I believe, at two thousand pounds or there-abouts. And all this property he had left to a man who, with his wife, had looked after him for some time. This man had been a farm labourer, and his name was Turk; an odd sort of name for an English labourer. We drew near the residence of the late Campo Tosto; a house removed a little way from the road on a slight hillside; a place rather pretentious in a small way without being in the least interesting; about fifty or sixty years old, I suppose. And just then we ran into Mr Turk, the happy heir of mediaeval art. He seemed worried. Men with cameras and long sticks buzzed about him. They wanted him to be photographed in the interests of the public, but he denied them, and did so with considerable irritation. I jumped out of the trap, and put my business before him. He stood still for a moment; and that was enough. Four cameras clicked at once, as Mr Turk firmly declined to have anything to do with me. Turk declared that he would tell me nothing, show me nothing. 'This is the only thing I'll do for you,' he said. 'Give me that paper,' I gave him my paper, open, at the 'leader page.' He deliberately turned it upside down, and read out nine or ten lines of inverted type with the greatest ease, and with absolute correct-ness.

'You see,' said Turk, cunningly, 'I used to be a farm labourer, but of late I've had a lot to do with fuller's earth.'

He was evidently convinced that he had furnished me with a com-plete and lucid explanation of his singular feat; a matter which is no feat at all to those engaged in the technical side of newspaper produc-tion, but not an accomplishment of the ordinary man.

I walked beside him on the path leading to his hall door. I was endeavouring to wheedle and persuade; without the faintest result. Now and again, he would stop to emphasise his denial with a blow of his fist on his open palm; and again the cameras went click, click. Finally, we got to the hall door, which was half glass. I had just caught a glimpse of a huddle of strange things within; Madonnas dim and rich, in curious frames of carven gold, great brass candlesticks that had stood before Flemish altars and had heard the holy mutter of the Mass, carved chests with linen-fold panels, saints in oak, grey with age—

when Mrs Turk appeared, terrible as an army with banners. Not even the men of the cameras could abide her onset. We all fled, as sheep before the wolf.

And then I went home and set down everything, just as it had happened. But it never got into print. People in authority at the newspaper office sidled into my room and looked at me quietly, keenly. They took counsel together over the matter. I think it was lucky that my engagements for the next few weeks were of an entirely ordinary kind, for if I had lit on anything remotely resembling the wonder world that had been disclosed to me at Burnt Green, I feel sure that I should have had an interview with a specialist; a specialist in the affairs of the mind.

The moral is obvious. We do not hear of 'Characters' now, because men are not suffered to write about them. They have become incredible, owing, as I believe, to a certain grossness and thickening of the power of apprehension. I have known many characters myself: there was the case of the lady, a member of a wandering company of entertainers, whose sentimental and pathetic ballad usually touched all hearts at the seaside. One afternoon she perceived to her amazement and indignation that the ballad was not going at all well. She heard some gasps of horrified wonder, then chuckles, then open mirth. Furious, and rightly so, for she was a most delightful and accomplished singer, she turned to leave the stage, and, turning, she saw the cause of this altered reception. On the floor, against the backcloth depicting a happy valley, bowered in roses, there crawled on his stomach another member of the company. One eye was upturned, and it was bloodshot. Between his teeth he held a gigantic carving knife. Years afterwards, this same gentleman caused some little commotion in Holborn, between two and three in the morning. He was reposing on his back in a horse-trough, calling loudly for his solicitor, declining to move till his legal adviser should attend. And the resident in a southern suburb who demanded in a formal and serious letter that his next door neighbour should chain up the bees in his hive, 'because your bee hass stung my baby's bottom'—he deserved fame, but the age denies it him.

It was otherwise of old. 'Characters' were once a literary genre; and I have often wondered as to those who compiled these chronicles of odd and whimsical lives. There is a certain style which was evidently considered appropriate to the matter; for the manner of these biographies never varies. The stranger the tale, the more stolid, flat and insipid does the chronicler become. I feel sure that every word is true; no liar could write with such dullness. Take the case of Betty Bolaine, born at Canterbury, in the year 1723. She was of 'a covetous turn.' She smiled on many suitors for the sake of the presents they gave her.

'At an assembly at Canterbury, when large hoop-petticoats were universally worn, the ladies, complaining of the inconvenience of the fashion, agreed to lay aside their hoops for awhile. Miss Bolaine objected to this proposal, fearing her saving contrivances would make her laughed at. However, her objections were overcome by her companions, and instead of a cane hoop she exhibited a straw one stitched with pack-thread and red tape and covered by an old dirty apron of her father's.'

Miss Bolaine found a man after her own heart, a Mr Box, with whom she set up housekeeping on the most economical principles.

'With this man she could eat a mouldy crust, with frowsy or stinking meat, sometimes picked up in the road, and cooked on cabbage stalks, burnt with turf, which was constantly stolen from the commons by night. These, with dried furze bushes, and dead stalks from their garden, constantly supplied fuel all the year round. . . . At this time, she was sometimes seen in a jacket crimped round her waist, and made of bed furniture, having monkeys, macaws and frogs depicted in needlework. . . . Her upper bonnet (for she wore two) consisted of thirty-six pieces of black stuff, curiously joined together; the under one was an old chip hat she once found on a dunghill in a garden, and which she was remembered to have worn nineteen years at least. Over this covering sometimes she would throw pieces of gauze, silk brocade, and tiffany, to make herself fine, as she thought . . . in this manner did she call every Sunday evening on the Dean of Canterbury, stumping through the hall and up the great staircase into the drawing-room.'

There is something stupendous about this bundle of unsavoury rags calling on the Dean of Canterbury; and Miss Bolaine's will was also picturesque. A dozen or so of people had endured her and bribed her for long years; and she left the whole of her fortune of £20,000 to a Prebendary of Canterbury, whose acquaintance she had just made.

The miser was a great favourite with the depicter of 'Characters,' as the friends of Mr Boffin and of Silas Wegg will remember, but he had other strings to his bow. There was the Reverend George Harvest, 'a lover of good eating almost to gluttony, extremely negligent in his dress, and a believer in ghosts, goblins, and fairies': there was the great painter, George Morland, who went through the ways of Marylebone, carrying a pig which he matched against every dog he met; there was Thomas Topham who could roll up a large pewter dish with his fingers; the Cock Lane Ghost; and the Fasting Woman of Tutbury— for Mrs Nickleby, it seems, was wrong in alluding to this Character as the Thirsty Woman.

THE EUSTON SQUARE MYSTERY

DECIDEDLY; THE murder of Matilda Hacker in Euston Square, in the year 1878, is one of those cases that are to be marked with an 'and yet. . . .' No doubt the verdict of the jury was the right verdict, according to the rules of the law; but . . . Miss Hacker, if she had lived in an earlier age, would undoubtedly have been one of those 'Characters,' of whom we were talking. Like Miss Betty Bolaine, she lived at Canterbury; like Miss Bolaine she had an aversion from the spending of money. But, born in a later age, she did not appear in polite company as an animated and malodorous rag-bag, nor did she make her meals of rotten meat picked up in the gutter and roasted on a fire of cabbage stalks. We have long lost the courage of our opinions; and Miss Hacker expressed herself in a purely negative way—she would not pay her rates at Canterbury. She was a well-to-do old woman, but she did not like paying rates. Accordingly, she absconded. She took various names, and lived in various places, so as to avoid being traced and proceeded against by the Canterbury authorities. At length, she called herself Huish, and took lodgings at 4, Euston Square—the place changed its name in consequence—a house kept by a Mr and Mrs Bastindoff. Like many other 'Characters' of the chronicles, she was accustomed to keep a good deal of money by her in a cash-box.

On the 10th of October, 1878, she wrote a business letter to her agent about some property, the reply to be addressed to 'M.B., Post Office, Holborn.' On Sunday, October 14, Mr and Mrs Bastindoff were out for the day, and Miss Hacker was alone in the house with the servant, Hannah Dobbs. Next day, Mr Bastindoff told the servant to go up to the old lady and get some rent due to him. Hannah, Mr Bastindoff declared, ran upstairs with alacrity, saying, 'I'll go,' and came down again with a £5 note. The note was changed, the rent owing deducted, and the balance handed to Hannah Dobbs; it does not appear why. But one would think that the lodger would have received the balance. And now a very singular point. Mrs Bastindoff said afterwards in the witness-box that on the morning of Sunday, October 14, Hannah had told her that she thought that Miss Huish (otherwise Hacker) was going to leave the lodgings that day; indeed, that she believed the old lady had already gone. This statement seems to have produced little effect on the Bastindoff family, since Mr Bastindoff sent up his servant to collect money from his lodger on the Monday morning, and collected it. It is not recorded that he said: 'So she hasn't gone, after all,' or made any remark in particular. But after the successful embassy of the £5 note, it would appear that the lodger's disappearance was gently allowed to steal on the family consciousness. Still, nobody troubled to go into the old lady's rooms for a couple of days, and then only to get them ready for a new lodger. In these rooms, Mrs Bastindoff declared, she saw a stain on the carpet, and also clear evidence that someone had tried to wash the stain away. Still, Mrs Bastindoff did not seem afraid with any amazement. A lodger had disappeared, probably on Sunday morning; had handed over five pounds on the Monday; her room, on the Wednesday, was found to be darkly stained; afterwards, analysis showed that this was, indeed, the stain of blood. But, so far as we can see, all these odd circumstances were accepted by the Bastindoffs as being completely in the natural order of things.

And there were other queer things, that appear to have aroused no particular comment at the time of their occurrence. Soon after October 15 Hannah Dobbs showed one of the Bastindoff children a Dream Book, which, she said, had belonged to Miss Hacker. She gave another child a funny toy, the lodger's cash box—with a broken lid. She also mounted a watch and chain which no one had ever seen about her before. But she explained that the watch and chain had been left her by an old uncle, lately dead at Bideford. She pawned them, later, under a false name, and it turned out at last that they were originally the property of Miss Hacker. It was found that there was no uncle at Bideford, and, naturally enough, therefore, that he hadn't died. Soon after the disappearance of the old woman, Hannah Dobbs left the

Bastindoff service, and went into lodgings. She could not pay her rent, so left her box as security. Eventually it was opened, and several articles in it were identified as having been the property of Miss Hacker.

So much for Miss Hacker's disappearance; now for her reappearance. Seven months later, in May, 1879, the cellar at No. 4, Euston Square, was cleared out, as one of the lodgers wanted to store coal there. Then Miss Hacker reappeared; very dead down in that cellar, with a rope about her neck. But the body was identified beyond doubt, and some pieces of jewellery found by the body were known to have been the property of the dead woman. A pretty strong case, as Montagu Williams observes, and yet Hannah Dobbs was acquitted. The judge was Mr Justice Hawkins, who was not generally supposed to be unduly favourable to prisoners at the bar. But the point, it seems, was technical. Hannah Dobbs was, undoubtedly, in possession of various pieces of property that had belonged to Miss Hacker; but that was no proof that she had murdered Miss Hacker; it was not even proof that she knew that Miss Hacker had been murdered. I do not know whether it were proved that Hannah Dobbs must have seen the watch and chain (for example) in the dead woman's possession; even so, they might have been given to her by another person and that other person might have assured Hannah that they were a gift to him from Miss Hacker.

Then followed a very odd sequel. Hannah Dobbs became a popular heroine. The proprietor of the *Police News* took up her case, and issued a pamphlet, which pretended to tell Miss Dobbs' true story. Miss Dobbs declared that there had been certain relations between herself and Bastindoff, before she entered his service, and during her residence in his house. Then Mr Bastindoff filed an affidavit, denying these allegations. And on that affidavit he was indicted for perjury. Again the Judge was Hawkins. Hannah Dobbs, who had been rather shabby at her own trial, turned up smartly dressed in the witness-box. She swore that the relations between herself and Bastindoff began in the autumn of 1877, when she was in service at 42, Torrington Square. Hannah and another girl were cleaning windows, and Mr Severin Bastindoff spoke to them.

'In consequence of that conversation he and I went out together that night or a night or two afterwards, and from that time until I entered his service we frequently went out together. The relationship was kept up during the time I was an inmate of his house.'

This story was corroborated by Hannah's fellow-servants. Two of them said that one night they were waiting for Bastindoff and that all three fell asleep before the kitchen fire, leaving the area door open. Two policemen noticed the open door, entered, woke the girls up, and partook of a little coffee with them. The girls identified the prisoner as the man they had seen, but explained that when they had met him below stairs his beard was differently cut. Mr Justice Hawkins then directed that a witness, once a partner of Bastindoff's, should be recalled, and he gave a description of the prisoner's beard, old style, which confirmed the statement of the servant girls. A Mrs Carpenter, keeper of an inn at Redhill, swore that in the year 1877 Dobbs and Bastindoff passed the night together at her hotel. It was observed that this Mrs Carpenter was violently antagonistic to the accused man. Hannah Dobbs was cross-examined. It appeared that she had been convicted of theft, and her little life story led Mr Justice Hawkins to declare her 'a most infamous person'. The defence was that on the day on which Bastindoff was said to have been at Redhill with infamous Hannah, he was really fishing in quite a different part of the country; and that the man who was with Hannah was really brother Peter Bastindoff, who was just like Severin. But, unfortunately, the people who swore that Severin was fishing, swore that Peter was fishing too, a statement making confusion very much worse confounded, but not helpful to the defence.

There is only one gleam of light in this strange, tragical, most horrible case: Severin Bastindoff's best witness was his mother-in-law. One would have thought that this affecting circumstance would have melted brassy bosoms and hearts of flint; but it was not so. In the result, Severin Bastindoff was found guilty of the crime of perjury, and sentenced to twelve months' hard labour.

There is no happy ending to this queer story. Nobody was hanged, though it seems pretty clear that somebody, perhaps several somebodies, would have been 'nane the waur for a hanging,' as the humorous Scots justice observed on one occasion.

MORE INNS

THERE IS A certain 'framework' to one of Dickens's Christmas Stories which, I suppose, is not as well known as many of his occasional works. It is called 'Somebody's Luggage,' and is, as a framework, tolerably artificial. The scheme of it is, that a certain unknown traveller comes to an old-fashioned London Inn, situated (I gather) in Holborn or the Strand, writes a great deal in the coffee-room, sends the porter on errands to publishing quarters, stays a night, and vanishes the next evening, leaving all his luggage behind him. Christopher, the head waiter, a most delightful character, becomes curious about this abandoned luggage. He buys it from the proprietress for the amount of the unknown's bill, and discovers that the luggage is full of manuscripts.

'He had crumpled up this writing of his everywhere, in every part and parcel of his luggage. There was writing in his dressing-case, writing in his boots, writing among his shaving tackle, writing in his hat box, writing folded away down among the whalebones of his umbrella.'

Christopher first of all disposes of the luggage to a dealer not far from St Clement Danes in the Strand. 'On my remarking that I should have thought these articles not quite in his line, he said; 'No more ith a manth grandmother, Mither Chrithtopher; but if any man will bring hith grandmother here, and offer her at a fair trifle below what the'll feth with good luck when the'th thcoured and turned—I'll buy her."

And then Christopher disposes of the Writings to the Editor of the *All the Year Round,* otherwise Mr Dickens, and the Christmas Number begins with the manuscript that was found in the traveller's Boots—and I am afraid that it had been better to have left it in his boots.

But what concerns me for the moment with 'Somebody's Luggage,' is the Bill of the man who went away. It is entered under the heading:

'Coffee Room, No. 4—the number of the box occupied by the traveller—Feb. 2nd, 1856.' It contains some curious items.

	£	s.	d.
Pen and Paper	.	.	6
Port Negus .	.	2	0
Ditto	.	2	0
Pen and Paper	.	.	6
Tumbler Broken	.	2	6
Brandy	.	2	0
Pen and Paper	.	.	6
Anchovy Toast	.	2	6
Pen and Paper	.	.	6
Bed .	.	3	0

Feb. 3rd	£	s.	d.
Pen and Paper	.	.	6
Breakfast	.	2	6
Broiled Ham	.	2	0
Eggs	.	1	0
Watercresses	.	1	0
Shrimps	.	1	0
Pen and Paper	.	.	6
Blotting Paper	.	.	6
Messenger to Paternoster Row and back	.	1	6
Again, when No Answer	.	1	6
Brandy, 2s. Devilled Port Chop, 2s. .	.	4	0
Pens and Paper	.	1	0
Messenger to Albemarle Street and back	.	1	0
Again (detained), when No Answer .	.	1	6
Salt-cellar broken	.	3	6
Large Liqueur glass Orange Brandy .	.	1	6
Dinner, Soup, Fish, Joint, and Bird .	.	7	6
Bottle old East India Brown .	.	8	0
Pen and Paper .	.	.	6
	£2	16	6

The oddest item is the charge for breakfast. Nominally this was
half-a-crown, but this sum covered, it is evident, merely the tea or

coffee, the bread and toast and the butter. Everything else is an extra, and these bring the total up to seven-and-sixpence; the profits to the establishment amounting to about 1,000 per cent or more; since I do not believe that the water-cress cost more than a penny. The breakages were also charged excessively, but the bed is cheap at three shillings, and the dinner most reasonable—provided that the dishes were good of their kind. Unfortunately, it is impossible to compare Christophers' inn with any hotel of our day, since the old kind has ceased to exist, save, perhaps, in a few old hostelries, lingering in small out-of-the-way country towns.

I have stayed at all sorts of houses of entertainment in my day in all parts of this island. I have lodged at small country 'pubs' and have been very comfortable; I have stayed at Palatial Hotels in big towns and have been hideously uncomfortable. I remember especially one of these latter. It had a Louis Quatorze, or Quinze, or Seize Tea room, furnished with the utmost luxury. There was marble everywhere, and hot air and cold air, and bathing arrangements that recalled the later Romans at their worst. And they kept me waiting twenty-five minutes for the bacon and eggs at breakfast; and when this rare and exotic dish did appear it was by no means excellent.

A great contrast to this was the Bell at Driffield, in that part of Yorkshire splendidly called the High Wolds. It is an extraordinary country; a great part of it ploughland when I visited it about eight years ago. The fields are huge; some of them, I believe, a hundred acres in extent. There are hardly any trees; they want to grow corn (they told me) not trees. The hedges are about three feet high by a foot broad, and if a hedge shows signs of becoming luxuriant, it is torn up. No weeds were suffered to grow in these hedgerows; not a flower appeared. But the lie of the land was the strangest thing about this strange region. It rose up before you with a great surge and swell; not precipitously, but gently and yet mightily, climbing up and up to the sky line; the white road rising perhaps for three or four miles, and in such a way that one felt that there must be a sudden and tremendous descent on the other side. Indeed I was strongly reminded of the Graveyard Scene in Sir John Martin Harvey's production of 'Hamlet,' the finest piece of scenic illusion that I have ever seen, where there was just such a gradual upward surge of the stage to the panorama cloth of the sky, with the like imperative suggestion that beyond the line of meeting, a thousand feet of sheer, precipitous cliff fell to the sea. But the Wolds were as deceptive as the theatre. The summit of the long wave gained, there was no violent, abrupt fall. The land went slowly down as it had slowly ascended; and then, far away, rose again into another climbing billow, marked by the white chalk road.

But the Bell at Driffield. It is a small, old coaching inn, and I did not suppose that its resources would be very varied. So when the landlord asked me on my first evening there what I would like for breakfast, I said, 'Oh, bacon and eggs, I suppose.' Instantly my host was roused. His manner became combative, his chin advanced with a sort of side-toss, peculiar to Yorkshire. And he said:

'Ah don't know about that. What about devilled kidneys?'

I assented gladly. Next morning, the devilled kidneys came and were admirable. Soon after they were served, the landlord came into the coffee-room. I expressed my high approval of the kidneys. He pointed to the sideboard, on which were a magnificent ham, just cut, and two plump fowls, golden brown from the roasting.

'Now mind you help yourself, Mr Machen,' said he, in an admonitory manner; implying that he would think very little of me if I did not help myself. 'And if there's anything else you would fancy, I hope you'll mention it.'

I left early the next day, and bid good-bye to this good host of the Bell. He relaxed a little.

'Coom again, Mr Machen, coom again. Coom next time for your pleasure, not for your business. As far as I know, you can get oop when you like, and go to bed when you like, and do anything you like for that matter.'

And he wagged a genial finger at me, as if he would say that he had imparted the great secret of life. Driving to the station, I found myself thinking of Shenstone's lines. I quote from memory:

> Whoe'er hath travelled life's dull round,
> Whate'er his fortunes may have been,
> Must sigh to think he still has found
> His warmest welcome at an inn.

MORE INNS

I have other good inns of pleasant and grateful memory. It is a great thing to stay at the Swan at Wells in summer weather; to look out across the street over the green turf of the close, to see the marvellous imagery of the west front of the cathedral against a sky of such a glowing and luminous blue as one only sees in the west. The inn at Dunster, too, the Luttrell Arms; that has a warm welcome and one of the loveliest prospects in England to commend it. And the Vine at Stafford has an old and flourishing vine making all its front green and living; and within there is the most delightful bar parlour, shaped like a boat. Here the boots brought a bag of list slippers at ten o'clock at night, and we all suited ourselves with slippers, as men who are too comfortable to stir in a hurry. We sat up talking to one another, and to the landlady and her daughter, who sat in the boat-shaped room with us in the old, friendly fashion. It was two o'clock in the morning before we stirred. The next morning, the landlady apologised for keeping me up so late. 'But really,' she said smiling, 'when one once embarks on these literary conversations, time seems to fly.' I agreed that literature was an absorbing subject; but what I remembered chiefly was some very old bottled ale which, to quote Mr Bob Sawyer on the brandy at the Blue Lion, Muggleton, was too good to leave in a hurry.

How I wish somebody would open a Bell or a Swan, or a Luttrell Arms, or a Vine—in London!

THE ADVENTURE OF THE
LONG-LOST BROTHER

IN THE SECOND week of November, 1803, a play called *A Bold Stroke for a Wife* was running at the Theatre Royal, Drury Lane. Miss Mellor was playing Anne; Bannister, Highwell; Atkin was Simon Pure; and Grimaldi, Aminadab. One night the prompter, otherwise the assistant stage manager, had put his head in at the green-room door and had summoned Mr Grimaldi, and as the actor was going on the stage a messenger told him that two gentlemen were waiting to see him at the stage door. The stage must never wait, so Grimaldi sent a message to the gentlemen, to the effect that he would come down to them as soon as the business of the scene was over. Accordingly, he went to the stage door and found there two gentlemanly young men.

'Here's Mr Grimaldi—who wants him?' said the actor, and one of the young men turned swiftly about and accosted Grimaldi in a very cordial manner. Grimaldi looked at him. He was about his own age and had the appearance of a man who had lived in some tropical climate. He wore the fashionable evening dress of 1803: a blue coat with gilt buttons, white waistcoat, and tight pantaloons, and a gold-headed dress cane was in his hand.

'Joe, my lad!' exclaimed this person, holding out his hand, with something of emotion in his manner, 'how goes it with you now, old fellow?'

Grimaldi was confused. To the best of his belief he had never seen the young man before and, hesitating, he replied that he really had not the pleasure of his acquaintance. 'Not the pleasure of my acquaintance!' repeated the stranger, with a loud laugh. 'Well, Joe, that seems funny, anyhow!' He appealed to his companion, who agreed, and they both laughed heartily. Grimaldi grew perturbed and uneasy; he suspected that the two men were rather laughing at him than with him, and he was turning away offended, when the first young man said, in a tremulous voice: 'Joe, don't you know me now?'

Grimaldi looked at him again. The man had opened his shirt, and was pointing to a scar upon his breast. By this scar Grimaldi recognised the young man as his only brother, John, who had gone to sea, had not been heard of many years, and was supposed to be dead. Grimaldi was very much moved. The two 'embraced again and again, and gave vent to their feelings in tears.' Men embraced each other in Dickens' earlier books. It is odd; but in the days of the Napoleonic War, when John Bull is supposed to have been most John Bullish, he had ways which we should call 'Continental'.

'Come upstairs,' said Grimaldi. 'Mr Wroughton is there—Mr Wroughton, who was the means of your going to sea—he'll be delighted to see you.' The two were hurrying off, when the other young man, who had been quite forgotten, said:

'Well, John, then I'll wish you good-night.'

'Good-night, good-night,' said John Grimaldi, shaking his friend's hand. 'I shall see you in the morning.'

'Yes,' replied the other, 'at ten, mind!'

'At ten precisely; I shall not forget,' answered John.

So the friend went away, unintroduced and unknown, so far as the actor was concerned. The brothers went first on the stage and then to the green-room; and the tale was told of this wonderful return, and the sailor was introduced to the actors. Still, the business of the stage continued, and the actor-brother had to leave the sailor-brother, gathering bits of his story between exits and entrances. The sailor said he had made a very successful trip.

'At this moment,' he boasted, slapping his pocket, 'I have six hundred pounds here.'

'Why, John,' said his brother, 'it's very dangerous to carry so much money about with you.'

'Dangerous!' replied John, 'we sailors know nothing about danger. But, my lad, even if all this were gone, I should not be penniless.'

Grimaldi was convinced by this and the knowing glance that the sailor gave him that he was, in fact, a wealthy man. But before he could get more exact information the prompter's voice was heard again, and the actor had to hurry away. In the meantime Mr Wroughton talked to John, making kind enquiries as to his doings and his success. John replied as he had replied to his brother, and brought out a coarse canvas bag, stuffed full of coins. The comedy was over at last, and Grimalidi asked his brother how long he had been in town. He replied only two or three hours; that he had had his dinner and come on at once to the theatre. What did he intend to do? He had not considered the matter; his only object had been to see his brother and mother once more. The two had a long talk. Joe told his brother that he, his wife, and his mother all lived together. But there was plenty of room in the house; why should not the sailor come and live with them, and so they would all be happy together. John was delighted with the notion. But he said that he knew he would not be able to sleep unless he saw his mother that very night; what was her address? The address was given, but the actor suggested that they had better walk home together. He had finished for the night, and would be ready as soon as he had changed his dress. The sailor assented, and Joe went off to his dressing-room.

And then the strangeness of it all came with a sudden onset on Grimaldi. 'The agitation of his feelings, the suddenness of his brother's return, the good fortune which had attended him in his absence, the gentility of his appearance, and his possession of so much money; all together confused him so that he could scarcely use his hands.' He seems to have fallen into the state which the Scots call a 'dwam,' a manner of waking vision, in which actualities are taken for dreams and the man wonders when he will awake and recognise that he has been amongst the shadows of the night. 'He stood still every now and then, quite lost in wonder, and then suddenly recollecting that his brother was waiting, looked over the room again and again for articles of dress that were lying before him.' In consequence, he took much more time than usual in getting off his make-up and changing his dress; but at last he was ready and ran down to the stage. On his way he met Powell, one of the Company. Powell congratulated him on his brother's return, and Grimaldi 'asked him more from nervousness than for information if he had seen him lately.'

THE ADVENTURE OF THE LONG-LOST BROTHER

I think the phrase is curious. It must be remembered that Grimaldi wrote his own *Memoirs*—they were severely sub-edited, it is true—and, likely enough, the phrase in question is the old actor's own. Taking into account the odd things that came upon him in the dressing-room, I am inclined to think that he had begun to suspect that his brother had never returned, had never been introduced to the actors, had never spoken of his wealth; that the whole thing was an illusion, a phantasm of his mind. That, I believe, was what he meant by 'nervousness'; he wished to be reassured by Powell, to be told that there was an actual brother waiting for him below, and that he would see him in a moment. But the events that were to come give this part of the story a very strange interest.

But Powell was reassuring enough.

'I saw him,' he replied, 'but a moment ago; he is waiting for you on the stage. I won't detain you, for he complains that you have been longer away now than you said you would be.'

Grimaldi hurried down to the spot where he had left his brother—it must have been the green-room, surely, not the stage, since there was an after-piece to follow *A Bold Stroke for a Wife*—but he was not there.

'Who are you looking for, Joe?' inquired Bannister, as he saw him looking eagerly about.

'For my brother,' he answered. 'I left him here a little while back.'

'Well, and I saw and spoke to him not a minute ago,' said Bannister. 'When he left me, he went in that direction (pointing towards the passage that led towards the stage-door). I should think he had left the theatre.'

Grimaldi rushed to the stage-door, and asked the door-keeper whether his brother had gone out. The man said he had gone out not a minute before, he had not had time to get out of the street. Grimaldi ran out, and ran up and down the street; not a sign of his brother. He wondered what had happened. Then it struck him that John might have gone to look up some old friend or neighbour—the Grimaldis had been brought up close to the Lane. There was Mr Bowley; he and John had been bosom friends when they were boys together. Forthwith Joe knocked at Mr Bowley's door.

Mr Bowley himself opened the door, and was evidently greatly surprised.

'I have, indeed, seen your brother,' said he. 'Good God! I was never so amazed in all my life.'

'Is he here now?' was the anxious inquiry.

'No; but he has not been gone a minute; he cannot have gone many yards.'

'Which way?'

'That way—towards Duke Street.'

Grimaldi thought on this that his brother must have gone to call on Mr Bailey, the Grimaldis' landlord, when they lived in Great Wild Street. Away to Mr Bailey's house in that street; again he knocked at the door. No one answered; he knocked and rang again with increased fury, and at length a girl put her head out of an upper window, and said in a voice both sulky and sleepy:

'I tell you again, he is not at home.'

'What are you talking about? Who is not at home?'

'Why, Mr Bailey. I told you so before. What do you keep on knocking for at this time of night?'

In great bewilderment, Grimaldi begged the girl to come downstairs, as he wanted to speak to her, telling her his name. She came down after a short interval.

'I'm sure I beg your pardon, sir,' said the maid. 'But there was a gentleman here knocking and ringing very violently not a minute before you came. I told him Mr Bailey was not at home; and when I heard you at the door I thought it was him, and that he would not go away.'

Then Grimaldi asked the girl if she had seen the gentleman's face. She had not; she had looked out of the upper-window, and all that she noticed was that the gentleman had a white waistcoat, whence she inferred that he might have come to take her master out to a party.

Back went the amazed and frightened actor to the theatre. There nothing had been seen of the lost brother; and then Grimaldi began a sort of mad midnight tour of the houses of old friends round the Lane, knocking and ringing people out of their beds and enquiring after his brother. Some of the people thought Grimaldi was mad; and said so.

His manner was wild, and nobody had heard of John Grimaldi for fourteen years. They had long given him up as dead.

One more call at the theatre; nothing had been seen of the missing man. Perhaps, Grimaldi thought, his brother had gone to the house in Pentonville. He had seemed so anxious to see his mother that very night; and between the calls of the prompter the two had been making plans of happiness of a family reunited after the passing of many years. But there was no brother at the house; but his mother sat in the supper-room, looking much paler than usual, so that Grimaldi thought she must have seen him.

'Well, mother,' he said, 'has anything strange occurred here tonight?'

'No; nothing that I have heard of.'

'What! no stranger arrived! no long-lost relative recovered!' exclaimed Grimaldi.

'What do you mean?'

'Mean! Why, that John is come home safe and well, and with money enough to make all our fortunes.'

The mother screamed and fainted. John Grimaldi was never seen again, never heard of. A great noble, a frequenter of Drury Lane, used his influence at the Admiralty; some people thought that John had been pressed for the Navy. He was known to have gone under another name, and when no news came, it was suggested that he might well have fallen in one of the great sea fights of those great wars; it was two years before Trafalgar. Then a police officer, who had made enquiries in the neighbourhood of the Lane, had his theory of the boastful sailor with his bag of gold being decoyed into some black den, there to be robbed and murdered. And Grimaldi himself was inclined to suspect his brother's companion, the smart young man in the white waistcoat, who made the appointment with his brother for ten o'clock the next morning. Why had this man not come round to the theatre, to make enquiries after his vanished friend? But John Grimaldi was seen no more.

It is an extraordinary tale. It may be true in every particular. But there are strange circumstances in the history. For example: why should John knock up his old friend, Mr Bowley, only to dart away from his door in a minute's time? Note that minute in advance all through the chase. It persisted up to Mr Bailey's house. The servant-girl there said, 'there was a gentleman here knocking and ringing very violently not a minute before you came.' I do not quite know why; but this fixed period of a minute inspires me with distrust.

But if the story be an invention, I am sure it was not Joe Grimaldi's. The famous clown was a worthy, stolid, solid man outside of his clowning. The lie, if it be a lie, must be the work of Mr Thomas Egerton Wilks, Grimaldi's friend during his life, editor of his *Memoirs* after the great clown's death.

But many of the actors at the theatre had seen John Grimaldi and talked to him on the night of his return? Possibly; but that was in 1803. Bannister died, I think, in the 'twenties; was any one of the company alive when the *Memoirs* were published in 1838?

And yet, in spite of all, I incline to believe in the truth of the tale.

THE POWER OF JARGON

NOT SO MANY years ago, fifteen or sixteen, or seventeen, perhaps, we were all following the Druce Case with immense interest. Stated baldly, as I remember it, the general thesis was that a Mr Druce, keeper of big furniture shop in Baker Street, who in due season died, and was buried in Highgate Cemetery, was not Mr Druce at all, but the Duke of Portland; the famous Duke who caused to be constructed the underground mansion at Welbeck, and was thought to be more than a little eccentric. Now, I have forgotten the detail, I regret to say, but if this Mr Druce could be proved to have been, in fact, the Duke, then somebody would come in for a great deal of money. The original claimant went mad and died, and then another claimant appeared, and turned himself or herself into a company, and found some hundreds of people ready to subscribe quite large sums so that the legal proceedings should be taken and the recovered treasure distributed amongst them. This monstrous bubble of a story was finally burst by leave being given to open the Druce vault at Highgate; whereupon the body of poor Mr Druce was disclosed and found to be undoubtedly the body of Mr Druce, and not a lump of lead, as (I think) was alleged by the Claimant. But in the course of litigation one extraordinary witness was called in support of the Claimant's case. She was a very old lady, over eighty, to the best of my recollection, and she had been brought all the way from New Zealand to tell the most outrageous cock-and-bull story that was ever heard in an English law court. She knew all about the secret of the Duke of Portland, who had the odd humour, according to the fable, of pretending at intervals to be an upholsterer in Baker Street; she knew, because in her youth she had been 'outside correspondent' to him, Charles Dickens, and Lord Lytton. She did not explain what an 'outside correspondent' was; she placidly babbled her imbecilities in the witness-box, and was finally prosecuted for perjury, convicted and let off very lightly.

But it is her phrase that interests me. I am convinced that it was a great attraction to the people who were persuaded to back this crazy imposture, just because it was idiotic, which, after all, is not surprising, since the persons concerned who parted with their money in such a cause were undoubtedly idiots, and so it was, I think, with the amazing case of Benson and the Turf Frauds, an old tale of the 'seventies.

Benson was a man of Jewish race. He was only twenty-six, but he had been in grave trouble before. He was perfectly well-mannered, well-educated, well-dressed, and had contrived, one gathers, by gig-keeping on a magnificent scale, to associate with the very best people in the Isle of Wight. He drove a splendidly equipped carriage and pair; therefore, he was a good man. He had collected about him a remarkable gang of assistants; and in the year 1876 Benson and his friends laid a remarkable trap, and baited it in the oddest manner. This bait was taken, and taken eagerly, by one Madame de Goncourt, a wealthy French widow. Benson, no doubt, had marked her down; it is the business of men who follow his difficult and dangerous craft to know everything—everything that may at all concern them. At all events, Madame de Goncourt received an odd number of an English paper called *Sport*. Of course, there was no such paper. But Madame de Goncourt, reading this journal which had fallen on her from the clouds, learned from it that it was the property of an immensely wealthy Englishman, a Mr Montgomery. This Mr Montgomery had mysterious and masterly access to turf and stable secrets that had enabled him to win, not thousands, but millions of pounds on the race-course. Not unnaturally, the bookmakers were enraged at the disastrous science of Mr Montgomery. They refused to take his bets. *Sport* was enraged. It pointed out a way. Though Mr Montgomery could not make bets in his own name, he could pay a slight commission to foreign agents, who would back horses for him in their own names. All this impressed Madame de Goncourt immensely, and she was impressed still more by the receipt of a letter from the great Mr Montgomery. This gentleman—*alias* Benson—wrote as follows:

'Your name has been favourably mentioned to me by the Franco-English Society of Publicity, and I consequently repose in you the most esteemed confidence. What I require of you is very simple indeed. I will send you for each race the amount which I desire to put on the horse which must, in my opinion, win. You will have to forward the money *in your name,* but *on my account,* to the bookmaker, and thus will be able to get the real odds, which, on account of my success and great knowledge, are denied me. The bookmaker will, on settling day, send you the amount, added to the stake originally forwarded to him. This you will please remit to me, and, on its receipt, I will forthwith forward to you a commission of five per cent.'

Madame de Goncourt had more money than she knew what to do with; naturally, therefore, she wanted to make more. She became Mr Montgomery's agent, and received cheques of 'The Royal Bank of London, Charing Cross.' There was no such bank, to be sure; but, then, there was no Franco-English Society of Publicity. Sham cheques came raining on Madame de Goncourt, and she forwarded them to various agents of Benson, who were supposed to be English book-makers. Then Mr Montgomery sent her a Bank of London cheque for £1,000, which was to be put on a certain horse and sent to a book-maker named Francis, who, said Mr Montgomery, was a 'sworn-book-maker.' And he advised the lady, very strongly, to invest a like sum on her own account. She did so, and in a few days she had sent £10,000 to various sworn-bookmakers.

Then, of course, the inevitable mistake. The gang did not know when to leave the board. They put it to Madame de Goncourt that a vast fortune was to be made if she could venture £30,000 with a sworn-bookmaker named Ellerton; and Mr Montgomery said that if the lady could not command the whole sum he would gladly advance the difference himself. She was only too ready to find the whole sum required; but before this could be done she had to have a talk with her banker—and then all was spoilt. Madame de Goncourt came over to England, and characteristically enough, applied to the Lord Mayor, telling him, no doubt, that she had suffered wrong. Her confidence in the French Legend of the Lord Mayor of London was justified; Benson and his rascals were caught, and the lady recovered almost the whole of her money. I do not think I am in the least glad to record this fact. On the whole, I think Benson and his pirates deserved the money quite as well as Madame de Goncourt, if not better. Poor men, men of large families and small means, may be readily excused if they are over-ready to accept idle tales of immense gains: but the rich should not be covetous. But this is not a moral tale. Its point lies in the highly successful use of absurd jargon, of the 'outside correspondent' order. Mark the 'Franco-English Society of Publicity,' non-existent, of course but interesting as containing an early example of the ugly word, 'publicity.' Note 'The Royal Bank of London'; note, above all, the 'sworn-book-maker,' a great creation. There is no surer bait than pompous and unmeaning gibberish of this sort. You remember 'The Anglo-Bengalee Disinterested Loan and Life Assurance Company.' In England we require the moral touch implied in 'Disinterested.' Benson was baiting his hook for Continental victims, and so did not appeal to the ethical issue. It is well known that they are not really moral on the Continent. I shall call my swindle 'The All-British Orphans' Benevolent Protection and Reconstruction Company, Ltd.' Reconstruction is one of the most blessed of these blessed words; and what good man could resist the temptation of benevolently protecting and reconstructing an All-British Orphan—especially if he were promised interest on his money at the rate of twenty-five per cent?

THE LITTLE PEOPLE

I HAVE BEEN looking into a very odd book, and I am going to tell the story of the Asiki, or Little Beings, first observing that the singular is Isiki. Well, it is said that the Asiki were once ordinary, human children, but were caught, when young and defenceless, by wizards or witches, and were dragged into the black depths of the forest, where there was no help for them, where no one could hear their cries. The wizards cut off their tongues as a first measure; and so they never speak again, and cannot inform against the magicians. They are then carried away, and hidden in a secret place, where they are subjected to magical processes which change their whole nature, so that they are no longer mortal. They forget their homes, their fathers and mothers and all their kinsfolk. Even the hair of their heads changes. Instead of being crisp wool, it becomes long and straight and hangs down their backs. At the back of their heads they wear a curious comb-shaped ornament, made of some twisted fibre. This they value almost as part of their life, just as in another quarter of the world there are people who drive motor-cars and cherish little images and idols and grotesque figures, which are believed to constitute a most powerful protection. These Asiki will sometimes be seen walking on dark nights, and are occasionally met on their walks. It is believed that if a person is either naturally fearless, or made fearless by charms and spells, and dares to seize an Isiki and snatch away the comb, the possession of this mascot will bring him great wealth. But he will not be allowed to remain in peaceful possession of it. The Isiki, in a state of misery and desolation, will be seen wandering about the place where the magic comb was taken from it, endeavouring to get it back. And as late as the year 1901 strange things were told of these Little People in Libreville, French Congo. A certain Frenchman, known to be a Freemason, returning from his restaurant dinner to his house one evening, noticed a small figure keeping pace with him on the other side of the road. He called out, 'Who are you?' There was no reply; the figure kept on walking, advancing and retreating before him.

A few nights later, a negro clerk in some trading house met the Isiki near the place where the Frenchman had encountered it. And the Little Being began to chase the negro. He ran for his life, and told his master, the trader, what had happened. He got laughed at for his pains, and the next night the trader told the tale to a select company of white men and black women, the Freemason being present. And he said, 'Your clerk did not lie; he told the truth. I have myself met that Little Being, but I did not try to catch it.' Then the black women spoke of the odd comb-ornament, and of how the Asiki treasured it, and of the good fortune it would bring to anybody who could capture it. Where-upon the Frenchman—otherwise the Freemason—said, 'As the Little Being is so small, the very next time I see it I will try to catch it and bring it here, so that you can see it and know that this story is actually true.'

Soon after, the Frenchman and the trader went out at night and tried to find the Isiki. No Little Being was to be found, but a few nights later the Frenchman met it near the place where it had been seen before. He ran forward and tried to catch it, but the Isiki eluded him. However, he succeeded in snatching the comb, and ran with it towards his house. The Little Being was displeased and ran after him to recover the charm. Having no tongue, it could not speak, but holding out one hand pleadingly and with the other motioning to the back of its head, it made pathetic sounds in its throat, thus pleading that its treasure should be given back to it. It followed the Frenchman till the lights of his house began to shine, and then it disappeared. The Frenchman showed the comb to his friends, both black and white, and all agreed that they had never seen anything like it before. From that night the Isiki was often seen by negroes, who were afraid to pass that way in the dark. It followed the Frenchman persistently, pleading with its hands in dumb show, and making a grunting noise in its throat. The Frenchman got tired of all this, and made up his mind that he would give the comb back. And so next night he took it with him; and also a pair of scissors. The Little Being appeared and followed him. He held out his hand, with the comb in it. The Isiki leapt forward and snatched at the talisman and secured it, and the Frenchman tried to catch the Isiki. The Little Being was too agile, however, and escaped; but the Frenchman snipped off a lock of the long straight hair with his scissors, and brought it home and showed it to his friends.

Such is the story told by Dr Robert H. Nassau, an American missionary, who had worked for forty years in Africa. He seems to fear that his tale will be regarded as incredible. It seems to me, on the contrary, highly probable. Naturally, one dismisses that part of it which relates to the process by which these Little Beings are made, and that part of it which ascribes to them immortality. The Little People were not made out of little woolly piccaninnies by the magic arts of the wizards; and probably, if one could be caught and examined, it would be found that it had a tongue in its mouth, like any other human being. The fact is that here, in all likelihood, we have a pretty exact parallel to the Little People of our own folk-lore: the Daione Sidhe of Ireland, the Tylwyth Teg of Wales. The substratum in both cases is the same: an aboriginal people of small stature overcome and sent into the dark by invaders. In Britain and Ireland the dark meant subterranean dwellings made under the hills in the wildest and most remote parts of the country; they will point you out the place of these dwellings in Antrim to this day, and tell you that they are Fairy Raths. And in nine cases out of ten you may accept the statement with entire confidence; so long as you define 'fairies' or 'the People' as small, dark aborigines who hid from the invading Celt somewhere about 1500-1000 B.C. And in Africa the dark meant the blackness of the forest; places hidden in the thickest tangle of trees and undergrowth, protected, perhaps, from all outsiders, black or white, by a maze of narrow paths winding in and out of a foul swamp. And as to the legend of the torn-out tongues, of the guttural noises made by the Asiki; is it not the case that the Little People of the genuine Celtic tradition are also silent? I will not be sure; but I incline to think that this is so. They beckon, they gesticulate, they are seen by Irish countrymen playing at hurly: but they say nothing— the reason being that they do not speak the language of their conquerors. I have seen a monoglot Englishman in Touraine behaving much as the Isiki behaved to the Frenchman at Libreville, even to the making of unearthly sounds and the indulging in antic gestures. But he only wanted milk with his tea. And there is this further parallel between the Little Beings of Africa and the Little People of Ireland. Both are on a curious borderland between the natural and the supernatural. Both are able to 'propagate procerity'—I use an elegant phrase of Dr Johnson's. This is formally asserted of the Asiki; and in Celtdom we have the legends of the changeling, the little, dark creature found in the cradle of the big, red-haired Celtic baby. And both are material and capable of dealing with material things and of making use of them. Miss Somerville has strange tales of them which are of our own day. Miss Somerville herself had seen the shoe that was found on the lonely hill. It was of the size that a child of about a year old might use, but it was heavily made, in the fashion of a workman's brogue, and had seen hard wear. And, again, she tells the story of two servants sent on a sudden errand at night. They were driving a car, and at the entrance of a certain town, the harness broke. And there they found a little saddler's shop, open in the dead of night, and two little men within—described with a shudder as 'quare'—to whom the servants told their trouble. They were terrified almost out of their senses they would not stay in the shop: but the work was done, and done well.

We have here a state of mind which is very hard to understand. What can an Immortal want with a workman's leather shoe? And how should Beings of another order from that of man, Beings to be beheld with awe and dread of the spirit, undertake saddlery repairs on demand? One would say that the belief that such things are so is impossible; but yet it exists in Ireland, probably to this day; and it is much like the negro belief as to the Asiki.

It is interesting to note, by the way, that Fairyland in Ireland seems strongly associated with leather. There is the matter of the fairy brogue, there is the adventure of the fairy saddlers; and then there is the Leprechaun, who is a fairy cobbler. He is, clearly, a distant cousin of the Asiki. And if, in spite of all his efforts to distract you, you continue to regard him with a fixed gaze, your reward will be a crock of gold.

THE CAMPDEN WONDER

MR WILLIAM HARRISON was steward to the Viscountess Campden, of Campden, in Gloucestershire. One afternoon—to be precise, on the 16th of August, 1660—he walked out from Campden to Charringworth, a place about two miles off, to receive some rent due to the Viscountess. He was late getting back, and between eight and nine in the evening his wife, feeling a little uneasy, sent the man, John Perry, to meet his master and bring him home. That night neither master nor man returned. Early the next morning Mr Harrison's son, Edward, went towards Charringworth to enquire after his father. He met Perry coming from Charringworth, and was told by him that his father was not there. Then Edward Harrison and Perry went together to a village called Ebrington, between Charringworth and Campden, and at Ebrington a man named Daniel told them that Mr Harrison had called on him on his way home from Charringworth the night before, but had not stayed. On this, the younger Harrison and the man turned back home, and on their way heard something of a hat, a band, and a comb found on the road between Ebrington and Campden by a poor woman, who was harvesting. They sought out the woman, they identified the hat, comb, and band as being the property of Mr William Harrison. The hat and comb were hacked and cut, and the band—the broad round collar, ancestor of the legal bands of today, for which the bandbox was designed—bloody. Crowds came to look for the body of Mr Harrison—his properties were found by a great brake of gorse—but no body was found. Mrs Harrison was grievously alarmed. It struck her as highly suspicious that Perry, the manservant, had stayed out the whole night, instead of coming back, with news or without news. So Perry was haled before a justice of the peace, and told a very odd story. He said he set out for Charringworth, but soon met one

111

William Reed, of Campden. It was getting dark, and Perry told Reed that he was afraid to go to Charringworth afoot, and so he would turn back and get his young master's horse, and ride to Charringworth. So Perry turned back, Reed being in his company, and came to the gate of the Harrison demesne. Reed went on his way, Perry stayed still by the gate. Then one Pierce came by, and Perry went with Pierce 'a bow's shot into the fields,' and again-returned, Pierce being of his company; and so Pierce went on his way. And then Perry went and lay about an hour in the hen-roost, but could not sleep. Then the clock struck twelve and for the third time Perry sallied forth on his errand. But a great mist arose, and he lost his way, and lay the rest of the night under a hedge. At daybreak the next morning he at last ended his journey and came to Charringworth. Here he heard from William Plaisterer that Mr Harrison had called the afternoon before and had received three-and-twenty pounds. And William Curtis had heard that Mr Harrison had called at his house; but he was out and did not see him. And so Perry turned back and met young Edward Harrison, as we have heard already. Reed, Pierce, Plaisterer and Curtis were called and confirmed Perry's story so far as it concerned them.

The justice asked the man why he was afraid to go to Charringworth at nine, and not afraid at twelve. The answer was that it was dark at nine, but moonlight at twelve. Then he was asked why he did not inquire whether his master had come back after his first return and his second return. He said he saw light in his master's bedroom window, 'which never used to be there so late when he was at home.' It was considered wise to keep Perry in custody, and so he was held at Campden, sometimes in the prison, sometimes in an inn—a genial age!—and there he told all sorts of stories. He told some people that Mr Harrison had been murdered by a tinker, others that he had been robbed and murdered by a gentleman's servant, others that he had been killed and his body hidden in a bean-rick. The bean-rick was searched and nothing found. Finally, Perry confessed that William Harrison had been murdered by his mother and his brother. He declared that the two had 'lain at him'—note the nearness of the seventeenth-century idiom to our 'had been at him' ever since he entered the service of Mr Harrison. They had pointed out how poor

they were, and how simple it would be for John to tell them when Mr
Harrison was going to receive rents, so that they could waylay and rob
him. These pleadings won at last upon John Perry's filial and fraternal
heart, as he said, and on the Thursday morning—the day of Mr Harrison's disappearance—he met his brother in the street of Campden and
told him where his master was going in the afternoon, amiably
remarking to brother Richard that if he cared to waylay Mr Harrison
he might have his money. That evening, Mrs Harrison sent John Perry
to meet his master, as we have heard, the time being about half-past
eight. He met his brother Richard close at hand, and the two prowled
about in the dusk of the evening till they came to some private grounds
of Lady Campden's, called the Conygree. Certain persons were
allowed to have a key which gave them passage through these grounds.
Mr Harrison, the agent, was, naturally, one of these persons, and he
was accustomed to use the Conygree as a short cut to his house. Good
son and brother John Perry saw a figure going into the Conygree, and
told Richard Perry that this figure was probably his master, and that he
could have his money. For his part, John observed, he would take a
short walk in the fields. So John communes with nature, and then
strolls into the Conygree. He finds his master on the ground, brother
Richard upon him, and his mother standing by. William Harrison then
cried out, 'Ah, rogues, will you kill me?' John Perry, shocked, observed
to Richard that he hoped he would not kill his master. Whereupon
Richard, exclaiming briefly, 'Peace, peace, you are a fool,' strangled
old Mr Harrison—the agent was a man of seventy. The prudent Richard then took a bag of money out of Mr Harrison's pocket and threw
it into his mother's lap. The two Perrys carried the dead body into the
garden adjoining the Conygree, and consulted what they should do
with it. It was finally determined that it should be thrown into 'the
great sink by Wallington's mill, behind the garden.' At this point John
left the little family party, taking with him his master's hat, band, and
comb, which he laid for the moment in the hen-roost. He then
mooned about, in the manner described by him at his first examination, meeting Reed and Pierce. Finally, he took the hat, band, and
comb, and after slashing them a little, laid them on the high-road,
where the harvesting woman found them. And as to his master's body,

said John, if it were not in the great sink, he did not know where it was.

The great sink was searched, the fishponds of Campden Vere searched, the ruins of Campden House, burnt in the Great Rebellion, were searched, but the body of William Harrison was not found. Nevertheless, Joan and Richard Perry, the mother and brother of John, were arrested; and the whole three charged with the murder of Mr Harrison. Joan and Richard denied the fact with imprecations on themselves if they had any share in the deed alleged against them: John persisted in his accusations and declared he would maintain them to his death. All three prisoners were committed. On their way to prison, Richard, at the end of the procession, 'pulling a clout out of his pocket, dropped a ball of inkle, which one of his guard taking up, he desired him to restore, saying it was only his wife's hair lace.' But the guard showed it to John, who said sorrowfully that he knew it very well; his brother had strangled his master with it. Next day, being Sunday, the prisoners were taken to church. On their way, they passed Richard's house, and two of his children ran out to meet him. He took the smaller child on his arm, and led the other by the hand; whereupon both the children's noses began to bleed. This was thought to look badly for Richard.

There was another point. The year before Mr Harrison's house had been broken into while he was at 'lecture'—the Puritans were still in power in 1659—and £140 had been taken. The justice of the peace, finding John in a confessing mood, asked him whether he knew about the robbery. Certainly, John knew. Richard had taken the money and hidden it in his garden. The garden was searched; nothing was found.

At the September assizes, the three were indicted for robbery and for robbery and murder. The Judge, Sir Christopher Turner, refused to try the latter charge, for the very good reason that no body had been found. On the charge of robbery—the robbery of 1659 they at first pleaded Not Guilty, but on advice altered the plea to Guilty, and enjoyed the benefit of the King's pardon and Act of Oblivion. Later, they denied any part in the robbery.

At the spring assizes of 1661, the three were tried again for murder, Sir Robert Hyde being the Judge. John's confession was put in evidence. Whereupon John said that he was mad when he uttered it, and knew not what he said. All three were found guilty of murdering William Harrison, condemned, and executed on Broadway Hill, in sight of Campden. Joan Perry, the mother, was hanged first. It was thought that she was a witch, and had cast a spell upon her sons, so that they could not confess while she lived. Richard then took his turn on the ladder, and died, protesting his innocence, and imploring his brother to tell all he knew about Mr Harrison. John, the last to climb, wore 'a dogged and surly carriage,' and told the people he was not bound to confess to them. But at the last he said he knew nothing about his master's death; but, he added, they might, possibly, hear hereafter.

They did. In a little under two years Mr Harrison came back to Campden.

He told the story of his adventures, in a letter addressed to Sir Thomas Overbury, Knight, of Bourton (near Campden), in Gloucestershire. He begins from the beginning.

'One Thursday in the afternoon, in the time of harvest, I went to Charringworth to demand rents, due to my lady Campden; at which time the tenants were busy in the fields, and late ere they came home, which occasioned my stay there till the close of the evening. I expected a considerable sum, but received only three-and-twenty pounds and no more. In my return home (in the narrow passage, amongst Ebrington Furzes), there met me one horseman, and said, 'Art thou there?' And I, fearing that he would have rid over me, struck his horse over the nose, whereupon he struck at me with his sword, several blows, and run it into my side; while I (with my little cane) made my defence as well as I could; at last another came behind me, run me into the thigh, laid hold on the collar of my doublet, and drew me to a hedge near to the place. Then came in another; they did not take my money, but mounted me behind one of them, drew my arms about his middle, and fastened my wrists together with something that had a spring lock to it as I con- ceived, by hearing it give a snap as they put it on; then they threw a great cloak over me, and carried me away. In the night they alighted at a hayrick which stood near unto a stone pit by a wall-side, where they took away my money, about two hours before day (as I heard one of them tell the other he thought it to be then). They tumbled me into the stone pit, they staid (as I thought) about an hour at the hayrick. When they took horse again, one of them bade me come out of the pit; I answered they had my money already, and asked what they would do with me; whereupon he struck me again, drew me out and put a great quantity of money to my pockets, and mounted me again after the same manner. And on the Friday night, about sun-setting, they brought me to a house . . . where they took me down almost dead, being sorely bruised with the carriage of the money. When the woman of the house saw I could neither stand nor speak, she asked them whether or no they had brought a dead man? They answered no, but a friend that was hurt, and they carrying him to a chirurgeon. She answered that if they did not make haste their friend would be dead before they could bring him to one. There they laid me on cushions, and suffered none to come into the room, but a little girl; there we stayed all night, they giving me some broth and strong waters. In the morning, very early, they mounted me as before, and on Saturday night they brought me to a place where were two or three houses, in one of which I lay all night on cushions, by their bedside. On Sunday morning they carried me from thence, and about three or four o'clock they brought me to a place by the seaside, called Deal, where they laid me down on the ground; and one of them staying by me, the other two walked a little off, to meet a man, with whom they talked; and in their discourse I heard them mention seven pounds, after which they went away together, and about half an hour after returned.

'The man (whose name, as I after heard, was Wrenshaw) said he feared I would die before he could get me on board; then presently they put me into a boat, and carried me on shipboard, where my wounds were dressed. I remained in the ship (as near as I could reckon) about six weeks, in which time I was indifferently recovered of my wounds and weakness. Then the master of the ship came and told me (and the rest who were in the same condition) that he discovered three Turkish ships; we all offered to fight in the defence of the ship and ourselves, but he commanded us to keep close, and said he could deal with them well enough. A little while after he called us up, and when we came on the deck we saw two Turkish ships close by us. Into

116

one of them we were put, and placed in a dark hole, where how long we continued before we were landed, I know not. When we were landed they led us two days' journey, and put us into a great house or prison, where we remained four days and a half. And then came to us eight men to view us, who seemed to be officers; they called us and examined us of our trades and callings, which everyone answered; one said he was a chirurgeon, another that he was a broadcloth weaver, and I (after two or three demands) said I had some skill in physic. We three were set by and I was chosen by a grave physician of 87 years of age, who lived near to Smyrna, who had formerly been in England and knew Crowland, in Lincolnshire, which he preferred before all other places in England. He employed me to keep his still house, and gave me a silver bowl, double gilt, to drink in; my business was most in that place; but once he set me to gather cotton wool, which I not doing to his mind, he struck me down to the ground, and after drew his stiletto to stab me; but I, holding up my hands to him, he gave a stamp, and turned from me. . . . I was there about a year and three-quarters, and then my master fell sick on a Thursday, and sent for me, and calling me as he used by the name of Boll told me he should die, and bade me shift for myself. He died on Saturday following, and I presently hastened with my bowl to a port about a day's journey distant. . . . When I came thither, I addressed myself to two men who came out of a ship of Hamborough, which (as they said) was bound for Portugal within three or four days. I enquired of them for an English ship, they answered there was none. I entreated them to take me into their ship; they answered they durst not for fear of being discovered by the searchers.'

To abbreviate Mr Harrison a little: he at length prevailed on another man of the same ship to take him on board; the effective argument being a sight of the gilt bowl. He was placed below in the vessel 'in a very uneasy place,' and so well hidden that he escaped the Turkish searchers and was finally landed at Lisbon, free but moneyless. Here he fortunately fell in with an Englishman, a native of Wisbech, who paid for his passage to Dover, and so, with some pious and becoming expression of gratitude, Mr William Harrison ends the story of his adventures, perils and deliverances.

Now, it may or may not have been noted, that I have told the whole story without comment or expression of opinion of any kind. And I have not commented, because I have no notion whether there is a single word of truth in the story. My authority is the State Trials, and one might think, on the face of it, that no more solid foundation of fact could be desired. But this is not so. The account in the State Trials is merely a reprint of a pamphlet issued in London in the year 1676:

'A True and Perfect Account of the Examination, Confession, Trial, Condemnation and Execution of Joan Perry, and her two sons, John and Richard Perry, for the Supposed Murder of William Harrison, Gent. London, printed for Rowland Reynolds, next Arundel Gate, over against St Clement's Church in the Strand, 1676.'

The pamphlet gives as its authority a letter sent by Sir T.O. [Thomas Overbury] to T.S. [T. Shirley], a London physician; but as both these gentlemen are far beyond all cross-examination, nothing is established thereby. Of course, the story reeks with improbabilities. At first sight, the most improbable circumstance of all is the conduct of John Perry in swearing away, not only the life of his mother and his brother, but his own life as well. But his conduct is not without precedent. To this day, people give themselves up for murders which they have not committed, and in John Perry's day women confessed freely to having shared in the monstrous horrors of the Witches' Sabbath. If the story be true, John Perry was a hysterical madman. And there is another point: the condemnation and execution of these people for murder, there being no *corpus delicti*—otherwise the body of the dead man or some identifiable part of it—producible; was such a thing possible? Unfortunately, it was. It was against all legal principle. The Civil Law forbade it. Lord Hale said: 'I would never convict any person of murder or manslaughter unless the fact were proved to be done, or at least the body found dead.' But, apparently, this was a matter left to the taste and fancy of the judge, for Lord Hale supports his principle by citing two cases in which men were hanged for the murder of persons who proved afterwards to be alive. So there is no improbability in this part of the story. As we have seen, the judge at the first assize, Sir Christopher Turner, held with Lord Hale and refused to try the Perrys, 'because the body was not found.' At the next assizes, the judge, Sir Robert Hyde, made no difficulties on the ground of the lacking body.

The big difficulty lies in Mr Harrison's story. Why was he abducted, and who were his abductors? He speaks of other people on the ship as being in the same condition as himself. Was there a Little Syndicate which operated in old gentlemen, selling them to master mariners at seven pounds apiece? This seems unlikely. And could you transport this sort of goods from Campden, Gloucestershire, to Deal, Kent, without fear of interruption? I do not know; the tale must remain the Campden Wonder, so far as I am concerned.

MORDUCK THE WITCH

THE BELIEF IN witchcraft died very hard. Indeed, it is not dead yet; but we call the thing and our belief in it by other names. It is not difficult, if you are so disposed, to consult both men and women who have a familiar spirit, in the year 1926.

Richard Hathaway was the defendant in an odd trial in this matter of witchcraft in the first year of Queen Anne. He said he had been bewitched by Sarah Morduck, and twenty years or so earlier, Sarah Morduck would, no doubt, have been hanged for the fact. But it was getting a little late, and so Richard was convicted of being a cheat and impostor, and pilloried in Southwark and Cornhill and at Temple Bar, and imprisoned for six months, and handsomely flogged—for being too late. Indeed Sarah Morduck had a narrow escape. Richard had vomited nails and pins, he could not speak nor open his eyes, great noises were heard in his house; all these troubles being due, as he said, to the spells of Sarah. Accordingly he went to the woman's house and scratched her savagely, and immediately experienced great relief. But there was a clever clergyman then at Southwark, where the persons of the story lived. It seemed that Hathaway, after the relief brought about by his scratchings, had relapsed, and Dr Martin, rector of St George's, calling on the man, found that he could neither speak nor see. So Dr Martin told Hathaway that he had heard of his troubles, and had brought Sarah Morduck with him that she might be scratched again, and another cure effected. But in the background Dr Martin had another woman, not visible to Hathaway, and when a hand was held out to be scratched, the Doctor had seen to it that it was the other woman's hand. Hathaway's eyes opened, and he began to talk, but, of course, the believers in witchcraft said that proved nothing. It has been laid down by high spiritualist authority that if a ghost is seized at a séance, and is found to be the medium swathed in white muslin, that proves nothing. Consequently, Sarah Morduck was haled from Southwark to the City, and set upon by the rabble, and scratched again in full court, but as luck and the turn of the tide of opinion would have it, acquitted in the end. Hathaway should have taken the hint. But he still persisted that he was bewitched, and now a spell had been laid upon him which prevented him from eating. He was consigned to the care and observation of a surgeon and in public kept up a tremendous fast. But crafty holes had been bored in the walls of his room, and through these holes he was observed to eat and drink most heartily. And so he was put upon his trial as a cheat and an impostor; whereupon the 'prayers of the congregation' were asked for him in many churches, and good people collected money to support him in his trials. And poor Sarah, as counsel observed, was in grave danger of being torn in pieces by the mob. Dr Martin, the Rector of Southwark, told the Court how he managed his ingenious device. There had been some difficulty, he said, in getting a woman who was willing to be scratched.

'I had before met with a poor woman, whom I ordered to follow me, who received alms of the parish, designing she should be the person the experiment should be tried on. . . . I told her I would give her a shilling if she would let this man scratch her. She flew off, and said she would not suffer it for all the world. At last somebody said, "Here is a woman who will suffer herself to be scratched"; and this was one Johnson.'

The Doctor goes on with his story; tells how his plain demonstration that Hathaway was a humbug, a cheat, and a liar did not demonstrate anything to the people who had made up their minds. Nay; the man himself had the impudence to speak to his parish priest in this style:

'Do you not believe,' he said to Dr Martin, 'that I am bewitched?'

'No, I do not.'

'Then,' says he, 'I may as well not believe what you say in the pulpit; I may say to you as our Saviour said to the Jews: Though you see miracles you will not believe.'

The logic is almost modern.

The good Rector went down to Guildford Assizes, where Sarah Morduck was charged with the capital offence of witchcraft. He gave his evidence, and Sarah was acquitted. And the result to the Doctor?

'When I came to town, I was abused by many people, both openly and privately: "You have the blood of that innocent man to be at your door; the woman had been hanged if you had not saved her; the judgments of God will fall on you." '

And the general opinion was, added Dr Martin, that he had been bribed, and the judge had been bribed, and the jury had been bribed, and that on the whole, mercy, and truth, and justice were fled out of the land since Sarah Morduck was not hanged, and oh! what must the feelings of poor Mr Hathaway be in this dreadful trial?

Mr Bateman, of Pembrokeshire, gave an entertaining account of Hathaway's great performance of vomiting pins.

'I said to him, "I hear you vomit pins!" "Yes," says he. Says I, "Prithee let me see thee." So he sat on a low seat, and they gave him something in a cup, and by drinking this I was to see him vomit pins; and he took some drink; but, as far as I could perceive, he did not swallow any. He pretended then to be in an agony and vomited several times, and there were pins on the ground. I had the room swept very clean, and gave him the same again. He vomited again, and there were abundance of pins on the ground again. I believe he vomited fourteen or fifteen times, and I believe there were some hundreds of pins on the ground; but I thought the pins were dropt from one or other; and I took up some of them, and they were dry.'

Mr Bateman searched Hathaway, and found pins by the parcel in his pockets. The man from Pembrokeshire concludes, sanely enough, that rascal Hathaway had some trick of dropping the pins on the ground, but he confesses that he could not catch him in the act, though he observed him keenly and closely. Then one Hearne, brother of the supposed witch, told how his sister was set upon and grievously used by the mob. Hearne applied for protection to Sir Thomas Lane, a magistrate, and that wise Solomon of a judge said there had been grievous provocation; and all the satisfaction Morduck and her brother received from the Court was that Sir Thomas ordered the witch to be scratched again. This done, Hathaway, supposed to be fasting under an evil spell, fell on some bread and cheese with enormous appetite, and 'brustled about like a cock sparrow.' Nobody could resist this, so poor Sarah Morduck was committed by Sir Thomas Lane to take her trial for witchcraft. Mr Kensy, the surgeon to whose care Hathaway was entrusted, then told, with much liveliness, how he had laid traps for the impostor, how he had feigned a furious quarrel with his servant in Hathaway's presence; and how this servant, instructed by him, arranged to bring the man food and drink in secret; and how the doctor viewed, through a secret hole in the wall, Mr Hathaway consuming fish, oysters, strong beer and brandy with immense relish, with so much relish, indeed, that he became extremely unwell. The maid-servant who was in the plot gave an example of the abusive language used by her master in the course of the sham quarrel: he called her 'presbyterian jade'; a phrase that shows that people had not yet forgotten Oliver's days in the first year of the reign of Queen Anne. And the maid relates how she gave Hathaway a bottle of stout—I did not know that strong porter was called so as far back as this—and this drink was so stout that the cheat became 'very merry, and danced about, and took the tongs and played upon them. But after that he was mighty sick'—details omitted. Strange noises were heard every night in the house where Hathaway slept. A psychical researcher, named Hunt, told how he had observed this side of the mystery. Hathaway was put to bed, 'three little things in black bags' called 'the charms' were sewed on his shirt, and Mr Hunt presently observed the man moving his hands about. 'Hunt struck the fellow's hands and told him to keep them still or put them out of the bed.

'Then I and the company sitting still about the bed, Welling (Hathaway's master) said, 'Hearken, you will not believe; hear what a noise there is; the like is heard here almost every night.' Whereupon all were silent. At last I heard a small scratching or rubbing at the bed's feet; and putting my head close to the bed's feet, listening, I heard something shriek; and perceiving the bed-clothes stir, I took hold of the fellow's foot, and said, "I have caught the witch that made the noise.' I thought it had been mice at first, but seeing the clothes move, I catched his foot.'

And so on, and so on. The defence called their witnesses who were sure, or almost sure, that Hathaway was bewitched. One of these, Mrs Willoughby, gives curious evidence.

LCJ: 'Do you think he was bewitched?'

Willoughby: 'I believe he was, my lord.'

LCJ: 'I suppose you have some skill in witchcraft. Did you ever see anybody that was bewitched before?'

Willoughby: 'My lord, I have been under the same circumstances myself, when I was a girl . . . I flew over them all . . . one held me by one arm, another by the other, and another behind, and I flew sheer over their heads.'

LCJ: 'Woman, can you produce any of these women that saw you fly?'

But they were dead. After the Lord Chief Justice had summed up, the jury found Hathaway guilty with all convenient speed, and he received the sentence that his crimes deserved.

And the odd thing is that when I began to unbury this old tale, I thought it might interest because it was so hopelessly obsolete. But it seems to me now that there are modern applications in it; enough and to spare.

THE MAN FROM NOWHERE

IN THAT HIGHLY picturesque, but quite un-Dickensian book, 'A Tale of Two Cities,' there is a curious chapter describing the reception at the house of Monseigneur—Monseigneur being a great nobleman, high in favour and power at Court. Dickens describes the company:
'Military officers destitute of military knowledge; naval officers with no idea of a ship; civil officers without a notion of affairs; brazen ecclesiastics of the worst world worldly, with sensual eyes, loose tongues, and looser lives; all totally unfit for their several callings, all lying horribly in pretending to belong to them, but all nearly or remotely of the order of Monseigneur, and therefore foisted on all public employments from which any living was to be got; these were to be told off by the score and the score.'

But there were still more remarkable people present at Monseigneur's reception.

'In the outermost room were half a dozen exceptional people who had had, for a few years, some vague misgiving in them that things in general were going rather wrong. As a promising way of setting them right, half of the half dozen had become members of a fantastic sect of Convulsionists, and were even then considering within themselves whether they should foam, rage, roar, and turn cataleptic on the spot, thereby setting up a highly intelligible finger-post to the future, for Monseigneur's guidance. Besides these Dervishes, were the other three who had rushed into another sect, which mended matters with a jargon about 'the Centre of Truth,' holding that man had got out of the Centre of Truth—which did not need much demonstration—but had not got out of the Circumference, and that he was to be kept from flying out of the Circumference, and was even to be shoved back into the Centre by fasting and seeing of spirits. Among these, accordingly, much discoursing with spirits went on, and it did a world of good which never became manifest.'

Dickens was thinking of a very curious sect, or occult fraternity, which existed in France in the later years of Louis XV. The founder of this fraternity or order (oddly enough, called 'The Elect Cohens,' Cohen being taken in its Hebrew significance of priest) was a mysterious person called Don Martines de Pasqually de la Tour, otherwise known as Martinez de Pasquales. Mr A.E. Waite, from whose most curious and most interesting 'Life of Louis Claude de St Martin' I gather these particulars, says that Martinez was probably of Spanish origin; but that nothing is known of his early life or of the sources of the occult knowledge which he professed, truly or falsely, to hold in his keeping. He said that he was a transfigured disciple of Swedenborg, 'and an initiate of the Rose Cross;' and one is tempted to infer from this latter claim that Martinez was either foolish or knavish, since all the story of the Rosicrucians is a dream about an order which never existed. However that may be, the evidence goes to show that Martinez, the Man from Nowhere, was in Paris in 1754, founding the Lodge—there was a Masonic connection—of the Elect Cohens. Later, the centre of the Elect Cohens was moved to Bordeaux, and here Martinez met Saint Martin, a young Tourainian of noble family, then a lieutenant in the regiment of Foix. Saint Martin became an enthusiastic admirer and disciple, and was initiated into the mysteries of the order. He was a valuable adherent; as a man of race he had access to the receptions of Monseigneur, and could propagate there the doctrines of his master. But the order of the Elect Cohens came to an abrupt end. It was understood by the faithful that Martinez had still certain secrets in reserve, that they had not yet attained to the highest grades of the order, when in 1772, the Grand Sovereign of the Elect Cohens was called by private affairs to the island of St Domingo. He never returned—in the body—dying there in 1774. And from that time Saint Martin gradually withdrew himself more and more from the world of occultism—which is a world where visible and sensible marvels happen or are supposed to happen—and attached himself to the teaching of Jacob Behmen, to the world of mysticism, where the signs and wonders are of the spirit, not of the body. Saint Martin ended as a

Catholic Quaker, if one may use such a term. He accepted all the doctrines of the Church, and denied the efficacy of all its Sacraments.

But there was another disciple of Martinez de Pasquales, the Man from Nowhere, to whom very strange things happened. This was the Abbé Fournié, who wrote a book called *Ce que nous avons été, ce que nous sommes, et ce que nous viendrons*, published in London in 1801, and now very rare. Fournie states that at an early age he conceived 'an intense desire for a demonstration of the reality of another life and the truth of the central doctrines of Christianity.'

After eighteen months of profound agitation—I quote from Mr Waite's life of Saint Martin—he met an unknown personage who promised a solution of his doubts, and pointing to the throng of a crowded thoroughfare observed: 'They know not whither they are going, but thou shalt know.'

This personage was Martinez. The Abbé speaks oddly of him. He left the disciples often in suspense 'as to whether he himself were true or false, good or bad, angel of light or fiend. This uncertainty kindled so strongly within me, that night and day I cried out on God to help me, if He really existed. But the more I appealed the more I sank into the abyss, and my only interior answer was the desolating feeling—there is no God, there is no life to come, there is only death and nothingness.' In spite of these desolations the Abbé continued in fervent prayer. He says that light came to him, but only in flashes, and now and then there were visions of things to come, which were afterwards fulfilled. In this manner he continued for five years 'full of agitation and darkness, consumed by the desire of God and the contradiction of that desire. At length, on a certain day towards ten o'clock in the evening,—I, being prostrated in my chamber, calling on God to assist me, heard suddenly the voice of M. de Pasqually, my director, who had died in the body more than two years previously. I heard him speaking distinctly outside my chamber, the door being closed and the windows in like manner, the shutters also being secured. I turned in the direction of the voice, being that of the long garden belonging to the house, and thereupon beheld M. de Pasqually with my eyes, who began speaking, and with him were my father and my mother, both also dead in the body. God knows the terrible night which I passed.' As

Mr Waite observes, it is clear that this proof of the life to come, so long and so fervently desired by the Abbé Fournié, almost frightened him to death. He describes an extraordinary sensation which accompanied the vision, 'as of a hand passing through his body and smiting his soul, leaving an impression of pain which could not be described in words, and seemed to belong rather to eternity than time.' The terror remained in the Abbé's soul as he wrote his story many years after the event; though he declares that he held with the figures of the vision an ordinary conversation, such as he might have held with the living. Then there was added to the ghostly assembly the appearance of his sister, who had been dead for twenty years, and, finally, there came 'another being who was not of the nature of men.' The vision returned again and again and became persistent.

It is an extraordinary tale. As Mr Waite notes, there can be no doubt of the Abbé's sincerity or honesty. There is one mark which distinguishes these apparitions from the apparitions of our modern spiritualistic séance. That is the mark of awe and terror even to the point of agony; of a dread so great that it could be described as a Hand piercing body and spirit. So Job spoke of his vision:

'Now a thing was secretly brought to me, and mine ear received a little thereof.
'In thoughts from the visions of the night, when deep sleep falleth upon men,
'Fear came upon me, and trembling, which made all my bones to shake,
'Then a spirit passed before my face; the hair of my flesh stood up.'

But, as I understand, the frequenters of the séance experience nothing of the dread of Job, nothing of the awful fear of the Abbé Fournié. They converse easily, familiarly, cosily with the spirits of the dead, and that Hand of Terror does not smite them.

And our conclusion? It is quite impossible to form any conclusion. Probably, I suppose, the long spiritual conflict through which the Abbé had passed had broken down the wall between perception and hallucination. There are all sorts of ways of breaking down this wall, one of them being brandy, the resulting visions being known as delirium tremens. Opium and haschisch also do the work in their manner; staring at a bright object such as a pool of ink or a crystal can induce visions in some subjects. And intense fatigue will now and then bring about like results. Amongst the nonsense and lies that gathered about the 'Angels of Mons' legend, there were certain veridical stories, which no doubt gave a true account of the experiences of those concerned. Worn-out men on that terrible retreat of August, 1914, found their way barred by spectral chairs and burning candles that were not there. A distinguished officer wrote to me, telling me how he, several of his officers, and several of his men watched for twenty minutes a ghostly army.

'As we rode along I became conscious of the fact that, in the fields on both sides of the road along which we were marching, I could see a very large body of horsemen. These horsemen had the appearance of squadrons of cavalry, and they seemed to be riding across the fields and going in the same direction as we ourselves, and keeping level with us.' A party was sent out to investigate. They found nothing. 'We were all dog tired and overtaxed,' said my correspondent; but he notes, very acutely, that all the observers saw the same appearance.

And so the Abbé Fournié may have hallucinated himself into that seeing of visions. Or perhaps not.

BEFORE WEMBLEY

IT IS TO BE gathered from all sorts of sources that the great Exhibition at Wembley did not go so prosperously as might be desired. I wonder why. I believe the reasons are composite. In the first place, I suspect that the Exhibition was much too big; the Great Exhibition of 1851 went into the Crystal Palace. Then it was too technical. I think I have heard that six acres—the area of Trafalgar Square—were devoted to engineering exhibits. Perfectly enchanting—to engineers. But how I should loathe seeing six acres of wheels going round. And, lastly, there is the matter of 'closing hours.' It is said that the first remark of the late Lord Tennyson on entering the Exhibition of 1851 was 'Can one get a decent bottle of Bass here?' It is deplorable, no doubt; but to the average male mind Exhibitions and the modern closing hours are incompatible.

It seems to me that we should begin by separating things which don't go together in the least. Let the Engineers hold their exhibition at Olympia, or at the Agricultural Hall, Islington; let the Builders follow them; let the Dominion Products have their due turn. But what London wants of a summer night is a place of moderate size where, amidst agreeable surroundings, it can sit and eat and drink and smoke in the open-air, and listen to a band or two and dance a dance or two, and perhaps see a revue or two, with a few variety turns now and then, and a cabaret performance and an occasional concert. Fireworks, of course; and I think a Grand Guignol theatre, with the audience in the open air on fine nights. I doubt whether there would be room for an Amusement Park. The fact is, I am for a return to Vauxhall, and all that sort of thing, with all the improvements that modern ingenuity can suggest. Here is a note of a pleasant evening spent at Vauxhall, just 175 years ago.

'I had a card,' writes Horace Walpole, 'from Lady Caroline Peter-sham, to go with her to Vauxhall. I went accordingly to her house, and found her and the little Ashe, or the Pollard Ashe as they called her; they had just finished their last layer of red, and looked as handsome as crimson could make them. . . . We marched to our barge, with a boat of French horns attending and little Ashe singing. We paraded some time up the river, and at last debarked at Vauxhall. . . . Here we picked up Lord Granby, arrived very drunk from Jenny Whims (a Chelsea tavern). At last we assembled in our booth, Lady Caroline in the front with the vizor of her hat erect, and looking gloriously jolly and hand-some. She had fetched my brother Orford from the next box, where he was enjoying himself with his *petite partie,* to help us to mince chick-ens. We minced seven chickens into a China dish, which Lady Caroline stewed over a lamp with three pats of butter and a flagon of water, stirring and rattling and laughing, and we every minute expecting the dish to fly about our ears. She had brought Betty, the fruit-girl, with hampers of strawberries and cherries from Roger's, and made her wait upon us, and then made her sup by us at a little table. . . . In short, the whole air of our party was sufficient, as you will easily imagine, to take up the whole attention of the Gardens; so much so, that from 11 o'clock till half an hour after one we had the whole concourse round our booth; at last they came into the little gardens of each booth on the sides of ours, till Harry Vane took up a bumper and drank their healths, and was proceeding to treat them with still greater freedoms. It was three o'clock before we got home.'

The company, as you perceive, was high, though distinctly jolly. Indeed, a contemporary writer describing Spring Gardens, as the place was then called, declares that they were laid out 'in so grand a taste that they are frequented in the three summer months by most of the nobility and gentry then in and near London; and are often honoured with some of the Royal Family, who are here entertained with the sweet song of numbers of nightingales, in concert with the best band of musick in England. Here are fine pavilions, shady groves, and most delightful walks, illuminated by above a thousand lamps, so disposed that they all take fire together, almost as quick as lightning, and with such a sudden blaze as is perfectly surprising.' In the generation before this Sir Roger de Coverley visited Vauxhall, 'exquisitely pleasant in summer,' as his friend, the Spectator, declares. 'When,' he says, 'I considered the fragrancy of the walks and bowers, with the choirs of birds that sang upon the trees, and the loose tribe of people that, walked under their shades, I could not but look on the place as a kind of Mahometan Paradise. Sir Roger told me it put him in mind of a little coppice by his house in the country, which his chaplain used to call an Aviary of Nightingales. He here fetched a deep sigh, and was falling into a fit of musing when a Mask, who came behind him, gave him a gentle tap on the shoulder and asked him if he would drink a bottle of Mead with her? But the Knight being startled at so unexpected a familiarity and displeased to be interrupted in his thoughts of the widow, told her she was a wanton baggage, and bid her go about her business. We concluded our walk with a glass of Burton ale and a slice of hung beef.'

The gardens lingered on, I believe, into the fifties of the last century, but the shady groves had got too shady to be agreeable. The Mask or Baggage still frequented the walks, but the nightingales had flown away, and with them Lady Caroline Petersham, the little Ashe, Horace Walpole, Lord Orford, the Marquis of Granby, Harry Vane, Sir Roger and the Spectator. The last real party who went to Vauxhall were Amelia Sedley, Jos. Sedley, George Osborne, Dobbin, and Becky Sharp; when Jos. drank too much rack punch and called Becky his diddle-diddle-darling.

Vauxhall had many competitors, on the large scale and the small. In 1740, Ranelagh was begun on a site near Chelsea Hospital. 'Vauxhall under cover' it was called: there was a Rotunda 'with balconies full of little alehouses.' Of course, Horace Walpole went to Ranelagh.

'Two nights ago Ranelagh Gardens were opened at Chelsea; the prince, princess, duke, much nobility, and much mob besides were there. There is a vast amphitheatre, finely gilt, painted, and illuminated, into which everybody that loves eating, drinking, staring, or crowding is admitted for twelve pence. The building and disposition of the gardens cost sixteen thousand pounds. Twice a week there are to be ridottos at guinea tickets, for which you are to have a supper and music.'

Horace was inclined to sniff in a languid manner when Ranelagh was opened. Vauxhall, he thought, was 'a little better.' But in two years the fashionable success of Ranelagh was assured, and the languid sniff has changed into a shrill squeak. 'Every night constantly I go to Ranelagh, which has totally beat Vauxhall. Nobody goes anywhere else—everybody goes there. My Lord Chesterfield is so fond of it that he says he has ordered all his letters to be directed thither.' One of the first of the entertainment gardens of London was old Spring Gardens, close to Charing Cross, and it is strange to think that this place, with its grave, late memories of the serious and salutary labours of the London County Council, owed its name to a piece of simple jocularity. There was a jet, or spring, of water there, and a German, travelling in England in Queen Elizabeth's days, writes:

'In a garden joining to this Palace (Whitehall) there is a jet d'eau, with a sundial, at which, while strangers are looking, a quantity of water forced by a wheel, which the gardener turns at a distance through a number of little pipes, plentifully sprinkles those that are standing around.'

The joke was improved later. A trap was contrived on the ground, and whoever trod on this trap was immediately deluged. There were other amusements, a bathing pond, a pheasant yard, and a bowling green. In the time of King Charles I:

'There was kept in it an ordinary of six shillings a meal (when the King's proclamation allows but two shillings elsewhere), continual bibbing and drinking wine all day under the trees; two or three quarrels every week.' There was also 'a certain cabaret, in the middle of this paradise, where the forbidden fruits are certain trifling tarts, neats' tongues, salacious meats, and bad Rhenish.'

Then there were Cuper's Gardens just opposite Somerset House, which became Cupid's Gardens in the famous old song, and Marylebone Gardens, and Bagnigge Wells, and Sadler's Wells, all popular in their day.

I believe I saw the last of the tribe one day in Camden Town. In a dreary street there was a drearier public house, with the dreariest little triangle of a garden beside it. Two dusty trees, six dusty bushes, four metal tables, and twice as many chairs, a small pipe from which a small jet of water might sometimes issue, traces of fairy lamps. . . . Such was the last echo of gorgeous, gay Vauxhall.

THE STRANGE CASE OF EMILY WESTON

THERE ARE CERTAIN resemblances between the affair of Grimaldi's brother and the disappearance and reappearance of Emily Weston at Stafford in the years 1849-50. Emily Weston was the only child of Samuel Weston, a shopkeeper and dealer in that pleasant town, which differs so happily from those other Staffordshire towns which make up the Potteries. Weston's shop was somewhere in that back quarter of Stafford which is near the eighteenth-century theatre; a very modest looking place, as I recollect seeing it about twenty-five years ago, with a bulging window divided into small squares of glass. Within, the stock was various; sides of bacon, large cheeses, mops and brooms, clusters of tallow candles hanging from a beam in the ceiling, rat-traps, tea in canisters, and some sacks of flour; in fact, as the old man who was my informant described it, the characteristic general shop of small country places, where, oddly enough, very solid sums of money were once made. Here, then, behind the little dark shop in the narrow street, lived Weston, his daughter Emily, and an old servant, who had been in the family for forty years. In 1849, Emily was twenty-three years old, and was considered to be, not exactly handsome, but decidedly attractive. She bore the best of characters, sang in the choir of the parish church, and was supposed to look favourably on the addresses of the son of the principal chemist of the town, named Elgie. One night in December, 1849, she told her father that she was going to a choir practice that was to be held in the church at nine o'clock. There was to be a new anthem for Christmas Day, 'Unto us a Child,' and the organist was rather anxious as to the solos. So the supper—bread, cheese, butter, and an openwork raspberry tart—was served at 8.30 instead of 9, the usual hour; and at five minutes to 9 Emily started for the church, which is about five minutes' walk from Weston's shop. Mary

Williams, the old servant, was to call for her at 10 o'clock. But Mary was delayed by some household business at the last moment, and it was eight or ten minutes past ten when she got to the church. The windows were all dark, and the rector was locking the door. The servant said she supposed Miss Emily had gone home by the other way.

'Indeed,' said the rector, 'she has not been at practice tonight. We feared she was ill. Do you say that she started from her home to come to practice?' . . .

Emily Weston did not come home that night. No trace of her was to be found. A woman said she thought that a person who passed her close to the church soon after nine was Emily; but the lighting of Stafford in those days was far from brilliant, and the veil that was then generally worn made identification difficult, if not impossible. Week after week went by; still no Emily. Her father offered a reward of £100 to anyone who would find the girl, living or dead: there was no result. The police seemed helpless in the matter.

It was almost a year—a year within three days, I believe—before Emily Weston returned, as her father always declared. It was late at night—for that household—actually about half-past ten, when old Weston, who had been sitting up over some accounts, heard a gentle tapping at the door. Mary Williams, the servant, had been in bed for half an hour or more, and Weston went to the shop door and slowly unbolted, unchained, and unlocked it. While he did so he had put down the candle on the counter. By the dim light he could see a woman standing on the doorstep. He took the candle and held it up, peering at the figure before him. He saw that the woman was richly dressed in silk and furs; but he did not recognise her.

'Who are you?' said the old man, 'And what can I have the pleasure of doing for you? It's rather late at night.'

The woman raised her veil.

'Father,' she exclaimed, 'don't you know me? It's Emily.'

'Even then,' the old man said afterwards. 'I didn't recognise her for a moment. Everything she wore was so splendid, and pearls and diamonds and all, that I could scarcely believe it was my Emily. But then when she smiled at me, I knew her to be sure, and brought her in, and lit the other candle in the parlour, and began to ask her all the questions I could think of. And all she would say was: "Wait a bit, father, wait a bit. I'll tell you all about it; but I've come a very long way, and I feel tired." ' Samuel Weston was overwhelmed with joy at his daughter's return. He was so excited, as he said, that he did not know what to do with himself. He could 'scarce believe his eyes,' and insisted on knocking up Mr and Mrs Dales, neighbours and old friends, who lived two doors off. According to his account, when he at last brought Mr Dales to his bedroom window, he called out that he and his wife must dress and come down at once, as Emily had come back. The two friends came down at length, heavy with sleep, and 'mazed' as they said; and Mr Weston opened a bottle of some very old sherry that he kept for great festivals, and the party sat together far into the night. At last the visitors went back to their beds, and Mr Weston kissed his daughter good night at her bedroom door. She told him that he should hear everything in the morning.

Now it seems odd that Weston, who knocked up the Dales, should not have roused the old servant. So it was, however; and the next morning when the old man came down to breakfast, he found the table laid for one, as usual.

'What are you about, Mary?' he said. 'Don't you know that Emily has come back? Lay her place, and tell her that breakfast is ready.'

Old Mary Williams shrieked and fainted. Mr Weston rushed upstairs, and knocked at his daughter's door. There was no answer, and when he went into the room it was empty. The bed had not been slept in. And Emily Weston was never seen again. And here is an odd circumstance. The Dales, the people who were roused from sleep by Weston, declared that to the best of their recollection, the old man did not mention his daughter. They thought he said, 'I have got somebody you would like to see,' but were not sure. They remembered going round and seeing a beautiful lady, beautifully dressed, who was very pleasant and talked about a wonderful country a long way off where she had been; but they didn't think it was Emily Weston, though as Mrs Dales said, 'There was a look of her.'

That is all. There is an explanation, but I leave that to the ingenuity of the reader.

THE GAY VICTORIANS

HERE IS A CERTAIN fable with which we greatly comfort our hearts in these days. And this is the fable of the mild, the tame, the old-maiden-ladylike Victorians. We know in our inner hearts that we, the Georgians, are the most regulation-ridden people that ever were. If we want a box of chocolates or a packet of cigarettes after eight o'clock at night, we cannot get either without breaking the law. In most parts of London, the greatest city in the world, a glass of beer after ten becomes a penal offence. We have the liberty to go to bed quietly; that is about all. I suppose it is the secret knowledge of all this, the knowledge that we have become a flock of rather pitiful sheep, driven tamely off to our pens by the sheep dog of the law, that makes us puff out our chests and pity the poor, limited, propriety-ridden Victorians, and pretend that we are desperate dogs, indeed. If a man would keep any spirit at all, it is necessary that he should look down on someone; rightly or wrongly. But the mid-Victorian age was not really what we pretend to think it. It was, probably, one of the jolliest ages in our history; and all the better for this, that a great deal of the jollity was above-ground, harmless, hearty mirth. There was the other side, of course; there always is that, and now more than ever, since the coming of cocaine—the nasty, underground, poisonous gaiety that is not gaiety at all, but rather ghastliness. But on the whole, the mid-Victorian who was resolved to 'keep it up' and 'make a night of it' could make a most tremendous night of it and be rather the better than the worse the morning after. A headache? Possibly. But an occasional headache does not do anyone much harm.

I was talking the other day to a man whose business it is, speaking generally, to know everything. I will not define his occupation more precisely; but I happened to mention to him the *Welcome Guest* and

Sala's 'Twice Round the Clock.' He had neither heard of the periodical nor the series of articles. And so, perhaps, I may safely quote this witness of the London world in the year 1858, when Queen Victoria had been reigning twenty-seven years. The period may fairly be called the mid-Victorian; and this was the fashion of it. The time is midnight; the people are coming out of the Haymarket Theatre, still laughing at the drolleries of the inimitable Mr Buckstone and—

'Supper is now the great cry, and the abundant eating and drinking resources of the Haymarket are forthwith called into requisition. By the ravenous hunger and thirst displayed by the late patrons of the theatre, you would imagine that they had gone without dinner for a week. . . Are you rich—there is Dubourg's, the Hotel de Paris, and the upstairs department of the Café de l'Europe. There is no lack of cunning cooks there, I warrant, to send you up pheasants and partridges *en papillote; filets* with mushrooms or truffles, culinary gew-gaws that shall cost five shillings the dish. Yes, and cellarers shall not be wanting to convey to you the Roederer's champagne, the fragrant Clos Vougeot, the refreshing Lafitte and the enlivening Chambertin with yellow seal . . . If your taste leads you still towards French cook-ery—though you wince somewhat at the idea of the claret, burgundy and champagne to follow—there exists a second-class French restau-rant or two where excellent suppers may be obtained at moderate prices.' Sala follows on the descending scale: a porkpie and a glass of ale at a bar for a few pence: 'trotters,' mysterious but succulent, for a penny; a potato from the can at the Coventry Street end of the Hay-market, with salt and pepper, for a halfpenny: and then reverts to oysters, as the refreshment most proper to the hour and the place.

'I will abide by the Haymarket oyster shop, rude, simple, primitive as it is, with its peaceful concourse of customers taking perpendicular refreshment at the counter, plying the unpretending pepper-castor and the vinegar cruet with the perforated cork, calling cheerfully for crusty bread and pats of butter; and tossing off foaming pints of brownest stout.' But a few oysters and a little bread-and-butter and stout at midnight were only the beginning of a mid-Victorian's night out. Refreshed, he strolled on to Evans's in Covent Garden, where, as Mr Sala assures him, Captain Costigan is no longer allowed to sing his

dubious songs, to the shame of young Clive Newcome and to the rage
and indignation of the immortal Colonel, his father.

'We have been to the play, we have consumed a few oysters in the
Haymarket; but the principal effect of that refreshment seems to have
been to make us ten times hungrier. The delicate bivalves of Colches-
ter'—I am afraid that Sala was the first to call an oyster a 'succulent
bivalve'—'have failed in appeasing our bucolic stomachs. We require
meat. Wherefore we walk till the piazza looms in sight. A low doorway, brilliantly lit with gas, greets our view. We descend a flight of
stone steps, pass through a vestibule, and enter the "Cave of
Harmony". The visitor finds himself in a vast music-hall of really noble
proportions and decorated not only with admirable taste, but with
something nearly akin to splendour. At the northern extremity of the
hall is a spacious proscenium and stage, with the grand pianoforte *de
rigueur,* the whole veiled by a curtain in the intervals of performance.
As for the huge area stretching from the proscenium to a row of
columns which separate it from the ante-chamber café, it is occupied
by parallel lines of tables. . . . See the suppers set forth for the strong
stomached supporters of Evans's. See the pyramids of dishes arrive; the
steaming succession of red-hot chops, with their brown, frizzling
caudal appendages seething hot tears of passionate fat. See the serene
kidneys unsubdued, though grilled, smiling though cooked, weltering
proudly in their noble gravy. . . . See the yellow lava of the Welsh
rabbit stream over and engulf the timid toast. Sniff the fragrant vapour
of the corpulent sausage. Mark how the russet leathern-coated baked
potato at first defies the knife, then gracefully cedes, and through a
lengthened gash yields its farinaceous effervescence to the influence of
butter and catsup. The only refreshment present open to even a suspicion of effeminacy are the poached eggs, glistening like suns in a
firmament of willow-pattern plate; and those, too, I am willing to
believe, are only to be taken by country gentlemen hard-pressed by
hunger, just to 'stay their stomachs,' while the more important chops
and kidneys are being prepared. . . Pints of stout, if you please, no
puny half-measures, pints of sparkling pale ale, or brownest Burton
moisten these sturdy rations. And when the strong men have supped—
or, rather, before they have supped, and while they have supped—and

indeed generally during the evening, there bursts out a strong smell of something good to drink; and presently you perceive that the strong men have ordered potent libations of spirituous liquors, hot whiskey and water being the favourite one; and are hastily brewing mighty jorums of punch and grog which they undauntedly quaff.'

There! What a jolly scene it is, and how entirely honest and free from blame. And while people are eating heartily and drinking heartily and smoking heartily, a choir of small boys sing eighteenth-century glees to them; or perhaps it is a nigger minstrel, some far-off precursor of poor Chirgwin; or it may be a comic singer who obliges. Perhaps, as I have hinted, there may be a headache tomorrow morning, perhaps a slight distaste for breakfast; but those stout fellows of the 'fifties care little for such trifles. And all this jollity, all this brown stout and steaming punch at one o'clock in the morning! To us 'daring' Georgians it seems well-nigh incredible.

There is one odd note in this tale of Sala's. It is well-known that Thackeray was a constant visitor at Evans's. Here is his portrait according to Sala.

'Thersites Theorbo (who is an assiduous frequenter of the Cave at hours when men of not so transcendent a genius are in bed), Thersites Theorbo, down yonder in the café ante-saloon, glowering over his grog, cannot forbear beating time and wagging his august head approvingly when he hears the little boys sing. May their pure harmony do the battered old cynic good!'

Now, I wonder. This was the very year of the famous Dickens-Thackeray-Yates quarrel. Thackeray had called Yates 'Young Grub-street' in print; I wonder whether he had called Sala 'Young Gutter-snipe' in conversation. Sala was a Dickens man; and led-captains fought valiantly for their chiefs in those brave days.

A CASTLE IN CELTIC MISTS

DOWN IN Pembrokeshire, far in West Wales, there are many noble castles: Pembroke, Carew, Manorbier; and Manorbier, I think noblest of all, not only for its building but also for its site. It stands on a high place or natural bastion that runs out from the land and makes the eastern wall of a little bay. On each side of this height, to right and left as you face westward, the ground falls away. On the right hand, a brook flows seaward from wooded hills, broadening out beneath the steadfast, lofty walls of the castle into a green marsh; once on a time fishponds where the lords of the castle caught the great pike they ate on fast days. And then again the marsh contracts and becomes a flashing brook that runs swiftly through yellow sand to the sea. On the left hand, the valley falls as green fields and rises abruptly past the church—there are arches there that spring not from piers or pillars but from the very pavement—past the church to a wild height, a place of bracken and gorse and heather through which you may have as rough walking as a man can desire, by miles of broken lands that overlook the enchanted sea, even to the green prehistoric walls of Old Castle Head.

Such is the site of Manorbier, and the limits of the bay are marked by rounded crimson cliffs on either side, glowing red in their depths where they meet the blue of the sea and the creaming foam, glowing green on their heights where they pass into the wild lands. Gerald Barry, whom the learned call Giraldus Cambrensis, played in the sands here with his brothers in summers of long ago, as near as I can tell without book, in the golden summers of the 'fifties of the twelfth century. The brothers made sand-castles, taking model from the strong place behind them; Gerald, looking at the church on the hillside to his left, made sand-churches and sand-abbeys, feeling truly that his heart was to be in such places all the days of his life. And Gerald Barry travelled far; but he wrote in his later years, echoing Ulysses, that he had never seen so sweet a place as Manorbier, his old home. And I would almost agree with him, and I think many would be on our side, excepting always and of course the people who love the intolerable, damned peaks and icy pits of the Alps, where no man (with any sense) comes or hath come since the making of the world. Talking once with a learned friend I questioned the existence of Switzerland. He allowed that there was a good deal to be said for my position. 'But,' he added, 'you must be wrong; if there were no such country as Switzerland, where would our aunts go in the summer?'

But—to return to more agreeable topics—Manorbier has always captured me, not only because of the splendour of the Castle and the beauty of its place, but also because it seems to me the most likely place for the emergence of the great legend of the Holy Grail from the doubtful Celtic mists into the light of European literature. I say advisedly 'emergence' not origin, for the legend which the Normans heard from the Welsh was already a complex; all of it old, and some of it age-old and pre-Christian. But here at Manorbier you had the exact circumstances demanded for such an emergence. On the one hand was the Barry, the lord of the Castle, a Norman noble; on the other his wife, a Welsh princess, daughter of the naughty Nest, the Helen of Wales. On the other side, the followers, knights, men-at-arms, priests and scholars; what more probable than that the strange tale of the land, known of old to the Welsh, should be told by them about the great hearth of Manorbier to their fellows, the Normans. And the dates suit the hypothesis; it was about thirty years after the marriage of the Norman and the Welshwoman that the word 'Grail' appears in romance.

Of course this is mere hypothesis, but it is with hypothesis that one must be content when one begins to investigate this extraordinarily complicated and curious legend; to which, I hold, all our English literature is indebted for that atmosphere of glamour, mystery, wonder that distinguish it from all other European literatures. It is even well with the hypothesis that it contains no wild absurdities. There is, for example, the theory which derives the Grail legend from the ritual of a

Gnostic sect, supposed without proof of the faintest sort, without even the shadow of a probability to have persisted in Wales up to the tenth, or even the eleventh century. This we may dismiss without putting ourselves to the pains of investigation; but with this negative act decision ends, and we must content ourselves with choosing the more probable rather than the less probable explanation.

The real difficulty lies in this: that the Legend is not one legend, but half-a-dozen legends at least. As I have said, the tale that the Norman clerks of Manorbier heard from their Welsh brethren was already a complex. There were pre-Christian elements in it, elements relating to sacred talismanic objects, on the safe keeping of which the prosperity of the tribe depended. There were Bardic, or Druidic myths of heroes who went questing in the underworld for mysterious treasure. There was the story of Peredur, or Percival, exiled, deprived of all, returning in triumph to execute vengeance on his enemies: a very ancient theme out of which Dickens quite unconsciously made the tale of *Nicholas Nickleby*. There was the tale of the Venerable Head, an age-old story, so old that it is known to the North American Indians. And then the Christian elements which shaped the whole, and coloured the whole, and made the Romance of the Holy Grail as we know it. We find traces of a missionary legend of the conversion of Britain by men from the East. Joseph of Arimathea being chief of the band. Then there is the legend of a sacred object, probably a portable altar, belonging to some Welsh saint, this object being fabled to have been given to the saint by Christ Himself. This altar was lost when the evil days came, and with it was lost the glory of the Britons. This altar is still an altar in the early German version of von Eschenbach; but in the other romances it has become a chalice. Finally, there is the struggle between the Celtic Church and the Church of St Augustine, between the Celtic Liturgy and the Roman Missal.

All this the Norman clerks heard from the Welsh clerks of winter nights—at Manorbier. It is likely enough.

A TALE OF A TURBOT

ONE OF THE chiefest marks of a truly great man is the capacity to confront sudden difficulties and emergencies and to overcome them and conquer them in triumph. I have never been able to rise to these heights myself. Indeed, I am so much a man of a past age and of quiet, country ways that, to this very day, the receipt of a telegram fills me with disquiet and alarm. It is certain that I belong in spirit to the times when a man was gratified on the receipt of a letter curiously folded and sealed, which might run somewhat as follows:

MY DEAR SIR—

It would give me the greatest Gratification, if you would do me the honour of dining with me on Thursday se'ennight at the Turk's Head in Fleet Street. The Hour is punctually at three o'clock, and I have reason to suppose that the great Dr Johnson will honour us with his Company. He will bring with him his young Scotch Friend, the ingenious Mr Boswell, whose work on Corsica we have both tasted. I confess that this Gentleman's Salleys, which, though gay are always free from all Tincture of Petulancy, give me great Enjoyment, arid provide, as I opine, the best Foil imaginable to the weighty wisdom of our illustrious Friend, Dr Johnson. Sir Joshua has also agreed to be of us: I know he is happy in the Possession of your Esteem and Admiration. I had thought of asking our chearful Friend Foote; but it must be confest that he doth sometimes exceed and abound overmuch in his Comick Vein. Mr Burke declares that he will not fail us, and he bids me assure Boswell that he will not *desert the diet,* a Term of Art as I take it among the Scottish Lawyers.

Si non Maecenas, aderit facundia Romae.

Trusting, Dear Sir, in your Acquiescence in these Proposals,

Believe me,

Your obliged, humble Servant,

OLIVER DELAME.

To Arthur Machen, Esquire, at his Lodging over the Mercer's, in Essex Street, by the Strand.

Now I could have grappled with all that with ease, and, I trust, in a satisfactory manner. After due consideration and a reference to my tablets, a letter would have been despatched on the following morning, witnessing to my delighted acceptance of Mr Delamere's proposals, and fortified with a Latin tag or two. But as things are now, a violent ring assaults the ear. The door is opened; a hurried boy stands without, holding up a bicycle. A rose-madder envelope is handed to me. My hands shake as I tear it open. I find within some such incoherence as:

dine tonight café royal seven friends.

And there is the blue reply-paid form, and the boy waits, and where is my pencil, and a plague on my spectacles, and haven't I an engagement tonight, and the boy waits, and—
WHERE ARE THOSE SPECTACLES?
That is not rising to an emergency; and thus, perhaps, my profound admiration for those whom no such fact appals.

I have just been reading a book by such an one; the delightful Brillat-Savarin, whose *Physiologie du Goût* is the classic of its subject, the supreme art of dining well, or as Doctor Johnson bluntly called it, 'minding your belly.'
Brillat-Savarin was bidden one day to dine with some relations in the country, and arriving soon before the meal found his cousins, a devoted husband and wife, almost ready to quarrel. It was the turbot, a magnificent fish, a superb fish—but far too large to go into any pot or kettle that the house possessed.
'There is no help for it,' said Monsieur. 'Send for the chopper and we will cut it in two.'
'Would you dishonour the poor creature so?' asked indignant Madame—evidently the intelligent partner of the household. A severed turbot is worth little; let no housewife buy 'a nice bit of turbot' for dinner.

Then the great man arrived. The situation was explained to him. He uttered, as he says, the solemn words:

'The turbot will remain whole, even to the moment of its official presentation.'

Thereupon, Brillat-Savarin demanded to be led to the kitchen. He saw nothing there fit for his great purpose. He passed into the scullery and saw the copper. Everybody was set to work. The servants put water in the copper and lit the fire. The great man prepared a sort of hurdle, of the exact size of the turbot, using for this purpose part of a wine hamper. Upon this hurdle he caused a bed of savoury roots and herbs to be laid. Thereupon the turbot, purged, dried, and salted, was laid in all his glorious breadth and length. A second layer of herbs was placed on top of the fish, and then all was covered with a wash-tub, morticed round the edges with sand, so that the steam should not escape. In half an hour the operation was accomplished.

Thus, then, do the truly great rise superior to all difficulties, and transmute apparent defeat into a glorious victory. Brillat-Savarin's book is full of things as good as this; and I am glad to know that an English version of it—the first complete translation, I believe—is to appear this autumn. I have a dim hope that it may make some of us wonder whether it is absolutely necessary that foreign meat, ill bred, ill fed, ill killed, ill chilled, ill cooked, and ill served should be the principal ingredient of the average English dinner.

CHIVALRY

WHEN I AM down in the county, I am sometimes taken to see castles, and I want to make a confession about them. I look about their walls, I mark portcullis and moat, newel stair and keep, I enter into the central court, a green space surrounded by walls half-whole, half-broken—and I cannot form the faintest conception of what these great places were like when they were inhabited; for, it must be remembered, what we see when we admire a ruined castle is a house without a roof, generally without floors or ceilings, always without woodwork of any kind or sort. Take the roof off Smith's villa at Surbiton. Burn every beam in the house, break in all the windows, make the kitchen and back garden a heap of confused stones overgrown with grass and weeds. Knock down every door and every party wall, blow up the stairs, smash the floors, make Smith's potting-shed and his fowl-house in the back garden into beautiful green mounds, turf-covered; and then bring along your post-historic New Zealander, and ask him to tell you what Laburnum Villa was like in the days of its pride, and what manner of life the Smiths led there. I don't believe the New Zealander would make much of the job; and so I make very little of the job when I pass into a twelfth-century castle. I can see that those high outer walls, sloping outward to the ground ('battered') for greater strength, were meant to keep people out; I conjecture that those windows, a narrow slit outside, a broad splay within, were handy for shooting without much chance of being shot; I have been told that the keep, or central tower, with walls six, eight, ten feet thick, was the last refuge of the De Somethings when a breach had been made in the outer defence; and that is about all. 'The great hall,' says somebody, pointing to a large space, where an inner wall half-stands, half-falls. It may be so; but it may be the chapel, or the great kitchen; all is so broken, so uncertain.

And then: 'Secret passage, communicating with the Abbey, five miles away,' and 'The black dungeon under the keep, where the objects of feudal oppression pined away.' It may be so, or it may be—the mere apparatus of drainage.

And as to how the De Somethings lived, where they slept, at what time they had their meals, what they ate at their meals, how they spent their days when the foe were not battering at the outer bailey, I have hardly the faintest notion. I except a few items of the castle bill of fare: a great deal of salt cod, a great deal of salt beef, a great deal of salt herring, venison pies, roast game, peacock and swan occasionally, buttered eggs, richly spiced dishes from the east, dishes in which meat, raisins, and currants were mingled—the mincepie is the only modern survivor of this school of cookery—pike and other fish from the castle pond; abundance of strong, thick ale—there were no clarifying hops then—and liberal Gascon wine; we may make out a fairly satisfactory bill for the table of our great lord. But that is about all, so far as I am concerned. Indeed, I once asked a man deeply learned in antiquity, a famous herald, to tell me what it was like, generally speaking, to pay a visit to a thirteenth-century lord at his castle. 'For example,' I said, 'when a Barry of Manorbier went to stay for a few weeks with a Bohun of Caldicot, how did the castle party begin the day? Was the Barry called for breakfast?' He considered the question, and finally declared that in his opinion there was no formal beginning of the day: 'I believe they all woke up like animals, and shook themselves.' It may be: but I would rather incline to think that a bell at six o'clock in the morning roused everybody for Mass in the chapel, and that afterwards people strolled to the buttery-hatch and broke their fast, lunching—in the proper sense of the word 'lunch'—on hunks of bread and chunks of salt beef or pasty, with quarts of ale for the simple and quarts of red wine for the gentle. And then to the stables, quite in the manner of a modern country house in the hunting shires, and a long discussion there as to the horses. And then, perhaps, a little tennis, the court being the castle courtyard with its lean-to wooden buildings (the penthouse of the game) the opening now called the grille—then the buttery-hatch aforesaid—and the odd projection of one wall which tennis players call the tambour. And so to a mighty dinner at ten, with

a very honest appetite, and a strong thirst. Of course, knight errantry
in the sense of the romances never existed; nothing at all like it ever
existed. The romances of chivalry that is, do not picture the thirteenth
century as Dickens, Thackeray, and Trollope between them very fairly
pictured the earlier and middle nineteenth century. The romances are
pure fantasies of the imagination: nothing more. I have just been
reading a curious document which bears on this point. It is a contract,
and is as formal and business-like a document as any contract between
manager and actor, or between author and publisher. It was executed
in the year 1297. It begins:

'An du rengne le Roy Edward fiz le Roy Hen' vintenne et quint ssi
accoumto p'entr Sire Johan Bluet Chevaler et Wylliame Martel.' Or in
English:

'In the year of the reign of King Edward, the son of King Henry,
one score and five, it was thus agreed between Sir John Bluet, Knight,
and William Martel.'

The fact was that the stout knight—to use the later Gothic
manner—Sir John Bluet, wanted a courtly squire. William Martel
applied for the engagement, and got it. A contract was then drawn up,
and duly sealed: it was a contract valid during the life of William
Martel, and it was binding on the heirs of Sir John Bluet. And the said
Sir John was to pay William sixty pence of silver yearly; payments due
at Hoekday (Eastertide) and Michaelmas. Provision is made for default
on the part of tenants who paid the rents from which William was to
draw his salary: it is expressly stipulated that the squire or his solicitor
may put an execution into the house of any such defaulting tenant.
Besides the money payment, the chivalrous (though businesslike)
squire was to have a robe at Christmas and another robe at Easter; the
value of each to be ten pence. Furthermore, William was to be maintained as long as he lived in sufficient meat and drink as a gentleman
ought to have 'E a sustenir le devauntdit Wyll' taunt come il vivera en
manger e en beovere avenauntement come a gental homme a peut.'
And his two servants are also to have their board and lodging, and his
two horses are to be found in hay and oats and shoes; the two horses
to have between them 46 bushels of oats a year. And, on his side, the
gentle William engaged himself well and faithfully to serve Sir John

Bluet as an esquire ought to do 'in the war now wageing between the King of England and the King of France; and also in England if war should break out there, which God forbid; and in Wales and all other lands on this side the sea, or beyond the sea wherever the said John may be (except the Holy Land), and in tournaments in time of peace with a great war horse—en tens de pees od en graunt chevall de armes—which the said John will find him and suitable armour without any default on his part.'

The gentle, the chivalrous William! He had evidently heard a thing or two about crusading; and I seem to hear a more modern voice speaking to much the same effect:

'No, dear old chap, I'm afraid we'll have to cut that clause about the Eastern Tour. I don't mind the Welsh smalls or the Scotch fitups, and I'm quite willing to go to South Africa or the States; but I've made up my mind I'll never play juvenile leads in the East again. You see, old man, if you come to cues, there's no bunce in it.'

Such was the actual Age of Chivalry. A little on the practical side, perhaps. Don Quixote would have been disgusted by the document which I have quoted; and, indeed, when Sancho Panza asked for a fixed salary—Teresa urging him—the Knight said there was no precedent in the books for such an arrangement. Not in *Amadis of Gaul* or in *Tirante lo Blanch*, perhaps, but we see how it was in actual life. It is clear that Sancho knew more about Chivalry than his master.

7B CONEY COURT

A GOOD MANY years ago the late Stephen Phillips, the poet and dramatist, got himself into a very queer piece of trouble. He had just left his house somewhere on the South Coast, I think at Littlehampton or near it, and rumours had got abroad that he had done so because the place was haunted. The rumours penetrated to Fleet Street, and some paper sent down a reporter to interview the poet. Stephen Phillips told the newspaper man his experiences in his late residence, and they were, indeed, most remarkable. I have forgotten the detail, and cannot recall the manner of the noises or voices or apparitions that had vexed the late tenant; but there was no doubt that the house was haunted, and haunted very badly. A sensational 'story' appeared in the paper—and then the landlord of the house sued everybody concerned for heavy damages. It had not occurred to Phillips or the newspaper that you could libel a house; but the owner of it pointed out that to call a house haunted made it unlettable, and that in consequence of the statements in the interview the place once occupied by the poet had been empty on his hands for the last eighteen months. How the matter ended has escaped my memory, but I believe somebody, the poet or the paper, had to pay, and I should think it was the paper. However, I am taking the affair as a warning, and so I declare that all names and places in the following history are fictitious. There is no such Inn of Court or Chancery as Curzon's Inn; there is no such square as Coney Court, though South Square, Gray's Inn, once bore that name. And therefore: no action will lie.

But assuming for the moment that names and places are as true as the tale, it may be said that Curzon's Inn lies somewhere between Fleet Street and Holborn. It is approached by a maze of crooked courts and paved alleys, guarded by iron posts, and it consists of a small hall—

note the very odd and elaborate 'sham Gothic' work about the principal doorway, date 1755—a huge and ancient and flourishing mulberry tree in a railed enclosure, a quadrangle called Assay Square, and another which is Coney Court. In Coney Court there are nine entrances in the buildings, which were rebuilt in 1670. All is of a dim red of ancient brickwork; the entrances are enriched with Corinthian pilasters, in the manner of the older doorways in King's Bench Walk in the Temple; and the carved wooden penthouses over these doorways have been attributed to Grinling Gibbons; somewhat doubtfully, as I am told, and on a misreading of an allusion in a contemporary diary. But, at all events, there are nine doors in Coney Court, and no more than nine, and hence the perplexity of Mr Hemmings, the Steward, when he received a cheque for £20, with a note to this effect:

DEAR SIR—

Please receive the enclosed cheque for Twenty Pounds (£20 0 0), being the quarter's rent due to you for my chambers at 7B Coney Court, Curzon's Inn.

I remain, Yours faithfully,

MICHAEL CARVER.

That was all. There was no address. There was no date. The postmark bore the letter N. The letter was delivered by the first post of November 11th, 1913, and by immemorial custom, of unknown origin, rents in Curzon's Inn are payable not on the English, but on the Scottish quarter days. Now, November 11th is Martinmas, and so far everything was in order, But there is no such entrance in Coney Court as 7B, and there was no such name as Michael Carver on the books of the Inn. Mr Hemmings was bothered, and nobody seemed to have heard of Mr Carver. The porter, who had been employed at the Inn for upwards of forty years, was quite positive that no such name had been on the doorposts during the time of his service. Of course, the Steward made all possible enquiries. He went round to the various tenants at 6, 7, and 8, but could get no information whatever. As is usual in the old Inns, the tenants were miscellaneous. The main substratum—also as usual—was legal. There was a publisher in a very small and young way of business, who thought that poetry could be made to pay. There were the offices of a few shy and queer companies and syndicates, with names such as 'Trexel Development Company, Ltd.,' 'J.H.V.N. Syndicate,' 'Sargasso Salvage: G. Nash, Secretary,' and so forth, and so forth. Then the private residents; some of these were initials on the doorposts, 'A.D.S.,' 'F.X.S.,' one 'Mr and Mrs Eugene Sheldon,' and names that were little more than names to the inhabitants of the Inn, since the owners of them were never seen during the day, but crept out at night, after the gates were shut, and prowled from Assay Square to Coney Court and back again, stealthily, silently, not looking at one another, never speaking a word. Among all these folk the Steward made his quest, but not one of them had heard of such a person as Michael Carver, and one or two had occupied their chambers for thirty years. The next day, 'St Martin's Morrow,' being the day appointed for the quarterly meeting of the Society, the 'Pension,' as they called it, the puzzled Hemmings laid the matter before the President and the Ancients, with the result that they decided that there was nothing to be done.

And from that date onward, quarter after quarter came the cheque for twenty pounds, with the formal note accompanying it. No date, no address, and the postmark still bearing the N. of the northern district, The matter was regularly laid before the Society: the Society as regularly decided that there was nothing to be done.

This went on till the Martinmas of November, 1918. The usual cheque was received; but the formal letter varied. It ran thus:

DEAR SIR—
    Please receive the enclosed cheque for Twenty Pounds (£20 0 0), being the quarter's rent due to you for my Chambers at 7B Coney Court, Curzon's Inn.
    There is a bad patch of damp on the ceiling of my sitting room; arising, I should think, from a defective tile.
    I shall be obliged if you will have this seen to at once.
            I remain, Yours faithfully
               MICHAEL CARVER.

The Steward was stupefied. There was no such number in Coney Court, or the Inn, as 7B; how, then, could there be a leak in the roof?

How could the Society see to a roof which did not exist? Next day, Mr Hemmings laid the letter before the Pension in silence: there was nothing to say. The President read it attentively; the ten Ancients read it attentively. Then one of them, who happened to be a solicitor, suggested that enquiries should be made at Mr Carver's bank. 'Sometimes you can bluff a bank,' he said hopefully. But Mr Carver banked at Tellson's, and the ancient should have known better. Hemmings received the curtest of letters from the House, informing him that Messrs. Tellson were not in the habit of discussing their client's affairs with outsiders; and so, for the time being, the matter dropped. Next quarter day, the usual Carver cheque was received, and with it an extremely stiff letter, pointing out that no notice had been taken of the writer's request, and that, in consequence the damp had spread all over the ceiling, and threatened to drip on the carpet. 'I shall be obliged if you will remedy the defect immediately,' the letter ended. The President and the Ancients again considered the matter. One suggested that the whole thing was the work of a practical joker, another uttered the word 'Mad,' but these explanations were considered unsatisfactory, and the Society, in the circumstances, resolved that there was nothing to be done.

The next quarter day brought no cheque. There was a letter, declaring that the tenant's furniture was covered with mould, and that in wet weather he was obliged to put a bowl on the floor to catch the water. Mr Carver said finally that he had determined to cease all payment of rent until the necessary repairs were seen to. And then something still queerer happened, and this is the point at which the history would have become libellous—if there were such a place as Curzon's Inn, or if there were such a court as Coney Court. The third pair chambers (right) of No. 7, Coney Court, had just been vacated by the tenants, solicitors or agents, and a widow lady and her daughter had moved in—'dingy, but so quiet,' as the lady told her friends. And now she found her chambers very far from quiet. Night after night, at twelve, one, two, or three o'clock, she and her daughter were awoke by thunderous piano music, always the same music, which rendered sleep out of the question. The widow complained to the Steward, and he came round, with the Inn carpenter, and said he couldn't understand it at all.

'We never had any complaints from Jackson and Dowling,' he declared, and the lady pointed out that Jackson and Dowling left the Inn every night at six.

The Steward went over the set carefully. He noticed a sort of crazy flight of steps, leading out of one of the rooms.

'What's that?' he asked the carpenter, and the man said it was a sort of lumber place, used by tenants for odds and ends.

They went up, and found themselves in a garret, lighted by one pane of glass in the roof. Here was a broken-down old piano with hardly a dozen notes sounding, a mouldy Gladstone bag, two odd men's socks, a pair of trousers, and some ragged copies of Bach's Fugues, in paper wrappers. There was a leak in the roof, and all reeked with damp.

The rubbish was removed, the place was turned out and whitewashed. There were no more disturbances. But a year later, the widow lady, being at a concert with a friend, suddenly gasped and choked, and whispered to the friend:

'That is the awful music I told you about.'

The distinguished pianist had just sounded the opening notes of John Sebastian Bach's Fugue in C Major.

Neither the Principal, the Ancients, nor the Steward heard any more of the tenant of 7B, Coney Court.

CONCERNING COCKTAILS

IT IS, PERHAPS, just that cocktails, which have mostly some infusion of bitterness in them, should have bitter things said of them. I often see the saddest reflections in the public Press as to these preliminaries of dinner. In the first place, it is declared that girls take cocktails freely, and this, it seems, is an unwomanly action, and a great innovation. And yet, when the girls of eighty, ninety years ago paid morning calls with their mammas, they saw nothing unseemly in taking a glass of sherry wine, with a slice of cake or a sweet biscuit; and there the folly, if not the unwomanliness, appears to reside in the cake and biscuit rather than in the wine. It is true that ladies of that age had certain polite conventions of eating and drinking. They are instructed in the hand-books of the period to decline liqueurs after dinner, and also to refuse snipe—that on account of the trail. Still, if grandmother took sherry at twelve, I see not why granddaughter should be debarred from a Martini at half-past one.

Then there is the other point of view, that of the gourmet, the lover of choice wine. He maintains that the cocktail destroys all flavour, aroma, or merit that the wine served with the meal may possess. This may be theoretically true; at all events, Professor Saintsbury is of this school, and I should be very sorry to dissent, obstinately and advisedly, from the lightest judgment of that great man, who has taken all litera-ture for his province, is faithful to Church and King, and a curious lover of good wine: in fine, such a gentle critic of life and letters that the men of our day seem beside him like brawling, unmannerly, untaught schoolboys. No doubt, if the wine is to be exquisite, we shall do well to refrain from cocktails before the repast; but, alas! How few of us have the chance of drinking exquisite wine in these sad years. This is not the age of the exquisite; rather of the pretty good if one is lucky, of the pretty bad commonly. It is a kindness to kill the flavour of many of the bottles of today. *Scelus est jugulare Falernum*, assuredly; but there is no Falernian left.

But, apart from these several lines of argument against the cocktail, there lies behind them both the assumption that the habit is wholly modern. Now this is certainly not true. The French have taken absinthe before lunch and dinner for ninety, or perhaps, a hundred years—I believe that this most admirable drink originated during the Algerian campaigns of 1820-30—and then there is the French phrase, 'tuer le ver,' meaning to drink white wine before lunch, which goes back to long ago. And then in Ned Ward's *London Spy*, published in 1700, we read how a certain company 'proceeded to a Whet of Old Hock, to sharpen our Appetites to our approaching Dinner.' And there is another, and a more singular instance of the cocktail habit, a cocktail to be used as a prelude, but not to a dinner.

' "But, pray," says he, "have you any wine for me in the morning, and some bitters, if I should want to carry any to the scaffold?" Upon enquiry, there was no bitters left in the bottle, and, therefore, his lordship gave the warder a shilling to send for a bottle of Stoughton's elixir! When the man was gone the warder recollected that there was some burnt brandy and bitters left in a bottle, which his lordship had with him to Westminster Hall, when on his trial, and informed him of it. "This very well, very well, Sir," says he; "pray take it in your pocket, and give me a sup if I should want it." '

Such is one of the details given in the 'Account of the Behaviour of Simon Fraser, Lord Lovat, from the time of his Death Warrant was delivered to the Day of his Execution.' This is in many ways a most curious document. I am not quite sure that it is wholly to be relied on as to high matters, such as Lord Lovat's religious views and pious sentiments; but, no man invents Stoughton's elixir! The little details, which I love most in history, are no doubt true. Thus, when the warrant for execution came down to the Tower, Lord Lovat 'smoked his pipe.' Smoking had become obsolete in good society for some years before 1747; but Lord Lovat was a man of eighty, and clung to old customs. A few days later, 'the Major' came to see him, and asked how he did.

'Do!' (says his lordship), 'why I am about doing very well, for I am preparing myself, Sir, for a place where hardly any majors, and very few lieutenant-generals, go.'

This may very well be authentic. It is quite in accord with the traditional story (which finds no place in the present 'Account') of the collapse of a sort of grand stand erected near the scaffold. Several people were killed, many injured, and Lord Lovat pleasantly observed: 'The mair mischief the better sport.'

On the night before the execution Lord Lovat sent for 'Mr P——, the barber, whose father, they tell me, is a Muggletonian.' Mr P—— was in the best tradition of barbers; that is, he was evidently talkative, and talkative in no usual measure. The circumstances, one would think, were grim enough to silence the most wanton chatterbox on earth: that place of doom and dreadful histories, the Tower of London, was the cell of the condemned, the old man of eighty who was to die the next day, the awful, instant shadow of the scaffold and the axe. Not so; Mr P—— was not daunted one whit.

'When his lordship was shaving, he talked a good deal about his father's principles; and when he was shaved, "Well" (says he), "pray give my service to your father, and tell him I shall go to heaven before him; for I find he does not expect to go till the day of resurrection, but I hope to be there in a few hours." '

I am afraid that Lord Lovat was not very well instructed in the faith of the Holy Roman Catholic and Apostolic Church to which he belonged—in a Jansenist, not a Jesuit way, as he carefully explained. Purgatory, perhaps, but Heaven—!

The strange old man continued cheerfully all through the evening, saw friends, talked about his funeral, feared that an old codicil to his will, providing that all the pipers from 'Johnie Groat's house to Edinburgh' were to be handsomely rewarded for playing before his corpse, could no longer be carried out. He dined well, wished grave stomachic trouble to all who favoured the bill then before Parliament for the abolition of the hereditary jurisdiction of the Highland chiefs, took a little wine and water, smoked a last pipe, and reminded his warders of the cocktail that was to be taken up the scaffold with him. In the morning there was an excellent breakfast of minced veal, and another little chat with Mr P——: first, as to the amount of powder to be applied to his lordship's wig, and, secondly, a further investigation of the theological principles of Mr P——'s father. And the barber, in return, 'wished my lord a good passage; for these were his words.'

Simon Fraser was, I suppose, a bad old man, since all the historians say so. But he was a brave Highlander; and before he mounted the scaffold, he duly partook of the famous burnt brandy and bitters—his last cocktail.

MOTHERS-IN-LAW

IN THE BOOK where I found the strange story of the Asiki, the 'Little People,' or fairies, of the African forest, there is an even odder tale of the woman who transformed herself by magic art into Three Things. And it happened like this. A man of the Batanga tribe had four wives, and one of them came from a tribe living in the interior of the country, the Boheba, a shade darker in its superstition than the Batanga. This lady belonged to the local Witchcraft Society, and attended its secret night meetings, which, it is hinted, were of a frightful kind. In fact, as we should put it, she was a regular attendant at the Witches' Sabbath.

The husband was not a sorcerer himself, but he knew a good deal about sorcery. He could not transform himself in the fashion of the true wizards, but he could see things done at distances far beyond the power of human sight. And one night, by this power, he saw the Boheba woman rise from her bed and go out to attend 'her witchcraft play.'

'She left her physical house, the fleshly body, lying on the bed, so that no one not in the secret, seeing that body lying there, would think other than it was herself, nor would know that she had gone out. In her going out she willed to emerge as Three-Things, and this triple unit went off to the witchcraft play. The husband happened to see this, and watched her as she disappeared, saw where she went, and though distant and out of sight, knew what she was doing. So he said to himself; "She is off at her play; I also will do some playing here; she shall know what I have done." '

Now, it seems that in the African forest, cayenne pepper is known to be a great defence against witchcraft. The evil powers whom the witches serve cannot prevail against it. So the husband gathered pepper-pods from his kitchen garden and pounded them to a fine

161

paste. This paste he smeared all over the body lying in the bed—the body from which Three-Things had, gone forth—and waited.

At the Sabbath, the night was far spent. The witches' bird, the owl, hooted to warn those at play that the dawn was at hand. So the woman set out on her journey home. Then came the first cockcrow of the morning, and she made still greater haste, 'lest daybreak should find her triple unit outside of its fleshly house. So the three came rushing with the speed of wind back to her village.'

And the Rev. Robert Nassau, who heard the tale from a native woman, notes that the confusion between 'they' and 'she,' as the narrator thinks now of the woman as a single entity, and then of her as a triple entity, is a strict following of the original language.

All the while the husband was watching. He heard a noise as of one panting for breath, and felt the breath of the wind as the Three returned to his house.

And Three-Things came to the body of the woman and tried to re-enter it. But the pepper barred the way. 'She searched long and anxiously, but in vain; and in despair they went and hid herself in a wood pile at the back of one of the village huts, waiting in terror for some possible escape,'

The husband watched till the sun rose. Then he knew that the body before him was dead, since the spirit had not been able to return to it before the morning light. Whereupon, being evidently self-controlled, he said nothing, but went off for a day's fishing. Finally, the dead body was discovered by some of his children, and they rushed to meet their father as he came back from his little excursion, and screamed to him: 'Father, we have found your Boheba wife dead.'

An amazing man, father; really, an example to many of us. He simply remarked:

'Let another one of my wives cook for me, I will first eat.'

For all we know he may have demanded a squeeze of lemon and the cayenne at dinner.

The dead lady's Boheba relations were informed of her death. They were wanting in father's admirable composure. They came with guns and spears and knives and uttered threats of revenge. Father begged them to wait a little and see what he had to show them. They saw the dead body, they searched for wounds or bruises, but found nothing. And they said: 'What then has killed her?' Then father told them that if they removed the sticks in the wood-pile they would find her. This was done, and they found Three-Things; and acknowledged, in a very gentlemanly manner, that father was not in the least to blame.

'In her terror at being unable to get back into her mortal body, the Three-Things, all the while she was hidden in the wood-pile, had shrivelled smaller and smaller, until what was left was three deformed crab-shaped beings, a few inches long, with mouths like frogs. These, paralyzed with fear, could not speak, but could only chatter and tremble.

'So the relatives seized these Three-Things, and also carried away the body; and, followed by all the people of the village, they burnt it and them on a large rock by the sea.'

A very queer tale, indeed, and in my experience, unique; so far as the Three-Things notion is concerned; the notion of the human personality being divided into three entities, which are yet to be spoken of as 'she'. The native narrator told the missionary that the calm gentleman whom I have called 'Father' was her great-grandfather, and possibly the story may have some kind of foundation. The woman may have died naturally in her sleep, or possibly the husband, disliking the queer ways of his wild Boheba bride, may have poisoned her. As for the Three-Things, like crabs, with mouths like frogs, I daresay it would not be difficult to find any quantity of nauseous little creatures beneath any pile of wood in Africa; and Father's ill-regulated imagination supplied all details.

Of course, negroes are, in a sense, confirmed spiritualists. I remember a Rhodesian magistrate telling me that no negro died a natural death. Poison was just a drink which had been filled with a devil by an incantation; a man might be found torn by a wild beast, but the wild beast was simply a wizard in a leopard's body—a were-leopard. Typhoid was merely 'overlooking' (as our English countryfolk called it), in a very severe form. So in Dr Nassau's book there is an account of a woman who was a very fine dancer, much in request at Fetich feasts, Witch Society entertainments, and similar agreeable festivals. Everybody thought that she was a fine dancer and nothing else; but it turned out that she owed all her abilities to certain spirits that she had summoned from the old graveyards.

All this appears strange enough to us; but at other points the African mind has curious parallels with our own. Take the famous mother-in-law business for example. With us it has become a sort of joke, a low comedian's 'wheeze,' though sometimes a London magistrate is heard to remark: 'In nine cases out of ten when there is trouble between young married people it is due to the mother-in-law.' But mother-in-law is no joking matter in Africa. My Rhodesian friend told me that amongst his people she was a savage tyrant, a burden hardly to be borne, and he told me also how the negroes coped with the difficulty.

'They put up with her,' he said, 'till she becomes a grandmother, and then they sew her up in a deerskin, and put her near the road to the next village. Presently a villager strolls along with a bow and arrows, ready for any chance sport. He sees a fine deer asleep by the track, and promptly shoots it. When he finds that he has shot a mother-in-law, he is quite vexed with himself, and apologises handsomely. Then the old lady's relations declare that accidents will happen in the best regulated families, and beg the villager to say no more about it.'

And I remember another pleasing parallel between the black forest and the white city. Two young people of New York City wanted to get married, but they were so 'advanced' that they really did not see how it could be done, marriage being notoriously reactionary and obsolete. So they were married in strict secrecy, and the bride kept her own name, and the two lived in different boarding houses, and all meetings between them were a matter of stealthy and hidden contrivance.

Poor young things! I hope they never found out that this little arrangement was an almost literal reproduction of the marriage customs of a rather backward negro tribe.

A PRETTY PARRICIDE

FRANCIS BLANDY, a well-to-do attorney, who lived at Henley-on-Thames in the first half of the eighteenth century, was a widower, with one child, Mary, the very apple of his eye. Mr Blandy bestowed every care on his daughter's education, and she grew up a charming girl, or, in the language of the period, 'genteel, agreeable, sprightly, sensible.' Her father's one thought was to see his daughter well-married and happily married; and in his desire to bring this end about he made a mistake which proved fatal to him and to her. He exaggerated his resources, and pretended that Mary would have a marriage portion of ten thousand pounds.

About 1745 or 1746, a Captain Cranstoun, a Scot of good family, was recruiting in Henley. He was a married man with children, but pretended to be a free bachelor, and made love to Mary Blandy, or rather, as counsel remarked afterwards, to her rumoured fortune. But old Mr Blandy had heard very ill-things about the gallant captain, and would have none of him.

Whereupon Cranstoun and the genteel, agreeable, sprightly, sensible Mary determined to put Mr Blandy out of the way and to enter on the enjoyment of the ten thousand pounds in company. They began operations in the August of 1750, and set about the black business oddly enough. The pair of them gave out that they 'heard music' in the house, and the Captain said, on the authority of a wise woman in Scotland, that this ghostly music was a sign that Mr Blandy would die within the year. Then the Captain declared that he had the Scots gift of second sight, and that he had seen the ghostly double of Mr Blandy. The wretched Mary told the servants about the music and about the wraith, and assured them that her father could not last much longer. Captain Cranstoun left Henley in November 1750, and soon after-

165

wards Mary began to give her father arsenic. The old man became very ill, and suffered great tortures. His teeth fell out of his gums, whereupon his genteel daughter 'damned him for a toothless old rogue, and wished him to hell.'

In April Mary's supply of poison was running low, so Captain Cranstoun sent some more with a present of Scottish pebbles. Mary Blandy put arsenic in her father's tea, and made a charwoman, who finished the pot, very ill indeed. For one reason or another, tea seemed an unsuitable vehicle for arsenic, and the Captain, on being consulted, advised putting it into a liquid 'of a more thickish substance,' and so the father began to take his arsenic in water-gruel; Mary Blandy warning the two maidservants not to touch the stuff, since, she observed, water-gruel was dangerous to some constitutions. Captain Cranstoun grew impatient. He wrote:

'I am sorry there are such occasions to clean your pebbles; you must make use of the powder to them by putting it in anything of substance, wherein it will not swim atop of the water, of which I wrote to you in one of my last. I am afraid it will be too weak to take off their rust, or at least it will take too long a time.'

This was a hint to Mary to increase the dose. She acted on it. Old Mr Blandy became much worse, and the two maids, cleaning out the pan in which the water-gruel had been standing, found at the bottom a white gritty substance. They collected some of the staff, and it was conveyed to a physician, who pronounced it to be arsenic. Thereupon Susan Gunnell, one of these maids, told her master that he was being poisoned by his daughter. And then:

'The father, with a fondness greater than ever a father felt before, cried out, "Poor, lovesick girl! What will not a woman do for the man she loves! But who do you think gave her the powder?" She answered, "She could not tell, unless it was sent by Mr Cranstoun." "I believe so too", says the master, "for I remember he has talked learnedly of poisons. I always thought there was mischief in those cursed Scotch pebbles." '

The girl was made to feel that she was violently suspected, or more than suspected. Her father came into the kitchen, and said to one of the servants in Mary's hearing: 'Molly! I had like to have been

poisoned twenty years ago, and now I find I shall die by poison at last.'
Thereupon Mary Blandy went upstairs, brought down Mr Cranstoun's
letters, together with the remainder of the poison, and threw them (as
she thought unobserved) into the fire. One of the servants put some
coal on the fire, and Mary Blandy left the kitchen. But Susan Gunnell
said to her fellow-servant, 'I saw Miss Blandy throw some papers in
the fire, let us see whether we can discover what they were.' The
letters were consumed, but there was a paper with white powder in it,
and on the packet, in Mr Cranstoun's hand, 'Powder to clean the
pebbles.' The powder was taken to the doctor, examined by him and
pronounced to be arsenic. Upon this Mary Blandy was kept apart from
her father by order of the physician, but after two days separation she
was allowed, at her earnest request, to see him, the servant, Susan
Gunnell, being present. And this strange conversation followed:

' "Papa, how do you do?"

' "My dear, I am very ill."

'She immediately fell on her knees and said:

' "Dear Sir, banish me where you will; do with me what you please,
so you do but pardon and forgive me. And as to Mr Cranstoun, I will
never see, write, or speak to him again."

'He answered, "I do forgive you, but you should, my dear, have
considered that I was your own father."

'Upon this she said, "Sir, as to your illness, I am innocent."

'Susan Gunnell, who was present, interrupted her at this expression, and told her she was astonished to hear her say she was innocent,
when they had the poison to produce against her, that she had put into
her father's water-gruel, and had preserved the paper she had thrown
into the fire.'

At last Mary Blandy fell on her knees and said, 'Dear Sir, your
kindness towards me is worse than swords to my heart. I must down
upon my knees, and beg you not to curse me.'

And the father replied:

'I curse thee, my dear! No, I bless you, and will pray God to bless
you, and to amend your life. So do, my dear, go out of the room, lest
you should say anything to accuse yourself.'

Two days afterwards, Francis Blandy died. Mary, who was in a kind of informal custody or detention in the house, made some wild and inefficient attempts to escape. She told the manservant that if he would help her, it would be £500 in his pocket. He refused the offer. In the middle of the night after her father's death she asked one of the maids to get a postchaise in order to go to London, telling the woman that she should have twenty-five guineas for her trouble. This servant also refused, in the blankest possible manner. The next morning Mary Blandy dressed herself for a journey, stole out of the house—she was evidently, loosely guarded—and went over Henley bridge. The mob were ready for her and followed her, so that she was forced to take refuge in the Angel, 'a little ale-house'. From this place she was removed in custody, tried for the murder of her father, found guilty, and hanged at Oxford on April 6, 1752. She suffered 'in a black bombazine short sack and petticoat, with a clean white handkerchief over her face. Her hands were tied together with a strong black ribband, and her feet, at her own request, almost touched the ground.'

And the strange thing is that she died almost a popular heroine, within a little of being held a martyr. People said that she behaved so nicely during her trial and in prison that she really couldn't be guilty. And then she was so orthodox in her attachment to the Church of England, so horrified at the rumour that Captain Cranstoun had perverted her to infidelity, so shocked at another rumour that she had committed suicide in gaol. Moreover, she wished it to be known that she had read the works 'of several of our most celebrated divines.' She mentioned this because 'the imputation of infidelity, in some of her last moments, had given her infinite uneasiness and concern.' And so the long agonies and tortures of poor, forgiving Francis Blandy were forgotten as a halo began to shine about Mary Blandy's head.

No doubt her punishment was well deserved. Her defence was that Captain Cranstoun had told her that the white powder would influence Francis Blandy in his favour; this will hardly do. But it is interesting to note that the evidence that hanged her, and the accounts of her cursing her father and longing for his death, all came from the two maidservants, and that this evidence has in it the savour of an intense and virulent personal hatred of Mary.

THE CRY OF A CAPTIVE

A WHIRL OF English and French cavalry soldiers, hand to hand battle, swords clashing, men pierced to the heart, cloven almost in two; the English dragoons break away; the young French sub-lieutenant charges furiously after them, far in advance of his men. Suddenly, he hears a loud 'Hurrah!' behind him. He is cut off, tumbled from his saddle, taken prisoner. Young M. de Barral is taken before a great personage.

'He is a tall man; dry, pale, with a long, grim face. He wears a crimson sash, his field-glasses are in his hand, his blue cloak falls down to his spurs, his plumed hat is of the kind called 'the Wellington.' He questions me as follows:

' "Are you an officer?"

' "Yes, general; I am a cavalry officer. I have been robbed and ill-treated; brigands could not have behaved worse than your soldiers."

' "It's the fortune of war," he replied, coldly. And then:

' "Is Massèna in command of the French Army?"

' "It is not my business to tell you about that, general."

Thereupon the great man, then Viscount Wellington, afterwards Duke of Wellington, uttered these remarkable words:

'God damn son of a . . . something.'

And this was the first stage of the long journey which led M. Octave de Barral, formerly page of the Emperor, from Torrequemada, Spain, to Abergavenny, Monmouthshire.

Decent Frenchmen are still enraged, decent Englishmen are still ashamed to read of the treatment of the French prisoners of war in England at the time of the Napoleonic wars. I fear it must be said that the brave French soldiers were so handled that the behaviour of the

German military authorities to our brave English soldiers during the late war seems generous by comparison. Thousands of private soldiers died of starvation or of something very like starvation. M. de Barral, being an officer, received the magnificent allowance of a shilling a day, and nothing found.

Young de Barral was dismal enough. He and his friends had to tramp all the way from Portsmouth to Abergavenny. When the procession of prisoners came into a town, the Frenchmen were greeted with cries of 'French dog! God damn you,' or 'Bony is dead.' They slept usually in stables, they lived on bread, potatoes, and sour beer. One night some of them bargained for a room in an alehouse. There were six beds in it, and one was occupied by 'a little gentleman,' and the landlady was not sure whether he would consent to sleep with five French prisoners. But he gave a genial permission; and in the morning it turned out that the little gentleman was 'a worthy Welsh beggar.' However, Abergavenny was reached at last. De Barral allows that the place was not without charm; as a matter of fact, it is of wonderful, of magic beauty. The day after the prisoners' arrival was market day, and they strolled about the town and viewed the scene. They did not like it. With few exceptions they found the women hideously ugly, so that they exclaimed:

'Beloved France, how proud we are to be thy children, when we look at these horrible monkey faces!' And then there was a quarrel with some local roughs, while the prisoners were cheapening potatoes, and the Frenchmen were so ill-advised as to 'put up their dukes'—with poor success. But as De Barral says, the English are mad about boxing.

He gives an odd instance. Some dragoons were quartered for a night at Abergavenny, In the morning, the ostler demanded the usual tip, in a very rude manner. The lieutenant in command refused to give one. Whereupon the ostler proposed that they should settle the matter with their fists. And then—following as closely as possible M. de Barral's idiom—

'To leap from his horse, to cast off his cloak, to fling his helmet to one side and his sword to the other was the work of a moment for our lieutenant. (Remember that all the while the squadron is drawn up opposite, in battle-array, sword in hand!) Thereupon the two champions pound one another scientifically, till both their faces are in a pulp and honour is satisfied, Then the son of Mars readjusts his uniform in silence, gets on his thoroughbred, and gives the word of command: "By the right! Quick! March!" '

There is a curious interlude in M. de Barral's account of life at Abergavenny. Near the town lived a certain Lord Kolborough—the name is, obviously, impossible, but I cannot proffer any emendation—who had a fine place in an immense park; possibly Llanover? On the gates of this park was written in letters of gold:

> *Ye who suffer, enter this abode,*
> *Ye who are happy, Pass along your road.*

And Lord Kolborough, not content with this general invitation, had publicly requested all the French prisoners of the neighbourhood to make use of his park at any hour of the day. Thereupon follows the strange history of Milord Kolborough. He had been very wild in his early youth, but at the age of twenty-five he had fallen in love with a beautiful Yorkshire girl. Unhappily, Lady Kolborough died in child-birth, and her little son did not survive her. And on the day of these two deaths, Lord Kolborough, who had been a great fox-hunter, gave orders that every horse and every hound was to die; even to Lady Kolborough's pet toy Yorkshire terrier, *Lovely*. The only animal left alive was coal-black *Blackguard*, Lord Kolborough's favourite mount.

It was *Blackguard* who led the funeral procession, which went on foot all the way from Yorkshire to Abergavenny. The horse's head was held low by a martingale, and he was led by the chief groom. Then came chariots draped in crêpe, containing the remains of the slaughtered horses and dogs. Twelve huntsmen followed, 'making the mountains echo with the saddest music that their horns could play.' Six stout footmen, in full mourning livery, drew the hearse.

I never heard his legend in my young days, spent not far from Abergavenny, and I should be grateful to any correspondent who would enlighten me as to its truth or falsity.

It must be said that if M. de Barral found his stay at the little Monmouthshire town dreary and unpleasant, it was largely his own fault. The Monmouthshire 'county families' were ready to welcome the French officers with open arms, and many of the prisoners took advantage of their invitations. And these, as M. Barral acknowledges, lived like fighting-cocks—'menaient une vraie vie de cocagne.' But De Barral considered such conduct as treason to France; and refused the most pressing invitations.

OUR FUNNY FRIENDS

THE PRACTICAL JOKE seems to have fallen very low indeed. I have just been reading a sad instance of it as it is practised today, under the heading of 'Hoaxing a Woman of 101.' The title is enough, but the 'joke' was even more stupid than might have been supposed. The lady who had attained these long years of life received a notification from the Town Clerk of her county town to the effect that she had been nominated as a candidate for the approaching municipal election. The nomination paper, it appeared, was in correct form, and there were ten assenters. Of course, the poor woman was terribly distressed. She had to be taken to see the mayor; to satisfy him that she had no intention of seeking election; and, as may be judged, that which is merely tiresome at fifty-one or sixty-one is tragical at a hundred and one.

The old practical jokes were sometimes ill-natured, but they were often on a magnificent scale. There is something splendid in the jest attributed, I think, to Theodore Hook, by which some harmless people were pestered all one morning by the arrival of cartloads of coal, sacks of flour, dozens of wine, sides of bacon, roomfuls of furniture, and so forth, with men in charge, producing their orders, and demanding that these vast piles of goods should be taken in by the wretched householders—who knew nothing of the goods and had no need of them. A spiteful trick, no doubt, but with something of the grand manner about it. And then there was an intricate, and, I think, meritorious joke of our own days, which was told to me not long ago by the perpetrator, Albert Diver, the black-and-white man, brother of John Diver, the tenor. A friend who had been in the United States for a couple of years, came to see Albert.

'Let me see,' said Albert, meditatively, 'you've never met my brother, have you?'

'No,' said the friend.

'Well, look here. You know he lives at Orchard House round the corner? Well, go there and ask to see him. Tell him you're a solicitor, that you've hunted him down at last, and ask him what he's going to do about those writs. Then I'll come round when you're in the thick of it, and we'll have a cheerful evening.'

The friend assented joyously, and began to feel himself in the part as he strolled round to Orchard House. He was not aware that John Diver had moved to another house twelve months before. A starchy, shiny, middle-aged man, of a somewhat pompous habit, came into the drawing-room of Orchard House, and stared interrogatively at the unknown stranger. The intruder nodded his head and winked—offensively—and smiled still more offensively.

'I beg your pardon, sir!' said the starchy one, with a hint of fury, and amazement, too, in his voice, 'I don't know you!'

'But I know *you*!' replied the amateur joker, with a simulated fury on his side. 'It's no good. We've run you to earth. We've got you at last. You're done. You know about those writs. What are you going to offer? I'm a solicitor and I'm acting for the other side. And about that fraudulent bankruptcy business?'

The passions of the starchy man swelled purple in his face. He foamed denials of everything. He pealed the bell for the butler. And Albert's friend found himself pushed, none too gently, into the street. Albert, as he imparted to me, told his friend that he had gone to the wrong house and insulted a wealthy linen-draper. But the friend is still wondering.

Montagu Williams gives a fine example of the practical joke as it flourished in the golden 'sixties. This matter was concocted between Toole, 'Dundreary' Sothern, and a friend of theirs named Addison. These three had made acquaintance with a retired insect-extirpator, named Tiffin, who took a strong interest in Spiritualism. Mr Tiffin had the two actors to dine with him at his St John's Wood villa one Sunday night, and they then imparted to him the secret that they were both Spiritualists, and that Toole was a medium of remarkable powers. It was arranged that they should all sup one night at Mr Addison's house in Regent's Park, where highly interesting manifestations were to be expected. Mr Tiffin said he would be delighted, and in the interval the three jokers arranged their programme, going so far as to fit the walls with concealed electric batteries. When the night came, Mr Tiffin saw and felt extraordinary things.

'When the fun had been going on for some time, the company sat down to supper. The meal was pursuing its prosaic course, when Sothern jumped up, and exclaimed: "Toole is seized with a fit! A Spiritualistic power has descended upon him, and he can't shake it off!"

'The face of Toole was horribly contorted, and he groaned piteously.

'Sothern, as though frightened out of his wits, jumped up from his seat, and got under the table. Mr Addison followed his example, and the old gentleman, with undignified haste; promptly joined them.

'Poor terrified Mr Tiffin peered at Toole from under the cloth. . . . Slowly, and with a savage gleam in his eyes, the comedian produced knives from all parts of his body.

'It was too much for the old gentleman. Scrambling to his feet, he rushed from the room; passed out at the front door, and fled for his life down the street. . . .

'Sothern and Mr Addison followed in the footsteps of the elderly vermin-destroyer, and Toole brought up the rear. It was between three and four o'clock in the morning.

'Mr Tiffin continued his flight through many streets. His pursuers gradually gained upon him, and apparently his alarm increased when he heard the footsteps behind him. Taking a sudden turn to the right, he entered some fields, ran across them, and presently came up to a brick wall. In his panic, he climbed over this obstruction, and then, his strength being exhausted, he sunk upon the grass on the other side.

There are fine things about this joke; but the mental and bodily distress of Tiffin, the victim, was past all the measure of joking. The scheme might very well have ended in an inquest and a verdict of manslaughter. The practical joke must never be cruel.

An example of the practical joke in all its classic beauty is told in 'The Bancrofts'. Mr and Mrs Bancroft were lunching in a famous Paris restaurant. Half way through the meal the head waiter who had served them was displaced by the *maître d'hotel*, who trusted that Monsieur and Madame were good enough to be satisfied with the repast, ventured to suggest more exquisite dishes, produced wines that most men have barely heard of. The actor and his wife were puzzled, amazed, intrigued by all this elaborated service. The bill was enormous; the whole staff bowed low as the Bancrofts went out.

It was the work of the villain Toole. Unseen; he had marked his friends' entrance, and, seizing his opportunity, he whispered in the ear of the *maître d'hotel* that the 'lady and gentleman at the corner table' were members of the English Royal Family, travelling strictly incognito.

And the Bancrofts tell the tale with huge relish: it was a flawless practical joke.

TWINS

THE OTHER DAY I cut out an odd piece of news from the morning paper and sent it to a friend of mine, interested in oddities, with the inscription: 'Astrologers, please note.'

It was a story, and a perfectly true story, of twins, small boys about ten or twelve years old. On a certain day, a fortnight or three weeks ago, Jack and Jim, or whatever their names were, were enjoying themselves in different quarters of their country town. And, at a particular hour, let us say three o'clock in the afternoon, Jack was run over by a motor-cycle and badly hurt, and Jim fell off a wall, and was badly hurt. They were photographed lying side by side in hospital; and I trust that by this time they are doing very well.

This queer circumstance brought out some singular facts of a like kind which had happened to twins; the authority being Galton, the eminent eugenist. Here, also, the twins (grown-up, these) were separated. In the first instance, Twin A, travelling in Yorkshire, saw in a shop-window some champagne glasses of novel decoration which pleased him so much that he bought a dozen as a present for Twin B. But at the same time Twin B, passing through Cheltenham, saw some champagne glasses of so excellent a design that he bought a dozen as a present for Twin A. And the pattern of the glasses was the same!

Then, another case. Twin C was having a small operation under an anaesthetic. Twin D, who knew nothing about the operation, found himself, at the hour when the doctors began their work on his brother, suddenly overtaken with severe fever and nausea.

And what are we to make of it all? Heredity might well account for the common taste in champagne glasses. I remember a lady of ancient race saying magnificently: 'We, as a family, have never cared for raspberry jam.' But not heredity, but rather a mysterious and occult sympathy must be brought in to explain that business of the operation. And what about the recent instance of the twins who were hurt at the same hour of the same day? Either it was a mere coincidence, or else astrology is a true science. I prefer the hypothesis of coincidence; for if astrology were true, and if we believed that it was true, then life would be intolerable. What mother could bear to look on her little child in his cradle, knowing that he would inevitably be hanged on his nineteenth birthday.

Coincidence is certainly the more tolerable supposition, and also the more probable, for, be it noted, by the nature of the case, we only hear of the strange event. We lack the complete history of Jack and Jim. For all we know, Jim may once have fallen into the canal, while Jack sat snug and unperturbed for the fire, eating a Christmas pie. There may have been an occasion when Twin A bought Twin B some napkin-rings which were received with ill-disguised aversion. And Twin D might have been thrown from his horse without in the least interrupting the flow of spirits of Twin C, a hundred miles away. And until we have these complete histories, let us take refuge in coincidence, rather than believe that our lives are predestined from the hour of our birth, and all our stories ended before they are begun, in the signs of the heavens.

It is coincidence, I have always held, that is the only possible solution of the Frost case, of which people were talking a good deal in the 'forties or early 'fifties of the last century. I cannot be sure of the date, since my source, a bound volume of a magazine—I think *Chambers Journal*—and I have long been parted. But, briefly, the matter was thus. Thomas Frost was a watchmaker's journeyman in Clerkenwell, where his family had long lived and worked at the local craft. He had a wife, and three children, and, so far as is known, the small establishment was reasonably prosperous and reasonably happy. One night in November, Mrs Frost and the children waited in vain for Mr Frost to come home from his work, at eight o'clock, his usual time. There was a dense white fog, and Mrs Frost thought at first that her husband must have missed his way, though the workshop was barely ten minutes off, and he had gone to and fro between home and workshop day after day for twenty years. She put his supper to keep hot in the oven and went round to the workshop to make enquiries. Mr Frost had left at the usual time; that was all she could hear. It was not till next day that a fellow craftsman came forward and said that he and the missing man had gone out together, and that he was a good deal surprised to see Frost turn to the right, towards St John's Gate, instead of the left, the way to his home. However, he did not think much of it; Frost, he supposed, might very well be going to buy something for his supper at the chandler's at the corner, where there was some very good Lancashire cheese to be had cheap.

And that was the matter. Thomas Frost never came home again. There was no evidence of foul play. His wife managed to support herself and the children by odd washing, odd charing, and a small shop of odds and ends. She always believed that her husband was still alive.

Now for the sequel. Five years after the disappearance of Frost, a Clerkenwell watchmaker was sent down to Devizes on an important job; the overhauling and repairing of the clocks of a big country house—Spy Park, I think it was called—in the neighbourhood, and also of the clock of the parish church adjacent to the country house. This man lodged in a small tavern in a Devizes by-street, and one evening, sitting in the old-fashioned 'parlour,' he astonished the quiet Devizes company by uttering a shout of amazement, as a newcomer entered the little room. 'You villain!' cried the Londoner. 'You black scoundrel! When are you going back to your wife and children?'

The newcomer was Thomas Frost. The London man, who had worked with Frost, swore that there could be no doubt of it; he knew him, he said, as well as his own brother; mentioning particularly a projecting upper tooth, and a scar above one eyebrow. The name of the man was undoubtedly Thomas Frost. He kept a small jeweller's and watchmaker's shop in Devizes; he had a wife and three children, like the missing man of Clerkenwell.

But Devizes, on the other hand, was quite sure that their Thomas Frost had been born in the town, and had lived there all his days. There could be no doubt of it. The London craftsman had to confess that he must be mistaken.

179

DREADS AND DROLLS

Some friends brought Mrs Frost of Clerkenwell and confronted her with the Devizes watchmaker. She is said to have 'gazed at the man very earnestly,' and to have murmured: 'Let bygones be bygones!'

But this Frost business was, no doubt, a case of coincidence.

HUNGRY WEATHER!

THE WEATHER HAS been growing keener of late. There is something appetising about the tang of it; more appetising than all the cocktails, including that cocktail of burnt brandy and bitters which Lord Lovat insisted on before execution. In fine, the hungry air suggests a good meal; let us begin with breakfast.

One of my favourite breakfasts is to be found in *Tom Brown's Schooldays*. Tom, it may be remembered, was going to Rugby. His father and he had come up from the Vale of the White Horse, and had put up at the Peacock, Islington, in order to catch the Tally-ho for Rugby, which started at three o'clock the next morning. There had been steaks and oyster sauce with brown stout for supper, and at ten minutes to three Tom was drinking coffee and eating a hard biscuit in the Peacock coffee-room, and so off he goes on the Tally-ho into the dark of a bitter November morning. At the fourth stage—the fortieth mile, I think—the guard tells Tom to jump down and have a drop of something to keep the cold out, and they have early purl. Brown stout and early purl for a mere child! It was a scandalous age. And at half-past seven, they stop at an inn, and there is twenty minutes for breakfast.

'There is the low dark wainscoted room hung with sporting prints. . . . the blazing fire, with the quaint old glass over the mantelpiece, in which is stuck a large card with the list of the meets for the week of the county hounds. The table covered with the whitest of cloths and of china, and bearing a pigeon pie, ham, round of cold boiled beef cut from a mammoth ox, and the great loaf of household bread on a wooden trencher. And here comes in the stout head-waiter, puffing under a tray of hot viands; kidneys and a steak, transparent rashers and poached eggs, buttered toast and muffins, coffee and tea, all smoking

181

hot.' A noble meal, indeed; but it is interesting to note that the coach-man and a sportsman in company have each a tankard of ale in place of tea or coffee. Indeed, tankards of ale formed part of the recognised breakfast furniture at Oxford, seventy or eighty years ago

Mr and Mrs Browdie had (as they would say) a pretty notion of break-fast. To begin with, there was a slight cocktail of a quarter of a pint of raw spirits; then the breakfast, composed of 'vast mounds of toast, new laid eggs, boiled ham, Yorkshire pie, and other cold substantials, of which heavy relays were constantly appearing from another kitchen under the direction of a very plump servant.' And Major Bagstock's 'camp fare,' as he called it, is appetising. He gave Mr Dombey a break-fast consisting of 'a devilled grill, a savoury pie, a dish of kidneys and so forth'—so forth apparently meant muffins. But if you feel that all these breakfasts are a little heavy for you; why not share Mr Trabb's simpler meal? Mr Trabb, the tailor in *Great Expectations*, was dis-covered 'slicing his hot rolls into three feather beds, and was slipping butter in between the blankets, and covering it up.' And Mr Trabb was more luxurious than the Prince Regent, whose breakfast-table, according to Tom Moore, was spread

> with tea and toast,
> Death-warrants and the *Morning Post*.

Well, we have breakfasted sufficiently: what about lunch? The Anglo-Bengalee Directors in *Martin Chuzzlewit* lunched on 'a pair of cold roast fowls, flanked by some potted meats and a cool salad.' The wine served was Madeira and champagne. Mr Guppy, in *Bleak House*, entertained Mr Jobling and Mr Smallweed to a meal which was, no doubt, dinner, though it was served at an unfashionably early hour. The three of them feasted on 'veal and ham and French beans—and don't you forget the stuffing, Polly,' three pints of half-and-half, summer cabbage (for Mr Jobling) 'without slugs, Polly!'—marrow puddings, Cheshire cheese, and three small rums (and another small rum for Mr Jobling). The bill, including threepence for Polly, was eight and six; very much what it would have been at an eating-house of like kind in the days before the War. The marrow puddings, by the way, appear to be an extinct delicacy: they were, I believe, a sort of paté, made of the marrow of meat.

So far we have done pretty well; indeed, I am afraid that 'A Physician' who sometimes admonishes us as to our diet in the morning paper, would say that we had grossly overeaten. But it must be remembered that we have gone a long way—to the best of my belief Nicholas Nickleby breakfasted with Mr and Mrs Browdie in 1825—and a hundred years' journey gives an appetite. But, however that may be, we are going to dine like men, and in the very best of company, whatever 'A Physician' may say. And the dinner, unlike the breakfasts and the lunches, is to be of fact, not fiction.

The place is Abbotsford, the time is October 28, 1820; our host is Sir Walter Scott. It is what Sir Walter calls 'a superior occasion,' the annual dinner of the Abbotsford Hunt. In the morning, the Abbotsford house party, the neighbouring gentry, yeomen and farmers went coursing on the moors and the hills, and brought back 'hares enough to supply the wife of every farmer that attended with soup for a week.' In the evening the whole party, thirty, forty or more, dined with Sir Walter, 'the Shirra;' as they called him. A genial Presbyterian Dominie said a grace on the text that the Almighty had given man dominion over the fowls of the air, and the beasts of the field, and expounded the matter at such length and with such rich references to coursing of hares that Scott responded, 'Well done, Mr George! I think we've had everything but the view holla!' And then the, feast.

'A baron of beef, roasted, at the foot of the table, a salted round at the head, while tureens of hare-soup, hotch-potch, and cockeyleekie extended clown the centre, and such light articles as geese, turkeys, entire sucking-pigs, a singed sheep's head, and the unfailing haggis were set forth by way of side-dishes. Blackcock and moorfowl, bushels of snipe, black puddings, white puddings, and pyramids of pancakes formed the second course.'

And they drank ale, port, and sherry, and swallowed quaighs—wooden cups—of Glenlivet as if it were water; and then the Ettrick Shepherd made great bowls of punch, and old stories of the hills and the border were told, and old Scots songs were sung . . . and times have changed a good deal since October 28, 1820.

THE MEDICINE-MAN'S MAGIC

A FEW YEARS ago Mr Joseph F. Rock was in charge of the American National Geographic Society's Expedition to the Yunnan province of China. In the course of his labours he came upon the strange tribe of the Nashi, who are to be found to the north of Burma, on the eastern border of Tibet. The Nashi had lived for many ages in this obscure corner of Asia, in valleys surrounded by high mountain ranges. They were once a kingdom; they were conquered by the Chinese in the eighth century of our era; they regained their independence, and were finally merged in the Chinese Empire at the beginning of the eighteenth century. Their race seems a mixture of Tibetan and Burmese; they have two scripts, one resembling the picture-writing of Red Indians, the other a character like Chinese, but so far undeciphered by Western scholars. Of all this and much more Mr Rock, who lived amongst this forgotten people for two years, gives faithful account in *The National Geographic Magazine* for November, 1924. And he also gives an account of Nashi medicine, which, being frankly incredible, is of the highest interest.

I do not gather that Mr Rock is a medical man, but he appears to have practised the simpler forms of medicine for the benefit of the natives, after the accustomed manner of explorers. And once a man came to him in a very bad way.

'His ailments, I found, were due to a black, ulcerated tooth, if such it could be called, for there was nothing left but a black hole in his lower jaw. His gums were swollen and intensely red, and pus was gathering within the palate; he was unable to swallow or close his mouth, and every movement of his lips must have caused him excruciating pain. I sent him away, as I had neither means nor skill to cure or help him.'

184

THE MEDICINE-MAN'S MAGIC

Whereupon the patient, finding that the West had failed him, betook himself to the clergy of his country.

Mr Rock was allowed to see every detail of the treatment. It was ten o'clock of a sultry night in July, and the thunder was rolling in the mountains, and the lightning flashing over the Yangtze gorge. A round bamboo altar had been set up in the courtyard of the sick man's house, and by it there squatted a blind priest beating a huge drum and uttering a weird chant. The other priests entered, wearing crowns that had the likeness of leaping flames. A cock was brought forward and set by the sick man. Its head and mouth were washed, and it was then taken away for a season. Then a small chick was produced and ceremonially slain, the patient choking it with flour. The little dead bird was washed and gently placed in a little coffin, and covered with rice, red paper, and perforated yellow paper. The lid was put on the coffin and the sick man pretended to hammer it down with a huge axe. All stood up and chanted funeral dirges; wine, rice, and potatoes were offered, and the patient knelt down and drank the wine and devoured the rice and the potatoes.

This was the first part of the service; the serious business was to come. Drums and gongs made a wild music, and a ploughshare was heated red hot in a bonfire kindled near the altar. A priest appeared with two dwarf trees, an oak and a pine. He took a sword from the altar, touched the oak with it nine times, and then cut it in two. The sick man, still kneeling, did the same office for the pine. Then the chief priest entered the house, changed his black robe for a blue one, and his flaming crown for a scarlet turban, and set flags, red and white, in his sash; these flags looking like bat wings, and giving the reverend gentleman a demoniacal appearance, as Mr Rock observes. Then the gong and drum music became wilder and wilder, and the priest danced madly, 'sword in hand, now between his teeth, now hurled against the ceiling from between his legs.' The unhappy cock reappears; 'his head is dipped in wine, his neck and legs are stretched simultaneously to the rhythm of the most devilish music ever invented. The gyrating, perspiring Tomba [priest] with a final cross-eyed look heavenward, gives one last jerk to the bird's neck, while a weird, long roll of the drum announces that life is extinct.'

More dancing, more furious banging of gongs—the Nashi clergy are, evidently, a hardworking body—and the congregation is visibly affected. A pot of oil is placed before the door of the house. The priest dances madly, with flaming strips of paper in his right hand, and suddenly leaps into the bonfire, scattering the burning logs all over the courtyard. The red hot ploughshare is set on end and the priest licks it with his tongue. The congregation hears the hiss of the burning metal as the tongue touches it. The oil in the pot is lit, and the Tomba dips his hand in the blue flames, and so with burning pot and flame-dripping fingers, his sword in his mouth, he goes all about the house, purging every room with fire, finally burning the bamboo altar. The rite is accomplished; the doors are closed.

And here is the incredible part of the story:

'Early next morning,' writes Mr Rock, 'I called for the sick man, who was the chief participant in all this weird ceremony. To my amazement, he showed no signs of ever having had a diseased gum or palate, although the bad tooth remained.'

What are we to say? The *Geographic Magazine* is a solid, responsible, almost an official publication, and Mr Rock writes as a responsible observer and explorer. He mentions that he induced the priests to repeat the ceremony in his own courtyard and by daylight. He took a series of photographs—the rector, if one may call him so, looks a delightful man with a sense of humour—with which his article is illustrated.

But how was it done? By a strong appeal to the imagination? We know that the imagination sometimes cures pain; toothache often disappears on the dentist's doorstep; but can the imagination change suppurating tissue into healthy tissue in the course of a few hours, leaving behind no trace of the disease?

THE BEST OF EVERYTHING

IN AUGUST, 1813, Mr Walter Scott, as he was then, met the Marquis of Abercorn travelling between Carlisle and Longtown. The two men had an appointment, and so Scott joined the cavalcade; the family and the household in four or five carriages drawn by the marquis's own horses, and the marquis last, mounted on horseback, and decorated with the ribbon of the Order of the Garter.

The noble party were dining at Longtown; which is rather a village than a town.

'The marquis's major-domo and cook had arrived there at an early hour in the morning, and everything was now arranged for his reception in the paltry little public-house, as nearly as possible in the style usual in his own lordly mansions. The ducks and geese that had been dabbling three or four hours ago in the village pond were now ready to make their appearance under numberless disguises as *entrées*; a regular bill-of-fare flanked the noble marquis's allotted cover; every huckaback towel in the place had been pressed to do service as a napkin; and that nothing might be wanting to the mimicry of splendour, the landlady's poor remnants of crockery and pewter had been furbished up, and mustered in solemn order on a crazy old beauffet.'

Scott loved to tell the tale of the marquis at Longtown. He thought that it was probably the last example of the manners of the old world.

All such trifles have a very strong interest to me. I like to cherish my recollection of Hereford on a market day, fifty years ago; all the old streets white with countrymen in smock frocks, that beautiful habit that had lasted a thousand years, and was to disappear in ten. And here and there elderly gentlemen strolled along in shiny broadcloth, and richly frilled shirts; and in the hall of the College of Vicars Choral there were still the great tables at which the Minor Canons and the

187

Priest Vicars used to dine together every day, till new ways came in with the 'sixties.

But to the lover of antiquity, who sees to his sorrow many old customs broken and many ancient things destroyed, there is this comfort; that the line of antiquity, as it were, perpetually advances. The commonplace of the past age becomes the curiosity of this. I often wonder whether any specimen of the 'knife-board' omnibus has been preserved; and to me the occasional surviving hansom cab is as pleasing as the spectacle of a man in knee-breeches must have been eighty or ninety years ago. And now listen to this. It is 'Advice on the Choice of a Wife'. It is only fifty years old. But it is as much a message from a dead world as the tale of the Marquis of Abercorn riding into Longtown with his Garter ribbon about him.

'Never dream of marriage with one of extravagant habits. A clergyman bent on marriage dined with a friend who possessed three marriageable daughters. Before dinner he had been at a loss as to which of the young ladies he should propose to. Towards the close of the meal, cheese was produced, and each of the three sisters took a portion. Before eating, the first pared her morsel, the second scraped hers, and the third took the cheese just as it was. The visitor was no longer at a loss; he proposed to the lady who, cleanly without being extravagant, scraped her cheese.'

And the next article in the admirable work from which I quote—it is entitled *The Best of Everything*—gives a receipt for cleaning marble chimney pieces with bullock's gall.

The Best of Everything was published in 1874; and I should have thought that the art of making wax flowers had fallen into desuetude by that time. But not so.

'Many of these imitations are exceedingly like the natural plant in all but perfume, and the manufacture of them affords all opportunity for the exercise of great neatness and good taste, as well as observation of the nature and structure of the flowers which it is intended to present.' And full instructions follow as to the materials necessary: the sheets of white and coloured wax, the pigments, the implements, finely pointed scissors, small sable brushes, boxwood tools, and so forth. Instructions for making a Camellia Japonica in wax follow, and those who wish to excel are referred to Mrs Peachey, 'whose address can be had at the Soho bazaar.'

I can remember the Soho Bazaar very well. It was founded in 1815, and lasted on into the 'nineties of the last century.

Turn haphazard to another page, which contains valuable hints on the decoration of the dinner-table. 'There are few houses,' says our author, where dinners *à la Russe* have not gained favour; and the 'looking-glass tables' are strongly recommended. These tables, save for the space taken by the covers, were sheets of glass, decorated by wreaths of flowers and drooping leaves set in narrow trays filled with damp sand. And there is one last point of elegance:

'Charming little bouquets, are laid on each guest's plate, or placed in the champagne glass. Everyone seems pleased to receive such a sweet welcome—and they are speedily transferred to the dresses of their fair recipients, or to the button holes of the sterner sex.'

'Fair recipients,' 'sterner sex'! And now they are all 'old beans' and 'priceless old things'—and everybody knows which is the sterner sex.

But how soothing it is to think that in 1975 the 'beans' and 'old things' will be with Nineveh and Tyre, with the 'fair,' with 'beaux' and 'belles,' 'gallants' and 'charmers.'

They had their amusements in those far off days. The young ladies decorated all sorts of objects by means of Decalomanie; I do not venture to say whether this were the same as Potichomanie. And they played Bézique—I have played Bézique—and Drole. Drole was a brand-new game and 'Cavendish'—the great authority on cards—had written a text-book on it. There were 'privileged cards': the Emperor, the Empress, Beautiful Nell (Queen of Spades), Jack Drole, and the Four Beggars (the Aces). Beautiful Nell had the power of interceding, and Jack Drole (Knave of Diamonds) could rob in any suit.

And compared with this jargon, 'two for his heels,' and 'Basto, ma'am, you have spadille, I believe,' sound fresh and new and green.

THE MERRY WIDOW

MRS VANWICKE, a widow, was some time ago the cause of very grave trouble, which ended in the violent deaths of two of her friends. One of these friends was Dr Andrew Clenche, of Brownlow Street, High Holborn; the other a man named Henry Harrison, described officially as 'gent,' and unofficially as a bully. And the trouble was that Dr Clenche was found strangled in a hackney coach near Leadenhall, and that Henry Harrison was hanged for the murder.

I wish we knew more of Mrs Vanwicke; but though she plays so important a part in the story, she hardly makes any appearance in it. It is stated that there was 'a great kindness' between her and Harrison; and apparently there was a kindness, on one side at all events, between her and the doctor. Dr Clenche had lent her £20, whereupon Mrs Vanwicke asked for £80 more, and offered a mortgage on her house in Buckingham Court, Strand, as a security. The doctor lent the money, but was finally obliged, in default of payment, to foreclose, bringing an action for ejectment against the widow. Whereupon the gallant Harrison breathed flames and threats against Dr Clenche, laid his hand on his sword in the doctor's presence, and vowed that the amiable physician deserved to have his throat cut. Mrs Vanwicke tried the doctor again for a little loan, but, not unnaturally, met with a refusal. Whereupon Harrison uttered worse threats than ever, and proceeded to dissemble.

The dissembling began by his changing his lodgings. On Christmas Eve, 1691, he moved into lodgings at Mr Garraway's, at the Hand and Apple, Threadneedle Street. I do not know whether this was the original Garraway's Coffee House, where tea was first sold in England in the year 1657; I suppose not, since that was in Exchange Alley, and was never known, I think, by any sign. However, Henry Harrison, attended by a footboy, and pretending to be a parliament man just up from the county, took up his abode at the Hand and Apple, and slept there till the night of January 1. And it was at Garraway's that there occurred the odd incident of the pocket-handkerchief.

One evening Mr Harrison was sitting in his room, and Mrs Jackson, Mrs Garraway's daughter, was attending to his fire. She noticed that the lodger took out his pocket-handkerchief and held it before the fire, and she noticed also that it was not at all the kind of pocket-handkerchief that an M.P. would be expected to carry. It was coarse and dirty, 'not fit for the quality,' being made 'of ordinary Indian stuff.' That was a fatal handkerchief for Henry Harrison since it was found at last twisted around Dr Clenche's neck, and in a sense round the bully's neck also when death came to him at Tyburn. Here, then, the dissembling broke down badly, and it was not much mended by Harrison sending a letter to himself from an imaginary friend in the country, this friend alleging severe illness and an urgent need of Harrison's comforting presence. By this time Mrs Vanwicke found herself in a debtor's prison. Harrison visited her there, and uttered more threats against the doctor, and, still dissembling in an altogether clumsy and futile manner, took new lodgings at Mr Jones's, a cane-chair maker's of St Paul's Churchyard.

Two men, said John Sikes, the coachman, got into his hackney coach soon after nine, on the night of January 4, in Fleet Street, by the end of Fetter Lane. They ordered him to drive to Dr Clenche's in Brownlow Street, and a woman who had come out upon an errand saw a coach stop at the end of Brownlow Street and heard one of the men bid the coachman go to Dr Clenche's and tell him that a man was very ill, and that a coach was waiting for him.

'There were two lamps burning,' said the observant Mrs Ashbolt, the interested female in question, 'one in Brownlow Street and the other in Holborn over against the end of Brownlow Street, and they lighted quite through the coach; and the men pulled themselves backward when they saw me look on them.'

But it was too late. Mrs Ashbolt swore that one of the men was Harrison.

Then John Sikes takes up the tale. He relates how he found the doctor in nightgown and slippers, how he dressed on hearing of the sick man, and got into the coach. Then the order was given to drive to Leadenhall Market, 'and when it came about Holborn Bars, one of them called to me and asked me why I drove so slowly. So I drove fast and came to Leadenhall, and then one of them bade me drive to the Pye Tavern without Aldgate.' From the Pye Tavern that fatal coach was directed back to Leadenhall, and sixpence had to be given on the watch at Aldgate, because the gate was shut. Outside Leadenhall the coach was stopped, and the coachman was given three-and-six and told to buy a couple of fowls in the market.

The clever coachman got a pair of fowls for three shillings: but when he got back to the coach the two men were gone. One man remained, and that was Dr Andrew Clenche, at the bottom of the coach, strangled, with a coarse handkerchief twisted about his neck. The doctor's hat was found next morning in Holborn, by Fetter Lane, and there it was judged the deed was done.

Harrison, 'gent,' and 'bully,' and, occasionally, 'captain,' tried to set up an alibi, but the jury disregarded it, and he was hanged, protesting his entire innocence.

But who was the other man in the coach? That mystery was never solved. Some months after Harrison had been duly hanged, one John Cole, a labourer, was indicted for the murder of Dr Clenche, and the only witness against him was the prosecutrix, one Mrs Milward, who told the court that her late husband had told her before he died that he and Cole were the murderers of Dr Clenche. The court very properly ruled that what Mr Milward had said was not evidence, and Cole was acquitted.

KNOCKING LEGENDS TO SMITHEREENS

NOT VERY LONG ago Lord Fyvie, of Fyvie Castle, died, and, as it happened, left no son to succeed him. In itself there seems nothing so very amazing in this circumstance, which is not of infrequent occurrence; but we soon learned that the case of Fyvie Castle and the succession to it was far removed from the ordinary.

It seemed that there was an ancient curse upon the place, if, indeed, there were not two or three ancient curses. Different versions appeared in the newspapers. By one account, Fyvie Castle had been built of the ruins of an old monastery; and this should have been enough for any reasonable person. To put anything set apart for holy objects to a common secular use is, evidently, sacrilege, and a curse seems the natural result of conduct so profane. But this was not enough. A single stone of the old abbey or priory or whatever it was had been accidentally dropped into the river, and according to one version of the legend in this lay the sting of the offence. The sacrilege it would almost seem might have been forgiven, but not the mad prodigality implied in wasting a single stone. The patron saint of the abbey was, evidently, every inch a Scot; and hence his curse issued against Fyvie Castle and its inhabitants—till that missing stone should be fished up and set to some useful service. And then there was another legend, of quite different origin, which explained the curse of Fyvie without any reference to the horrid sin of sacrilege or the more horrid sin of prodigality. In this second story, Thomas of Ercildoune—that famous bard of the thirteenth century who visited the Queen of Faerie—came one night to Fyvie in the guise of a poor, ragged beggar and was rudely and inhospitably treated and driven from the door. Hence, and hence alone, the Curse of Fyvie: it was True Thomas who uttered the doom of the churlish and unknightly castle.

And what was the curse? Simply this: that thenceforth no lord of Fyvie should be succeeded in his possessions by his son.

Now, one knows the attitude with which this sort of tale is received. We accord it a general assent: with certain reservations. We may hesitate as to the origin of the curse; we may doubt whether an act of sacrilege or waste, or both together, would really blight the succession of Fyvie for ever. And again, if we adopt the Ercildoune legend, we may boggle a little in accepting it literally. Still, there are the facts of the case; the story or stories are undoubtedly ancient traditions; the late Lord Fyvie did not leave a son to succeed him. What is one to say?

And such, I am sure, would have been the attitude towards the Curse of Fyvie—if it had not been for the intervention of a meddlesome scholar. This gentleman was so indecent as to consult his books of reference and to show that Fyvie passed from father to son about seventy years ago.

And in an instant the whole fabric of the Curse of Fyvie dissolves into mere nothingness. The facts—the circumstance of the broken succession—turn out to be non-existent; and the legends explaining the non-existent facts are probably about ten years old. We think we live in a scientific and rational age, and yet our credulity is immeasurable. Before a newspaper paragraph beginning 'There has always been a strange legend about Dunblather Castle' we are as helpless as black Africans in the presence of the medicine man.

Sometimes these fables may be traced to their source; and this is the case with the widely known legend of Glamis Castle. This was—nay, is—a vague but horrible tradition, supposed to be of vast antiquity. Briefly, the story goes that there is a hidden room in this ancient and mighty place. Awful are the surmises which whisper of the secret chamber of Glamis and of what dwells therein. I have listened to some of these mutterings, and they have made my hair shiver. And even the professed sceptic would probably remark: 'Of course, most of these legends are lies, but I happen to know for a fact that there is something very queer indeed about Glamis. A friend of mine staying there,' etc., etc.

Very fine indeed: but I doubt whether the 'legend' be a hundred years old. I should not be surprised to hear that it was invented in the fifties of the last century.

Here is the cold truth: In 1793 young Walter Scott spent a night at Glamis, the guest of the seneschal, Peter Proctor. Scott acknowledges that it was an eerie place; that as he heard door after door shut behind the steps of the man who had shown him to his room he felt 'too far from the living, and somewhat too near the dead.' But to the dread chamber, thus Walter Scott:

'It [the castle] contains also a curious monument of the peril of feudal times, being a secret chamber, the entrance of which, by the law or custom of the family, must only be known to three persons at once, namely, the Earl of Strathmore, his heir-apparent, and any third person whom they may take into their confidence.'

It was a secret strong room for the keeping of valuables, and, possibly, a safe hiding place in time of danger: that was all. Clearly there was no legend of terror, no tale of an awful Presence hidden in that secret place. For, if there had been any such legend, Walter Scott, that keenest of Scottish antiquaries and tradition-mongers, would most certainly have heard of it. But from this simple source all the monstrous mythology of Glamis has proceeded.

ONE NIGHT WHEN I WAS FRIGHTENED

MOST MOUNTAINEERS, I suppose, have had their moments of panic. Indeed, even to look at the photographs of their perils has often made me shudder. To see a man with his feet resting on a ledge a few inches broad, one hand grasping a craggy projection—and a thousand feet of space beneath him: there is horror in the very thought of such a pass. What the actuality must be I can scarcely conceive; and though the mountaineer clearly has nerves that are well-nigh superhuman, I suppose that once or twice in his awful sport he has known how terror seizes the heart. But the strangest fright that ever befell a mountaineer has been described lately by Professor J. Norman Collie, lecturer in organic chemistry at London University.

This was no case of physical peril. The Professor has climbed most of peaks of the world, and perhaps he has outgrown all common bodily terrors. At all events, he told some fellow mountaineers how the most intense fear of his life came to him on Ben Macdhui (or Mhuichdhui), the principal peak of the Cairngorn Range; a big mountain, no doubt, according to the standard of the British Isles, but a small affair to an accomplished Alpinist.

It was thirty-five years ago, the professor said, when the fright of his life befell him. He was coming down the mountain side in a mist, when he began to be aware of strange sounds. He heard a big crunch and then another crunch, as if someone were walking after him, but taking steps three or four times the length of his own. He said to himself, 'This is all nonsense.' But he walked on, and the eerie 'crunch, crunch' sounded behind him, and he was seized with terror. He took to his heels and ran, staggering blindly among the boulders for four or five miles nearly down to Rothiemurchas Forest.

And the Professor ends his tale by saying that this experience had made him quite resolved never more to climb to the Cairn of Ben Macdhui alone.

Now this tale of mountaineering strikes me as most impressive. It is much more impressive, to me at all events, than a kind of sequel added by Professor Collie. He had imparted his experience to a friend, a scientific colleague, I think, and this gentleman, Dr Kellas, had also encountered adventure on Ben Macdhui. He had seen a figure, ten feet high in appearance, walking near his brother, who was sitting down near the cairn on the summit of the mountain. The brother, it turned out, had seen nothing, but an old man of Rothiemurchas Forest, hearing the story, accepted the appearance as quite in the natural order: 'Oh, aye,' the Highlander remarked, 'that would have been Ferla Mhor—the big grey man.' That is very fine, no doubt, but is more in the Highland convention of the ghostly, and one cannot help reflecting that the imagination, helped by solitude and the grim height in the clouds, and the shapes of the mist and the shapes of the dim rocks, is quite capable of fashioning such giant shapes. Not that I would say a word against any well established Gaelic ghost; but each man has his own peculiar taste in the ghastly, and the footsteps of Professor Collier appeal to me more richly than the Ferla Mhor of Dr Kellas. And there is another reason for my interest: I have heard those footsteps myself, or something very like them.

It happened a little more than twenty-one years ago. My wife and I were touring with Sir Frank Benson, in the summer of 1904, and, amongst other places, we visited Marlborough. It may be mentioned, by the way, that the tour was a semi-scholastic one, the chief attraction being the famous trilogy, *Agamemnon*, *Libation Bearers* and *Furies* of Aeschylus. Hence Marlborough, hence other places of the same sort.

Well, it fell out that one night at Marlborough some other piece was put on, and neither my wife nor I was wanted at the show, and so towards dusk we strolled out of the little town, and climbed up a white road, and found ourselves on the Downs. And it came upon me as we strolled along that we were in a strange country. It was twilight and the distances were vague, but close at hand everything was clearly presented, and yet (as it seemed to me) not altogether in the light of the common world. As I remember the scene, the road we followed was terraced on the hillside; higher land was above us, and to the right the turf fell swiftly away to some valley that was but dimly visible. And here were little bent thorn-trees, very old and very crooked and very strange, and by them little narrow tracks wound in and out and crept away down the steep hillside to the unseen valley. And the night was still and not a leaf stirred, and, of course, those tiny paths were sheep tracks.

We strolled along this queer way for a couple of miles, perhaps, and then turned to go back to Marlborough. The night was now upon us, and all that was clearly visible was the road, white with limestone dust. And then we heard the footsteps. They came behind us, hurried, vehement, insistent, as if some one were walking for his life—if such a phrase might be allowed. We both heard but took no notice; it was merely somebody in a great hurry. And, I am not quite certain, but I think I half turned and gave a casual glance behind me as wondering why as fast a walker did not overtake us, who were strolling along in all leisure. And there was the stretch of road, a broad white ribbon in the darkness, and not a soul to see. I made some remark, and we both stopped dead and turned round. Nobody to be seen, and not a sound in the silence. Perplexed, we went again on our way back to Marlborough; in a moment those rattling, violent footsteps range upon the road behind us. An echo? Impossible; the road was thick with velvety limestone dust; our feet fell upon it in silence; we set out once more on our walk, and once more the loud steps beat faster and faster on our track. And so they continued till we came to the hill just above Marlborough, and then the night was silent.

To this day I have never been able to account for those footsteps on the Downs; but that is very far from saying that they were unaccountable.

THE WOOD FAMILY

A FAMOUS DRAMATIC critic has just declared that the condition of the stage in the provinces is well-nigh desperate. He gives his chapter and verse for this statement; at one big provincial town after another there is nothing to be found but musical comedy and revue. The legitimate drama is barely tolerated; the 'London play,' the play that appeals above all to the stalls of the London theatre, is not understood at Leeds or Birmingham, and if it were understood would not be liked. And so the country stage is in a very bad way.

But was it ever in any other sort of way? There is, of course, the point of view of the actor and the point of view of the audience. The provincial actor of today is very ill-paid, or rather, he is hardly paid at all, because, excepting musical productions, there are very few plays going out. But in the old days, say, a hundred years ago, the country stage by no means flourished. I remember Crummles. He saw in Nicholas Nickleby a most promising recruit.

'There's genteel comedy in your walk and manner, juvenile tragedy in your eye, and touch-and-go farce in your laugh,' said Mr Vincent Crummles. 'You'll do as well as if you had thought of nothing else but the lamps, from your birth downwards.'

And, besides acting, Nicholas was to draw up the bills and become the playhouse author, and:

'What should I get for all this?' inquired Nicholas. . . . 'Could I live by it?'

'Live by it!' said the manager, 'like a prince!' With your own salary, and your friend's, and your writings you'd make—ah! You'd make a pound a week!'

No doubt Dickens often paints with a full brush; but there is little exaggeration in this passage. 'Old Odell' once told me that in his young days a beginner could and did manage on nine shillings a week, and that fifteen shillings a week was regarded as solid comfort in the provincial theatre. And I heard from Mrs Keeley the terms of her first engagement. She was paid five shillings weekly. I know that these figures must be trebled, perhaps quadrupled to obtain their equivalents in modern money; still, when that has been done, the sums are not magnificent.

And the reason of all this, then and now, is the same. It is not that theatrical managers are villains. The fact is that the vast majority of people in the country stay away from the theatre, and, to the best of my belief, always have stayed away from the theatre. Why was Crummles unable to pay Nicholas and Smike more than a pound a week? Because the Portsmouth theatre was only attended by a handful of people. The audience, according to the old players' phrase, was principally composed of 'the Wood family'—empty benches. And why is the provincial actor of today usually resting in town instead of playing in the country? Because managers know that the average tour is a gamble, with the odds heavily against success—which is the empty Portsmouth theatre over again. If the pit be empty, the actor's pocket naturally will be empty, too. And in spite of Mr Cuddle; there never was any golden age of the country playhouse. Things were always pretty bad with the strolling player; in the eighteenth century they were often ghastly. Strange stories survive of those forgotten day's in memoirs which only a few have heard of. Mr King, if I remember, created an important part in 'The School for Scandal.' 'I remember,' he said once in Drury Lane green-room, 'that when I had been a short time on the stage, I performed one night King Richard, gave two comic songs, played in an interlude, spoke a prologue, afterwards harlequin, in a sharing company; and after all this fatigue, my share came to threepence and two pieces of candle.'

Sometimes an extra shilling or two might be earned by undertaking the office of 'orator,' or bill-distributor, or, in our modern phrase, advance agent. The orator called on the shopkeepers and at the back doors of great houses, where he tried to secure the good offices of the butler, who would sometimes lay the players' bills before his lord and lady. One of these poor players, a man named Ryley, tells of a night's adventure.

'After playing Touchstone, young Philpot, and dancing, I went home penniless. I had lodged and boarded with an old woman, who kept a creditable public-house; she was at the play: I was unavoidably in her debt. I never was more cast down and dispirited; I could with difficulty muster courage to open the door. When I entered I shall never forget my reception. I believe she saw my backwardness: "Come, Come along," says she; "bless your dear little legs." This was a wonderful cordial to my drooping spirits; I never stood in greater need of one; but she nor her husband would be satisfied till out of his friendly bottle I had taken two cordials; then told me there was a little fowl boiled and ready for my supper: not to be uneasy about anything but make myself comfortable.'

Such was the life of country actors in the middle years of the eighteenth century.

JUSTICE: A VIGNETTE

IN THE YEAR of our Lord, 1689, Ireland was very far from being the peaceful country it is now. King James II had fled from England and was supposed to have abdicated the throne, and William and Mary reigned in his place. But James was expected daily in Ireland, and that island was in a state of considerable unrest. The unrest took the specific form of stealing cows; and from the nature of things in those days in Ireland, the cows were mostly Protestant cows, and the cow-stealers, were Roman Catholics.

The whole country, indeed, was upside down; people roamed about in bands arresting one another, raiding one another's lands, nobody being quite clear as to who was king, or whose throat it was safe to cut! A perplexing state of things for the simple peasantry. Yet the King's writ—that is, King James's writ—still ran in a fashion, and at Wicklow, in March, 1688-9, Lord Chief Justice Keating and Baron Lynch held an assize, chiefly to try the people who thought of politics in terms of cows.

There was the case of Leaghlin Birne, and nine head of black cattle. No witnesses appeared to give evidence against him, and the Chief Justice, an evident disciple of Jeffreys, observed to the jury:

'Gentlemen, you have nothing against this man; he was born in the state of innocency; but the truth is, the parties dare not appear against him.'

However, witnesses were found who testified—with trembling knees, I suspect—against Maurice Cavenagh, Edmund Poor, and William Bowland. The Chief Justice, anticipating a little, told the witnesses not to spare 'any of these villains.' And then the evidence leaves cows for a while, and becomes concerned with 'skeans,' or knive, which, I think we spell 'skenes.' Thus:

JUSTICE: A VIGNETTE

L.C.J.: 'Sir, how durst you carry such an unlawful weapon?'

CAVENAGH: 'My lord, I am a butcher; it was a butcher's knife.'

L.C.J.: 'Ay, I do not question but thou canst butcher upon occasion.'

There was a wrangle about this knife, and Cavenagh said that he had been ordered to have one.

L.C.J.: 'Pray, sir, who ordered you?'

CAVENAGH: 'The priest of the parish.'

L.C.J.: 'A priest, sir?' (turning to his brother judge). 'Do you hear that brother?'

It should be mentioned that the Chief Justice was a Protestant, and Baron Lynch a Roman Catholic. So the Baron:

'What priest, sir? What priest? What is your priest's name?'

L.C.J.: 'Hold, brother. Come sir, I shall not ask your priest's name: I believe you will have occasion to see your priest soon, to do you a better office than to advise you to carry skeans.'

A grim jest this, in the purest Jeffreys manner. And then the Chief Justice looked at two priests who were sitting by Sheriff Birne on the bench, and said that priests should be ministers of peace. 'It is not for priests to arm or animate such villains as you are for mischief. I shall not ask your priest's name.

CLANCY (an Irish Gentleman): 'My lord, he belies the priest; he is a rogue.'

CAVENAGH: 'I do not. The priests of every parish did give orders to get half-pikes and skeans, and they were getting together in companies in every parish.'

L.C.J.: 'Who were they that were gotten together? Such fellows as you?'

CAVENAGH: 'No, my lord, better men than I; a great many that are here in court.'

Mr Cavenagh was probably telling the exact truth: and one can almost detect the perplexity of himself and his friends. They have stolen Protestant cows, they have armed themselves with pikes and skenes to fight for King James; and yet King James's justices are trying them, and doing their best to hang them. As a matter of fact, it would seem that the judges were doing their best to deal out pure justice, without fear or favour; and that, perhaps, was the most puzzling circumstance of all to Cavenagh and his companions.

Cavenagh got off. The jury found him not guilty, whereupon Keating, L.C.J., said: 'Gentlemen, you have acquitted the greater villain; at your door let it lie.' And then he turned to Poor and Bowland, who had been found guilty! It was their first offence, and they were entitled to Benefit of Clergy: to show that they could read, and then to be branded and released. As a rule, this was a mere formula. The criminal had learnt a verse from a psalm and repeated it, and the Ordinary, or Chaplain, made his report to the judge: *legit*, he can read, and Clergy was allowed. But on this occasion things did not go so easily. The Chief Justice observed that 'the times are so that men must forget bowels of mercy.'

'Ordinary, do your duty. What place do you show them?'

ORDINARY: 'My lord, I show them the fiftieth psalm.'

L.C.J.: 'Let them read the fifth verse.'

And the Ordinary returned them both, *non legit*. They had not been prepared for the fifth verse.

The judge spoke of the troubles of the country. 'On this side of the Cape of Good Hope, where are the most brutish and barbarous people we read of, there is none like the people of this country, nor so great a desolation as in this kingdom, at this day, anywhere to be found, and particularly in this country. It has come to that pass that a man, that looses the better part of his substance, chooses rather to let that and what he has besides go than come to give evidence, and why? Because he is certain to have his house burnt, and his throat cut, if he appears against them.' And so on to the dread conclusion:

'Mr Sheriff, let them have a confessor sent to them, for Saturday is the day of their execution.'

And the women, their friends, setting up their cry in the Court:

L.C.J.: 'They did not cry thus when the cows were brought home to them; they were busied then in the killing and the powdering them up.'

HOUSES

SOME TIME BEFORE the publication of a famous novel called *Waverley*, there was a little discussion between the author and the printer as to the sub-title. The author, Walter Scott, wished to call his book, *Waverley; or 'tis Sixty Years Since*, but Ballantyne, the printer, objected, because, as he said, this sub-title was uninteresting, unalluring. Sixty years ago, he declared, was too near to be attractive; manners were much the same then as in the beginning of the nineteenth century; there had been no vivid or picturesque changes in life or habit.

It seems odd to us that Ballantyne should not have perceived the gulf that yawned between the Scotland of the '45, and the Scotland of 1805; for it is as large as the gulf between the Old World and the New. But, on reflection, is it so odd? Are we, in our turn, aware of the depth of the gulf that separates the life of 1926 from the life of sixty, seventy years ago? I doubt it. The other day I was looking through an old magazine (dated 1858); and I glanced at a somewhat feeble story by George Augustus Sala. A feeble story, as I say; the only thing interesting to me was the status and habit of one of the characters. This gentleman had an income of £800 a year. He lived in a comfortable and well-appointed house in Brompton—which means, I think, South Kensington. His domestic staff consisted of a cook, a housemaid, a parlourmaid, and a boy in buttons. And I should very much like to know what income would be required in these days to support a similar mode of life. I suppose the £800 would have to be multiplied by three or even four, and Brompton would become, let us say, Wimbledon; so great have been the changes between 1858 and 1926.

This circumstance in this feeble story in an old magazine serves to illuminate a question which often perplexes me as I pass through the

205

older parts of London. I do not mean the quarters built in the seventeenth or eighteenth century; I never speculate, for example, on the housekeeping bills of the Beauclerks when they lived in Great Russell Street in the Johnsonian era. I know how sugar went up during the American War of Independence—even to eighteenpence a pound, as Mrs Thrale records with horror; and I have no doubt that patient enquiry could recover many such details; but all this is the province of the antiquaries. I am thinking of the age just before my own, the age that my father and my grandfather knew; and so I often wonder when I see the great houses that were built between 1840 and 1860 how the tenants managed to live in them. A basement, a ground floor, three, even four stories above it: and be it remembered, no water, hot or cold, laid on above the basement level. What a troop of servants must have been required to tramp up and down the multitudinous stairs of such a place, what an income—we should say—must have been needed to keep a house like this in the trim order that was the custom of those days. And, be it understood, I am not speaking of the houses of the great world, of Mayfair, or Belgravia, or of the squares of Tyburnia and Marylebone, but rather of the quarters a little beyond these, of the streets that were never within the circle of fashion.

And there are other even more perplexing quarters in the nearnorthern parts of London; all that neighbourhood to the east of Pentonville which was once Spa Fields and Islington Fields, grey, decorous and forgotten. And there are squares and habitations in Islington and Barnsbury, Canonbury, Holloway and Camden Town which give rise to questions and wonders of the spirit; but here the enigma is a little different. It is not so much, 'How did they live in them?' as, 'Who lived in them?' 'For what class were they built?' And of course there are distinctions between square and square, quarter and quarter. Just as in the bright London of fashion there is 'the right side of the Park' and 'the wrong side of the Park'; so in London the obscure there are eminences and depressions.. There are deep and leafy gardens about certain Canonbury houses which are as waterpools and palm trees in the desert in burning July weather; and then in Barnsbury I once came upon a square that froze me with amazement. It was built entirely of grey brick. Each house was the exact facsimile of its fellow;

and all, even to the iron bell pulls, was of the purest fifteenth-century Gothic, as that period of architecture was understood in the eighteen-thirties. What manner of man, what sort of family, first took up its abode in this grey, sham-Gothic place? What song did the sirens sing?

Sometimes a strange light shines on these forgotten ways. A few weeks ago a girl was found dreadfully murdered in an unfamiliar street of Camden Town. Then somebody recollected that in this very street Ford Madox Brown had once lived at one number, while the Rossettis were to be found at another. Mrs Rossetti tried to keep a school here, not with much success. But unprosperous academies for young ladies are quite in the tradition of the near-north. Mrs Micawber and Mrs Wilfer differed in many respects from the mother of Dante Gabriel Rossetti; but all three ladies kept school—or tried to.

THE PEOPLE OF THE WILD

I SUPPOSE THAT the day of the people of the wild, otherwise the gipsies, is pretty well over. I do not know whether it is a good thing or a bad thing that this should be so; but I do know that I am sorry that it is so. My feeling on the point is, I suppose, a selfish one. It is not of the welfare of the gipsies that I am thinking. Will they be a happier people when they have abandoned their tents for ever and sold their caravans so that well-to-do people may make-believe at gipsying in August? Will they be radically better off when they live in barrack buildings, and little upper parts of little houses, or amid the endless monotony of long, grey streets, when they have become labourers, mechanics, and commercial clerks? To my mind the benefit of the change is doubtful enough; but that is not the point; not my point. When I think of the reformation and civilisation of gipsydom I grieve, not for them, but for the advance of the dull wave of uniformity that threatens to over-whelm all the world.

Things are interesting, very largely, because they are different. As I have remarked elsewhere, a dull modern street owes its dullness not so much to the mean aspect and design of each house, as to the fact that every house is an exact facsimile of every other house: there is no difference. And I remember Mr George Moore saying to me quite gravely, and I think justly, that one of the chief horrors of the modern world was the prevalence of cosmopolitan cookery. As he put it, if you go to a big hotel in Paris, you will have exactly the same sort of meal as the dinner you ate in a big hotel in London the day before; and the menu is duplicated in the big hotels of Rome, Florence, Madrid, Seville, and New York. There is no difference; and the best sole is a dull fish when it is always done in the same way. The delight of life is, largely, due to a constant succession of surprises. I still find pleasure in the thought of a bowl of custard that I once had at a Japanese restaurant. Strange little green herbs were embedded on its surface, and beneath, the fork disclosed a lobster's claw.

And so with the gipsies. It seems to me surprising, wonderful, and, therefore, delightful, to know that there are still amongst us in this modern, electrified, urbanised, industrialised England, a people who preserve the habit of the earlier ages, perhaps of the earliest age of the world. They are still happy on the heath, the moor, the waste lands, and in the wood; and most completely at home when they have no home. The caravan and the horse are now, I suppose, the most popular mode in gipsydom; but the old barrel-like tents are still to be found in out-of-the-way lanes, and less than forty years ago there were gipsy families frequenting the Chiltern Hills that had not so much as a tent to shelter them. They bore about with them big bundles of old duds—clouts and rags of all sorts—and they camped for the night by turning themselves into rag chrysalides, rolling their monstrous bags and bundles about them—after all, the sleeping-bag of the explorer in a primitive state. I remember once being out early on a winter morning on the Chilterns, and coming across one of these parties. The frost was bitter, so that my moustache was frozen hard after I had been five minutes in the early air. The gipsies had found a dry ditch well lined with brown bracken on the snug side of a wild hedge, thick and high, bordering the common. Three or four of them lay in their bundles at the bottom of the ditch; but one, a man as wild as the hedge, was putting dry sticks on the fire that had glowed all night, and it blazed and crackled in the cold, still air of the dawn. A queer life, no doubt; but if you like it? It may seem strange to us; but to these folk four walls, blankets, sheets, mattress, and a gas fire might well seem a queer life. It sounds trite and more than tiresome to declare that it takes all sorts to make a world; but suppose it is true? Perhaps it does take all sorts of different things and people to make a world worth living in.

And hence I cannot feel really happy over the recent announcement that a tin school has been opened in the very heart of gipsydom so that the little Romanys may be turned into 'Kooshti Gorgers.' That means 'good Gentiles,' and I give the phrase phonetically, as it was once uttered to me by a man who dwelt in the tents. Will the gipsies be made better and happier thereby?

LAUGH WHEN YOU AWAKE

THERE IS A NEW cure before the public, and it has a pleasant and favourable sound. Many cures are dismal matters. You have to give up all the things you like: claret and bitter beer, veal cutlets and French beans, tea and coffee, and idleness. You must not dream of a roast fowl, and an omelette *fines herbes* is equally out of the question. They say that if you put away all these delights you will no more be troubled with rheumatism. This may be so, but, as Aristotle says, all action is a result of a balance of considerations, and, for my part, the rheumatism that should justify such a cure would have to be fierce, agonising, perpetual.

The new cure is not of that savage, abstaining kind. It is better than Couéism. Dr Coué says that if you say '*je peux*' fast enough and often enough then you will be able to do what you want to do; that if you mutter '*ça passe*' in the right way your toothache will go. Perhaps so; I have never given the system a serious trial. But the newest method is, as I say, better still. It is just laughter. You begin first thing in the morning. You think of the funniest things that you can as soon as you awake, and you lie in bed shaking with laughter for five or ten minutes. It is not necessary, I gather, to bellow, to utter any sound at all, not even that 'hoarse, internal rumbling' which attended old Weller's 'quiet laugh'. I am not quite clear whether the patient must quiver and shake, internally at all events; but I incline to think that this is desirable. But, according to the inventor of the treatment, the results are admirable. You get out of bed rejoicing, fit in body and mind, more than ready, eager to fight the battles of the day. Indeed, if I remember rightly, the prophet of the laughter cure, having explained the system, fell down a flight of stairs, burst into a roar of laughter, and said he felt ever so much better.

Well, he might be right. Rabelais said that laughter was the peculiar property of man, and it is like enough that many of us have neglected our prerogative of laughter of late, and are suffering for our neglect. But the propounder of the laughter cure interested me chiefly by his final remark to the effect that laughter is a mad thing, though a grand tonic. He is quite right: laughter is a mad thing. But are not all the best things in the world in a like case: the best things in a big way and the best things in a small way? In other words, should we not be very hard put to it to defend, rationally, the things which make up both the greater delights and the lesser delights of life?

I remember a most able and amiable American Ambassador being a good deal perplexed by a State banquet at Buckingham Palace. He noted the splendid golden uniforms, the blazing orders, the fire of the jewels, the rich service of the table, the intricate, stately, measured ceremonial. He was clearly inclined to ask himself at the end what was the good—or the sense—of it all; whether, in fact, it was not a gorgeous piece of nonsense, or, in other words, madness. Very well; but the Ambassador did not perceive that it is all a question of degree. We have just been hearing of some forlorn African savages who, when they are hungry, catch a mouse or two and a few lizards and eat them raw. This is a wholly rational proceeding: the savage eats to keep alive, without ceremony of any kind. But all beyond that simple limit is nonsense, madness. The cottager eats his grateful portion from a willow-pattern plate; but he cannot justify this proceeding. The pictured Chinese fairy tale makes his bread and cheese and onions no better, either in flavour or in nourishment. And, rising a little socially, is there any sense in a man's putting on a black coat of the fashion of 1830-40 because he is going to have his dinner in 1926? And so, by degrees; to the State banquet splendours: when once brutish savagery is left behind, the circumstances of every meal are irrational, and dinner is a madman's feast.

And this is quite a minor instance. How about the things that are veritably great: poetry, painting, music, sculpture, architecture, all the fine arts? It is quite evident that, rationally considered, they are all mad together; as mad as laughter. The practical reason can find nothing to say for the bird that charmed magic casements opening on the foam of perilous seas in faery lands forlorn. From any sane standpoint a cathe-dral is massive mania in stone, and a Bach fugue a piece of noisy delirium. And so on, through all the order of human life: and this conclusion being clearly absurd and intolerable, we are compelled to turn round and declare that it is the rational system which is the true madness, and that the highest sanity consists in doing things for which we can give no reason whatever.

Not long ago there was a mighty Yorkshire squire who was wont to make frequent and careful perambulations of his estate. Whenever he saw flowers growing in a cottage garden, he would beat roses and lilies and violets to pieces with his heavy stick. 'Grow potatoes,' he would say to the poor people, 'grow something useful.'

On rational principles, the squire was a man of admirable sanity. I believe him to have been a violent lunatic. This is a point for theologi-ans; but it seems to me that in Adam's fatal fruit there were the seeds of Rational Principles.

THE LITTLE BROWN THINGS

SURVIVALS ARE always interesting. There was a prosecution for witchcraft somewhere down in the country a week or two ago. The pig was ill, or the cream refused to turn into butter, or the victim was attacked by shooting pains: whatever it was, the suit was brought and the wizard and the witch appeared before the court. The Bench dismissed the case, and no more was said, though, to the best of my belief, the prosecutor might himself have been prosecuted. The Act of George II which abolished the laws against sorcery made it a penal offence to bring any such charge; or so I remember reading in that grave law-book, *Peregrine Pickle*.

But the point is this: here are people who still have a fervent and assured belief in witchcraft; that it is in the power of one human being to injure another human being by the exercise of a malignant will. You wish Smith to experience excruciating pains: and he has them. You wish Smith's pig dead: and the pig dies. This is what the country people who brought their grief before the magistrates believed; and the question is whether they were representative or whether they were rare exceptions to the general rule of incredulity.

A clergyman wrote to the papers about the case I have cited. He said that in a certain district which he named every other person was a firm believer in witchcraft. Whereupon a resident of the district in question—a General, if I remember rightly—wrote in his turn, saying that he had asked a number of his neighbours whether they believed in witchcraft, and that they had all denied the possession of any such belief with laughter and contempt. I remember a Scot telling me what would most likely happen to me if I toured the Highlands with a view to investigating the second sight.

'You would go,' he said, 'into some remote village and find out the oldest inhabitant and ask him if he knew any cases of second sight in the neighbourhood. The old man would tell you gravely that the Highlanders of the present day were an educated people who had long ago given up all belief in such superstitious nonsense. And the chances are that your old man would be the village seer!'

And I have always had my doubts as to the case of the late Principal Mills, of Jesus College, Oxford, and the Welsh farmer. Far in the west of Wales there is an ancient family of farmers who are the hereditary keepers of the skull of Teilo Sant, one of the most illustrious of the Celtic saints. And it has been believed through long ages that if the eldest son of the house draws water from the holy well of Teilo Sant near by, and administers this water in the skull of the saint, the sick will be healed. Principal Rhys went investigating this marvel. He interviewed the keepers of the relic. They laughed at the popular belief, but told the Oxford don that they kept up the old custom: 'just to oblige the neighbours.'

Then there was another case: a still odder case than the witchcraft trial. This was the business of the Little People in the Forest of Dean, down in Gloucestershire. A responsible London paper gave the story of these mysterious folk a couple of weeks ago. Two specimens of the Little People had been observed, one in the spring, another quite recently. There, were, perhaps, six or seven witnesses to the facts. In the first case the creature was observed in a neighbouring coal mine, the second and more recent specimen was seen in a house, creeping about the coals in the coal-scuttle. The Little Man of the mine was about fourteen inches long; a miniature human being, but covered with close dark hair or fur and lacking arms. The visitant of the coal-scuttle was perfect; 'just like a collier.' I forget how the first creature disappeared; in the latter case the whole family were so frightened that they tilted the coal-scuttle with its coals and its (possibly) supernatural visitant on to their garden path. This was at night: in the morning there was nothing but coals to be seen.

Coleford, the scene of these strange appearances, holds various theories as to the Little People. Some hold that they are fairies, others that they are descendants of a dwarfish race which, they say, lived long ago in the Forest, and was forced to go underground. And there are some who think that they are animals of some unknown and uncon-jectured genus, who, as it would seem, inhabit the coal mines.

The most interesting suggestion of the three is the identification of the little brown beings with the pre-Celtic inhabitants of the country, the underground dwellers who originated the Irish fancies about fairy raths. There was such a race of short, dark people, who did, in fact, live subterraneously, and survived far into the Celtic age. Put the people of this race must have been about four feet—not fourteen inches—high. As to the 'facts' of the Coleford case, I say nothing. But I think that there must be a mistake somewhere.

SHAKESPEARE'S 'BARE BONES'

THERE ARE debates which never end; and among them is the debate on the proper presentation of stage plays. Should the play be put on with the utmost degree of actuality possible; the Chippendale chairs warranted to have come from Chippendale's factory; the costly Persian rugs to be dated antiques; the pictures on the walls masterpieces of Velazquez, Reynolds, or Turner; the books on the shelves all first editions? That, in some exaggerated form, is the demand of one side; while the other camp holds that *As You Like It* is all the better by being enacted in a bare room with a few Windsor chairs for the characters to sit on, and a green shrub in a flower-pot on a deal table to symbolise the Forest of Arden.

I was reminded of this old quarrel by reading a criticism of a recent Sunday night revival of *Richard II*. The critic contrasts the splendours of Tree's production of *Richard II* with the austerity of the show at the Regent Theatre, very much to the disadvantage of the latter. He confesses that he does not care to see the great tragedies of Shakespeare in their 'bare bones'; and he declares that Shakespeare himself would have presented his places with the utmost elaboration of magnificence if he had been able to do so.

Now his last statement is highly questionable. Taking the plays as they were written, one finds a constant change of scene: 'A Battlefield,' 'Another Part of the Battlefield'; 'The Forest,' 'Another Part of the Forest,' 'A Meadow by the Forest,' and so forth. And, in many cases, these scenes consist of half-a-dozen or a dozen lines. Now it is quite clear that if the critic's opinions were to prevail, and each of these slight scenes were to be presented with elaborate scenic apparatus, the play would not be over till long after midnight. It seems clear that Shakespeare accepted the stage convention of his day and wrote his

216

plays to fit that convention. He could alter his scene as often as he would; since the set was changed only in the mind of the beholder, with the slight swift aid of a curtain raised or lowered.

And I do not think that a great play is affected in the slightest degree by the austerity or, if you will, the poverty of the setting. I remember the setting of *Lincoln* at the Lyric, Hammersmith. To the best of my belief the first scene, depicting Lincoln's sitting-room, differed very little from the Cabinet room at Washington, and both were like enough in their materials to General Grant's tent. Tables and chairs—the same tables and chairs, very likely—were set in various orders, and it didn't matter two straws. The play held you from the first word to the last; and the play that does that, does everything that a play can do.

But there are plays of another order, such as *A Midsummer Night's Dream* and *As You Like It*. In these, as it seems to me, the woodland is almost the chief character in the piece: each play exists to convey the spirit and the mystery of the trees. I am afraid that I could not make-believe a blank wall, or even a curtain, into the Forest of Arden or the Forest of Attica, and yet I cannot be beguiled by the contrivance called a 'cut-cloth': here is a problem for the scenic artist, how to suggest wood without making a pretty picture of a wood, which will be violently illuminated by floats, battens and limes so that it is seen to be a pretty picture, and nothing more.

And there are other plays in which the setting and the costume signify very highly. I do not think it would matter a bit if King John were dressed in Richard III costume, or if Richard II wore the robes of the twelfth century—save to the antiquaries, who, as I said, don't matter in the arts. But *The School for Scandal* must not lack a single curl of its wigs, not a ruffle, not a morsel of its lace. Sheridan's great comedy is definitely of the eighteenth century, it cannot be conceived to exist in any other age; and we all know what an eighteenth-century gentleman looked like. There is a mezzotint after Reynolds depicting Dr Johnson without his famous wig, wearing his own dark, close-cut hair. It is quite incredible; it is not the Doctor we all of us know and love; it is not a bit like him. So Charles Surface would be incredible: in evening dress of today, or in the costume of a Cavalier.

THE SIMPLICITY OF GENIUS

SOME READERS of *The Graphic*, I dare say, will remember certain articles in which I retold incidents in 'The Life of Grimaldi,' that king of all pantomime clowns, who left the stage a little more than a hundred years ago. There was the tale of Grimaldi and the mysterious house in Charlotte Street, Fitzroy Square. To this house Grimaldi went again and again at the invitation of a queer friend of his, finding on each occasion, as he arrived after midnight, a place all ablaze with light, resplendent with rich furniture and appointments, a gorgeous banquet served by gorgeous servants, crowned with the rarest wine; and always six ladies and six gentlemen, the same ladies and the same gentlemen, in company, welcoming him with open arms. A strange scene, and a stranger end. Grimaldi's queer friend was tried for his life and only saved by the evidence of the clown proving an alibi; and the six ladies and the six gentlemen were all inveterate criminals.

Then there was the old tale of Grimaldi and the Man with the Silver Staff, who suddenly appeared at the Sadler's Wells tavern and rescued an actor from the grip of the rascally constable, 'old Lucas.' 'Who this gentleman was,' said Grimaldi, 'I never could ascertain.' And best of all is the really amazing incident of the return of the actor's long-lost brother, given up as dead many years before. The brother reappears at the stage door of Drury Lane, talks to Grimaldi during the intervals of the play, gets tired of waiting in the green-room, strolls out into Drury Lane, calls on a couple of old friends—and disappears again; this time for ever.

Now, there is one circumstance which is common to all these stories, and that is the atmosphere of unreality in which each moves. Nobody can read the tale of Grimaldi and the Twelve Criminals without being violently reminded of the *Arabian Nights*; the Man with the

218

Silver Staff, though he appears in a tavern and reappears in a police court, might be a servant of Haroun al-Raschid—to see the staff is instantly to obey—and the tale of the Long-Lost Brother might be a modern ghost story of the most subtle artistry. In other words, there is something so strange about all three tales, more especially about the last, that one is strongly tempted to question their truth. They are 'too good to be true'.

But I have made up my mind firmly that every word of the tale is the purest truth. The fact is that it is not in life but in ourselves that dullness resides. We say a strange story is too good to be true because we are incapable of discerning the strangeness that is all about us. That is why genius is so very rare a gift; genius being the faculty of discerning mysteries, wonders, strange proportions, in all the scenes of life. Falstaff walked gloriously, uproariously, we may be pretty sure, through the taverns of Bankside and the taverns of Chepe; but it was only Shakespeare who saw him as he was.

Now, we are not for one moment to compare the famous old clown with the creators. But it would appear that in Grimaldi, an utterly simple soul (save in the technique of pantomime), there was that simplicity of vision which is found in some children and in all men of genius.

Grimaldi could not invent a wonderful tale, but he could tell a true one. Few of us can do that, through our obstinate preconception that the truth is always dull.

BOOKS THAT A QUEEN MAY READ

ONE FAMOUS evening more than forty years ago, Queen Victoria received a very distinguished visitor. This was Mr Gladstone, then Prime Minister, and his business with the Queen was to inform Her Majesty that Khartoum had fallen and that Gordon had been killed. I believe that it must have been a terrible interview. Gladstone was more than sure of his own virtue and wisdom, and now and then suspected himself of infallibility; but I think that he must have shuddered a little before the cold anger and black condemnation with which the Queen received his news. The Sovereign Lady was seen a little later, trembling somewhat as she leant on her stick, but perfectly composed. 'My usual remedy,' she is reported to have said as she made her way to her room that night—'a chapter of *Guy Mannering.*'

And, indeed, *Guy Mannering* is one of the finest books, one of the most gracious books in the world. It has a world of kindly humour and wisdom in it, and some of the best characters—Dominie Sampson, Councillor Pleydell, Meg Merriles, Dandie Dinmont—that are to be found in all the world of fiction. We have wonderfully clever novelists today; but not one could make such a book as *Guy Mannering*. I do not think they are to be blamed—I should not dream of blaming an Esquimaux, shivering in his icy darkness, for being unable to realise the genial airs and the eternal sunshine of the South Seas. It would be very hard to describe the difference between the atmosphere in which Sir Walter Scott had his being and the atmosphere of our day; but, no doubt, the, change has been a vast one. In many respects, this change may be for the better; and yet something very precious has passed away from the light in which we live, something which I cannot define. But, lacking it, I feel quite sure that we cannot hope for any book so brave and good and merry as *Guy Mannering* to be written in our age.

Cleverer books we have in plenty. Long ago Stevenson pointed out how the lamentable carelessness of Sir Walter's style went far to annul the effect of that beautiful scene in which the long-lost heir finds strange memories stirring within him as he hears a village girl sing one of the old country songs that he had not heard since he was a little child. And then, of course, there is the odd circumstance that while ridicule is poured on astrology, while Guy Mannering himself derides the horoscope that he casts, all the judgments of the stars are justified to the very letter. But that is not so much a fault as a curious image of the soul of Scott. His mind was always deriding astrology—and other things—in which his heart profoundly believed.

But these are trifles: *Guy Mannering* is like sunshine and good wind on the hills of a happy land. Strangely, the wind has chilled, and the sky darkened, and the fields are no longer happy. The people that Scott loved cannot live in our air. It may be, as, I say, that we are infinitely better off than they were; nevertheless, they had a relish for their poor crusts which we cannot bring to our high feasts. I have just read in *The American Mercury*—the magazine to be read by English-men who want to understand America—an account of *An American Tragedy*, by that distinguished novelist, Theodore Dreiser. The plot, as the reviewer says, is extremely simple.

'Clyde Griffiths, the son of a street preacher in Kansas City, revolts against the piety of his squalid home, and gets himself a job as bell-boy in a gaudy hotel. There he acquires a taste for the luxuries affected by travelling Elks, and is presently a leader in shop-girl society. . . . One day his father's rich brother, a collar magnate from Lycurgus, N.Y. is put up (at a club) by a member, and Clyde resolves to cultivate him. The old boy, taking a shine to the youngster, invites him to Lycurgus, and gives him a job in the factory. There ensues the conflict that makes the story. Clyde has hopes, but very little ready cash; he is thus forced to seek most of his recreation in low life. But as a nephew to old Samuel Griffiths, he is also taken up by the Lycurgus *haut ton*. The conflict naturally assumes the form of girls. Roberta Alden, a beautiful female operative in the factory, falls in love with him and yields herself to him. Almost simultaneously, Sondra Finchley, an even more beauti-ful Society girl, falls in love with him, and promises to marry him.

221

Clyde is ambitious and decides for Sondra. But at that precise moment Roberta tells him that their sin has found her out. His reply is to take her to a lonely lake and drown her. The crime being detected, he is arrested, put on trial, convicted, and electrocuted.'

Will Queen—or tweeny-maid—ever read a chapter of *An American Tragedy* as her 'usual remedy'? I hardly think so. It is not that the people in *Guy Mannering* are good and the people in Mr Dreiser's story bad. Glossin, attorney, conspirator, abductor, was a thoroughly bad man, and the character of Dirk Hatteraick, the smuggler, shows some serious moral flaws.

The difference is, I think, that in the one book we read of men good, bad, indifferent: in the other of reptiles, with two legs and some infusion of human cunning.

SOCIETY AND THE SAVAGE

ROUSSEAU AND HIS friends, the people who, according to Dr Johnson, had found that Truth was a cow that would yield them no milk,
and so were gone to milk the bull by way of a change—these advanced
thinkers of the eighteenth century were never tired of proclaiming the
advantages of savage as compared with civilised life. They were always
contrasting the utterly simple, unceremonious, free life of savagery
with the elaborate hierarchy of the society in which their lot was cast.
They showed on the one hand the simple Red Indian or South Sea
Islander, content with little, nourished at the cost of pleasant toil,
ignorant of conventions, untroubled by thoughts of rank and state;
and, on the other hand, the Court of Versailles, obsessed by convention, ceremonial, minute and tedious observances, unmeaning or
idiotic royal ritual; a life, as Dickens put it, so frizzed, powdered,
gilded and jewelled that it seemed like a perpetual fancy dress ball.

Johnson had sense enough to know that Rousseau and his friends
were talking nonsense. A gentleman quoted the reflections of a man
who had lived for some time in the wilds of America: 'Here am I, free
and unrestrained, amidst the rude magnificence of nature, with this
Indian woman by my side, and this gun with which I can procure food
when I want it; what more can be desired for human happiness?'
Johnson would not bear this for one moment. 'Do not allow yourself,
Sir, to be imposed upon by such gross absurdity. It is sad stuff; it is
brutish. If a bull could speak he might as well exclaim—"Here am I
with this cow and this grass; what being can enjoy greater felicity?" '

The Doctor knew well, then, that all the fine talk about the delights
of a savage life was sad stuff and gross absurdity; but the odd thing is
that he was quite ignorant of a fatal flaw in the Rousseau argument.
He accepted, as everybody did in those days, the proposition that

savagery was life reduced to its simplest elements. He admitted that, and boldly said that the simple life was a bad life and a brutish life, 'Were you to tell men who live without houses how we pile brick upon brick, and rafter upon rafter, and after a house is raised to a certain height a man tumbles off a scaffold and breaks his neck, he would laugh heartily at our folly in building; but it does not follow that men are better without houses.' And to the same effect again and again. The savage life is simple, our life is complex: therefore so much the better we, so much the more bestial the savage. Social conventions, social inequalities, all elaborations of living, all refinements, all luxuries of living, all the grades of the civilised order: these are the things that make happiness. We are blest, not in spite of these things, but very largely because of them.

And, no doubt, taking the ground he did; Johnson was wholly in the right. If there were a life of absolute simplicity, without elaborations or conventions of any kind, it would be a bestial life. But the amusing thing is that there is no such life, and, so far as we know, there never has been such a life. And the more primitive the savagery, the more elaborate, the more complex the system of rules, conventions, and regulations by which it is ordered. Or, as that eminent physician, Dr Haden Guest, said the other day: 'The elaborate taboo systems, fetish systems, and social observances of primitive people are extraordinarily more complex than the ideas of any well-trained modern man.' The savage, whose pure simplicity Rousseau praised, was, in fact, living under an order besides which the Versailles of Louis XV appears bald and crude. The marriage laws of the Australian Blackfellow are far more complicated than the marriage laws of England today.

There is this great difference between our social order and that of the savage. No doubt a levee at Versailles was a highly formal and ceremonial business; so it is at Buckingham palace today. But levees come to an end; and for all I know great lords may lounge in old coats and smoke pipes afterwards till it is time to dress for dinner. But in savagery the levee never comes to an end. There is no time for lounging. The Rule is with you in your simplest actions.

Mrs Green, the African missionary's wife, went to her kitchen to choose the dinner. She inspected some fruit. 'No,' she said to her black cook, 'we won't make them into a tart. They're too green.'

The black of the cook's face grew ashen. She waited for consuming fire to descend upon that wicked house and all within it. The missionary's wife had uttered her husband's name: a deadly sin. She should have said that the fruit was not ripe enough. If, on occasion, a paraphrase is impossible, and the awful Word must be spoken, then a child of five years or under must be summoned. The Name is whispered in his ear. He, in his turn, whispers it in the ear of the person to whom it must be communicated. That is real savagery, as distinguished from the imagined, nonexistent savagery of foolish Rousseau.

THOSE DOCTORS!

THE PHYSICIAN IS at his old games again. I suppose we all know who the Physician is. He is the man who writes to the papers or gets reported in the papers without incurring the grievous charge of infamous conduct. And he always writes in a most disagreeable vein. Everything that we do is wrong. We eat the wrong things, we drink the wrong things. We eat and drink a great deal too much. We should be much better if we did not smoke; but, perhaps, two cigarettes a day may not do us much harm. One Physician—a famous one—pointed out a few years ago that cooking our food was one of our worst blunders. He outlined a rational diet, and, greatly to my joy, I found it identical with the special diet ordered by Mr Squeers, of Dotheboys Hall.

Mr Squeers, calling on Ralph Nickleby, told that gentleman that he had been brought up to town by a bothering action, 'for what they call neglect of a boy. I don't know what they would have. He had as good grazing, that boy had, as there is about us. . . . When a boy gets weak and ill and don't relish his meals, we give him a change of diet—turn him out, for an hour or so every day, into a neighbour's turnip field, or sometimes, if it's a delicate case, a turnip field and a piece of carrots alternately, and let him eat as many as he likes.'

What a pity Mr Squeers lived before his time. In these present days the plaintiffs in such an action would not have a leg to stand upon. Some of the greatest names in Harley Street would be called and would show that meat is next door to poison, that cooking destroys all food values, and that raw vegetables constitute an absolutely perfect diet.

And, as I say, the Physician is still active amongst us. I have just gathered his latest maxim: it is as follows:

'Most of us would be better for being rationed and exercised as a racehorse is exercised and rationed.'

Which amounts just to this: That men would be much better if they could be persuaded or compelled to live like beasts. But let us consider. A racehorse is bred and maintained for one definite end, and for one alone. He is to win races . . . occasionally, at all events. And all the details of the horse's existence are regulated and allotted with this end in view. Further, the horse's nature is such that he submits himself readily to the regimen ordained. Air, exercise, food, drink are meas- ured out to him, and so far as we know he suffers all this rule gladly, and if his quality be good, wins the Rutlandshire or the Little Pedling- ton, or whatever he is set to win. Now and then, it is true, the race- horse develops whims and fancies, and is known as a queer horse.

Very well; but what possible analogy is there between the case of the racehorse and the case of the man? Oxford and Cambridge oars- men, it is true, have to submit to a certain regimen before their great race; for the time they are rowing men, and are trained accordingly. But the boatrace is not their lives; it is a mere interlude in their lives. The race over, they can eat pastry, drink whisky, smoke cigarettes, and go to bed when they please. The only human beings who are rationed and exercised like racehorses are convicts in gaol; and the common consent of humanity has pronounced their state to be far from gracious. In many cases, perhaps, the prisoner's bodily health is better when he comes out than it was when he went in; but the man is not better. He is much worse: because, he is not a racehorse, but a man.

We have just noted that the average racehorse submits peaceably and contentedly to the treatment which is given him; it is the excep- tional horse which has odd fancies, likes and dislikes, and is pronounced to be queer tempered. And the vice of the horse is the virtue of the man. No man who is worth twopence will order his life with the sole object of becoming physically fit. Fitness of this sort is, of course, highly desirable, but as a means, not an end; and sometimes physical fitness has to go by the board. Balzac is said to have shortened his life by his crazy way of living, by his toils continued day after day, night after night, without rest or sleep, by his monstrous draughts of the blackest coffee that could be made. Very good; if you admire the

'Comédie Humaine' you will say that Balzac was perfectly right to live as he did. His business in life was not to keep physically fit, but to write great books; and so he gave up the lesser good for the greater.

And, above all, the great things of life have been done by the men who may be fairly equated with the fanciful, 'queer-tempered,' horses; the men of dreams and visions, whose souls are full of wonders, and surmises of undiscovered lands in the world of matter and the world of spirit. You cannot shut up Pegasus in the training stable.

THE 'B' IN BACONIAN BONNETS

THERE ARE SOME delusions so remarkable that it is only by a strong act of the will that we believe in their existence. Of such is Baconianism: the wild legend that links the name of Lord Verulam, a great writer and a learned though corrupt judge, not only with the plays of Shakespeare, not only with practically the whole of Elizabethan literature, but also with the essays of Montaigne and the *Don Quixote* of Cervantes. Nay, with more than this. For Bacon, according to certain Baconians, was the founder of Rosicrucianism and inventor of Freemasonry. He was also the unacknowledged son of Queen Elizabeth, and the possessor of a secret doctrine, its nature not distinctly stated, which will be found in the watermarks of the paper of the period. Some hold that the watermark doctrine embodied the teaching of the twelfth-century Albigenses of Southern France.

I say it requires an act of the will to believe in the mere existence of so monstrous a belief, or set of beliefs. On the face of it, one would say that no sane human being could credit so wild a mass of nonsense. Yet it is so. A new Baconian book was published only the other day. The author, I am sure, is a well-read man, perfectly sane and sensible on all other matters. But he is quite certain that Bacon wrote *Don Quixote*. I do not know whether he confirms his belief by a curious circumstance alleged by another Baconian, who showed that the name Don Quixote should really be read: 'duun qui s'ôte'—concerning one who keeps out of the way: Bacon, of course. One wonders in a helpless, bemused sort of manner, whether it is really possible to credit such nonsense as this, and the nonsense of the, biliteral cipher, and the nonsense about the Rosicrucians and the watermarks. It is, indeed, amazing: and yet it is so. The late W.H. Mallock was a man of exceptionally brilliant and

sceptical intelligence; and yet he was a Baconian of the most extravagant kind. He wrote an article on the subject in the *Pall Mall Magazine*,
twenty-four or twenty-five years ago. One of the plates illustrating the
article was a reproduction of the title page of Florio's translation of
Montaigne: a florid and elaborate piece of work. In the centre was a
small vignette, with round Roman arches for a background. 'Turn the
page sideways,' said Mallock, 'and then say what you make of those
arches.' He meant that the arches became a capital B, showing that
Bacon wrote the *Essays of Montaigne*. It is quite impossible, you will
say, that keen, scholarly Mallock believed in that big B. I agree; it is
impossible. But he did!

That, I think, is very interesting; this impossibility which, nevertheless, has happened. And there is another matter which is interesting:
the immense difficulty of disproving, positively and absolutely, any of
these crazy statements. You are quite sure that *Don Quixote* was
written by Cervantes. All Spain knew that it was written by Cervantes.
It is obviously the work of a Spaniard, of a man deeply rooted in the
life of his country. You are as sure that Bacon did not write *Don
Quixote* as you are sure that *Pickwick* was not written by a Russian Jew
of Nijni Novgorod. But can you prove that Bacon had no hand in the
greatest of all romances? I doubt it.

So with Bacon-Shakespeare. You may show that a scholar like
Bacon would never have made Hamlet go to Wittenburg, a university
which was founded about thirty years before the production of the
play, and six or seven hundred years after the (presumed) date of
Hamlet's death. You will be told that Bacon was hiding behind the
mask of the ignorant playhouse loafer, Shaksper, and took care to drop
in plenty of blunders. You may go on another tack. The Baconians are
all agreed that Shaksper was an illiterate country bumpkin. Many of
them doubt whether he could either read or write. But all this must
have been well known to the world of the playhouse. Is it likely, you
may ask, that Bacon, desirous of concealing his playwriting, should
adopt as his mask a man who was notoriously incapable of writing so
much as his own name? But I am sure there is a Baconian answer to
this, as to all other objections.

And the only conclusion I can come to is a very odd one. It seems to me that looking at this Bacon-Shakespeare-Cervantes-Montaigne business from both sides, we are irresistibly led to the position that the human intellect is an intensely fallible instrument. On the one side, you have a brilliant man, an exceptional man like Mallock, believing in what we think to be frantic nonsense. On the other side, here are who are perfectly assured that it is nonsense, and nonsense of the worst kind; and yet we cannot prove it to be nonsense. To take an instance far removed from the particular controversy before us: I once read in some spiritualist publication that King Edward the Seventh is learning portrait painting in the next world, and that Queen Victoria is helping him to put in the eyes. I know that this is not so; but how am I to prove that it is not so?

It seems clear that when men are led aright, it is by virtue of some hidden faculty, remote from the intellect and infinitely superior to it.

231

THE SCHOLAR AND THE SUN-MYTH

THAT WAS A FALSE definition of Carlyle's when he said that genius simply consisted in an infinite capacity for taking pains. All human experience refutes it: we know men in every sort of craft and occupation who are willing to take incredible pains and yet remain dull and inefficient. However, the taking of pains is sometimes brilliantly justified. And so it is with the Heidelberg scholar, Dr Schoch, who has found out the exact date of the Trojan War, the Fall of Troy, the wandering of Ulysses and his slaughter of the suitors on returning to Ithaca. Here is Dr Schoch's Table of Events:

Trojan War, B.C. 1197-1187.
Fall of Troy, B.C. 1187.
Wanderings of Ulysses, B.C. 1187-1177.
Landing on Ithaca, B.C. 1177, April 12th.
Slaughter of Suitors, B.C. 1177, April 16th, 6-8.30 p.m.

To me this seems admirable, wonderful. Here is one of the great legends of the world, which we had thought a beautiful legend and little more, bearing, perhaps, some faint relation to actual events, but so transfigured by the imagination of the poet, by the glamour of the past, that the fiction was hardly more than a gorgeous shadow of the fact; here we have the *Odyssey* dated as if it were a record of the Great War, the Fall of Troy pinned to its exact year as if it had been the Battle of the Somme, and the Slaughter of the Suitors set down to the very hour of the day, as surely as the Armistice of eleven o'clock on November 11, 1918.

Now this feat is the result of great pains, and, I think we should add, of a certain brilliance and audacity of intellectual venture. Dr Schoch had noted the lines in the *Odyssey*:

Ah, unfortunate men, what horror is this that has happened?
Shrouded in night are faces and heads. To the hands it descendeth.
See, too, crowded with ghosts is the porch and crowded the courtyard....
Withered and gone is the sun and the poisonous mist is arising.

Now, ancient writers believed this passage to describe a total eclipse. Dr Schoch agreed with them, and proceeded to calculate backwards. He found that, making due allowance for the retardation of the earth, there was a total eclipse of the sun, visible at Ithaca, on April 16, at 11.41 a.m., local mean time. And from this one date all the other dates are derived.

There is something fascinating in this linking of age-old romance, of one of the greatest of the world's epic stories with the precision of year and month and day and hour. I get something of the same pleasure when I read in stories, which are perhaps even more ancient, how the hero of all the great and glorious deeds of the tale was the youngest of his family. For here you have the reflection of one of the oldest laws of succession in the world, perhaps the very oldest. The name of this law of inheritance is—oddly—Borough English; and until January 1, 1926, it was the customary law of many English manors. By it, the youngest, not the eldest son, succeeded to the copyhold of his father; it was the youngest son who was the hero of the family. Lord Birkenhead swept all this away: I am sorry for it. The law of faerie is law of England no more.

Dr Schoch criticises Homer from the right standpoint. When I was young, Homeric criticism and mythological criticism in general were in the hands of Max Muller. Max Muller had found out that the whole story of the Trojan War was a sun myth, as it was called. There hadn't been any Troy, it wasn't besieged, and it did not fall. The tale of Troy could not be described as a legend; it was a symbolical description of the daily march of the sun across the heavens. Most of the Greek mythology was sun-myth, but here and there was the decay of language element. For example: the story of Apollo and Daphne. Thus the

233

Greeks forgot in course of time that *daphne* meant the dawn, and so they invented a tale of the god Apollo pursuing the nymph Daphne. In reality 'Apollo pursues Daphne' only meant that the sun, as it rises, pursues, or chases away, the dawn.

And we all believed that stuff! In my youngest days nobody would have dared to say that there was once long ago a town called Troy, and that it was actually taken, sacked, and burned. And then, happily, came another German, Dr Schliemann, who believed that Troy had been, and had theories as to the site of it. And then he went and found the famous city, and found that it had been burned, and brought up rich golden vessels from the ruined palace of King Priam, And after that the sun myth sank, and the decay of language theory decayed.

And still we are credulous. For the last dozen years or more the place of the sun myth has been taken by the culture myth. Briefly and baldly, this theory holds that the one thought, the one care of primitive man, was for the crops. He meditated nothing else but crops; and these anxieties of his about crops explain all the legends of the world. I have read a most learned and ingenious work which shows that the legend of the Holy Grail is a culture myth. I have seen the Maypole explained on the same principle. The Maypole, originally decked with boughs, was an invocation to the real trees to come into leaf.

It would be harsh to say that this theory is all nonsense. No doubt primitive man, first a huntsman, then a shepherd, only last of all a tiller of the soil, was deeply impressed by the yearly symbolism of death and resurrection in the dying of the green things and their return in the spring. But the poetry and legend of all the ages has a deeper foundation than the furrow of the plough.

DR JOHNSON'S DISAPPEARING ACT

MOST READERS OF Boswell's *Johnson* are aware that there is a singular hiatus, a blank tract, in Boswell's minute survey of his hero's life, letters, and writings. Up to the year 1745, everything is carefully chronicled, and we follow the Doctor's doings almost month by month, sometimes from day to day. Business letters are put in, such as the following to Mr Cave, the founder of *The Gentleman's Magazine*:

> 'DEAR SIR
> You may remember I have formerly talked with you about a military dictionary. The eldest Mr Macbean, who was with Mr Chambers, has very good materials for such a work, which I have seen, and will do it at a very low rate. I think the terms of War and Navigation might be comprised, with good explanations, in one 8vo. Pica, which he is willing to do for twelve shillings a sheet, to be made up a guinea at the second impression. If you think on it, I will wait on you with him.
> > I am, Sir, your humble servant,
> > SAM. JOHNSON.
> Pray lend me Topsel on Animals'

This is not a letter of the highest importance, though the 'rates per thou.' (about 4s. a thousand words, with a problematic increase to 7s.) may interest the Author's Society. But Boswell put in every scrap relating to Johnson that he could find; nothing could be too trifling for his purpose. Hence the gap in the story during 1745-46 is all the more remarkable.

235

The year before, Johnson had published his life of Savage, a book that touched on a secret story and a bitter controversy and an extraordinary—and very bad—character. The *Life of Savage* probably did a good deal to get Johnson known, for he was still an obscure man and a very poor one. 'His circumstances,' in Boswell's words, 'were at this time much embarrassed.' And yet, with one trifling exception, Johnson, badly in need of money for himself and his wife, seems to have been totally idle all through the years 'forty-five and 'forty-six. The trifling exception was a pamphlet: *Miscellaneous Observations on the Tragedy of Macbeth, with remarks on Sir T.H.'s Edition of Shakespeare*. This was in fact a prospectus of a new edition of Shakespeare which Johnson meditated; it could bring in no immediate profit. For the rest: silence for two years,

Boswell conjectures at large: 'As we do not trace anything else published by him during the course of this year, we may conjecture that he was, occupied entirely with that work.' But his Shakespeare was not published till 1765; twenty years later. And, again under the date 1746: 'It is probable that he was still employed upon his Shakespeare. . . . It is somewhat curious that his literary career appears to have been almost totally suspended in the years 1745 and 1746, those years which were marked by a civil war in Great Britain, when a rash attempt was made to restore the House of Stuart to the throne. That he had a tenderness for that unfortunate House is well known; and some may fancifully imagine that a sympathetick anxiety impeded the exertion of his intellectual powers: but I am inclined to think that he was, during this time, sketching the outlines of a great philological work. None of his letters during those years are extant, so far as I can discover.'

It is certainly a puzzling matter, this sudden gulf of silence. Johnson seems to disappear utterly from the scenes of his activities; he neither writes 'copy' for the printer, nor letters to his friends. Nothing is known about him for two whole years. An explanation has been suggested. It has been said that he marched with Prince Charlie, that he was in the army of the Young Chevalier.

And there is, at first sight, some plausibility in the theory. In principle, Johnson was a Jacobite. He held that if a man had a right to his own property then the House of Stuart had a right to the throne of England. Moreover, he had an affection for the Stuarts. He would not suffer a word to be uttered against the Church of England—or Charles II! And, again, in his younger days at all events, he had an active hatred for George II, the de facto King of England in 1745. And in 'forty-five Johnson was a young man of thirty-seven, and a strong young man, perfectly fitted to bear the toils of a campaign. Did he, then, arise and follow Charlie; and is this fact the reason for the blank in his life?

The conjecture is plausible, but impossible. Johnson was a truth-telling man; and Boswell heard him declare that 'if holding up his right hand would have secured victory at Culloden to Prince Charles's army, he was not sure that he would have held it up . . . so fearful was he of the consequences of another revolution on the throne of Great Britain.' This is decisive.

Where then, was Johnson in 1745-1746? I believe it to be highly probable that his 'embarrassments' consigned him to the Fleet Prison, and that his sufferings there were such that he did his utmost to blot them out of his recollection, and to keep the dismal episode from his friends.

WHEN THE MUCH-TRAVELLED
MAN COMES HOME

THERE ARE VERY few dishes, I suppose, that are not obtainable in London. All the nations of the earth dwell in it, and in it a man may find whatever kind of cookery his heart desires. Not long ago I was speaking of the lobster's claw in custard that so gratified me in the Japanese restaurant, and I recollect that though I was once familiar enough with the kitchen ways of France, north, south, west and centre—both in hotels and private houses—the only occasion on which I had an opportunity of eating frogs was in Soho. Birds' nest soup and all the Chinese family of dishes are to be had here, there, and every-where in the West End of the town; those who will may eat in perfec-tion the chicken broth of Jewry and the fillets of plaice fried in olive oil and served with bloated gherkins of monstrous shape; and in Soho, somewhere in the Great Pulteney Street region, there is a choice Greek restaurant, where you may have pilaff and stuffed eggplants in hot oil, ripe, black olives, and sour milk.

This is all very well indeed; it is only right that the Bagdad of the West, as Stevenson called London, should have its rarities and curiosi-ties of cooking as of all else; but I think that one thing is lacking in this way, and I often wonder why it has not occurred to some ingenious man (with a little money) to supply the want. Why should not London, the capital of England, be able to support an English chop house? I am aware that many people may regard the notion as revolutionary; but, in spite of that, I am confident that it is quite a practical one, if taken in hand in the right way.

The first thing to be considered is the neighbourhood to be chosen for such an establishment. It should be somewhere in the centre of things, part of the town frequented not only in the morning, but at night; and that means in these days somewhere between Charing Cross and Piccadilly Circus, with a leaning in the direction of Leicester Square. If possible, an old house should be chosen. And when you enter, you should receive an impression somewhat of this kind:

'I glanced about the room which had its sanded floor, sanded, no doubt, in exactly the same manner when the chief waiter was a boy—if he ever was a boy, which appeared improbable; and at the shining tables, where I saw myself reflected, in unruffled depths of old mahogany; and at the lamps without a flaw in their trimming or cleaning; and at the comfortable green curtains, with their pure brass rods, snugly enclosing the boxes; and at the two large coal fires, brightly burning; and at the rows of decanters, burly as if with the consciousness of pipes of expensive old port wine below.'

That, I should think, should be the general effect aimed at; but, after all, these are but externals, important in their way, but not absolutely essential. I am willing to waive the sand on the floor, for example. But now for the vital part, the revolutionary part of our programme.

All the meat, all the poultry and game, all the fish consumed in our tavern should be the produce of Great Britain.

And this without evasion. We would have nothing to say to 'English killed' meat. We would have our contracts with Herefordshire farmers and Scottish farmers who would supply us with our prime beef; big fair men of the South Downs would furnish us with mutton of one kind, while another kind would come from small dark men living under hills with names like Skirrid Vawr and Mynyddysllwyn. So with the juicy fowls and the ducks; these latter being ducks that had clapped their wings in welcome of the rain, and had dabbled in clear, shallow brooks; not the miserable, tasteless captives of the narrow coop, fatted with pap. And so the salmon should be of the Severn, and the turkeys of Norfolk, and the geese of the county where commons are plentiful. Of course, we should get our pork from Mr Wardle of Dingley Dell— 'oh, don't he breed nice pork!' and so with all the meats and fowls and fishes.

And the roast meat and the roast birds should actually be roasted on the spit, before an open fire.

As for the vegetables; I am afraid we shall have to cultivate them ourselves. The market gardener thinks more of heavy cropping and size than delicacy of flavour; they know nothing of carrots that only London carrots knows. Our chophouse will have its own garden thirty miles from town, and every morning a motor van will bring up the day's supply. No more limp lettuces, and no more parsley hanging its head and showing the sallow hues of decay.

I say nothing of the beefsteak pudding, of the pigeon pie, of the game pie, of the fawn pie, the secret of which last rare delicacy shall be dragged from holy land in Edmundsbury: but each dish shall be a marvel.

Finally; roly-poly pudding shall once more be known. Not the pale pretence of today, with its dab of dubious jam beside it on the dish; but the veritable roly-poly, gushing richly with its veritable jam, the joy of all honest men.

ENGLAND'S LAST STATE LOTTERY

NEXT MONDAY is a notable anniversary in the records of the god of Chance, for on October 18, 1826, the State Lottery was drawn for the last time. At that time it had been enquired into, condemned, declared horrible, for the previous twenty years. It was abolished by an Act of 1823, and finally its end came without mourning or lamentation. In fact, I suspect, a worse thing than the condemnation of the virtuous and the fatal decision of Parliament had come upon the Lottery: it had gone out of fashion. Every age has its own vices; a Restoration rake would raise his eyebrows at some of ours.

The last drawing was held in Coopers' Hall, Basinghall Street, and, as the Press of the day puts it, 'such was the anxiety on the part of the public to witness the last drawing of the Lottery, that great numbers of persons were attracted to the spot, independently of those who had an interest in the proceedings. The gallery of Coopers' Hall was crowded to excess long before the period fixed for the drawing. . . . Only one instance occurred where a prize was drawn and a number held by an individual present. The fortunate person was a little man who no sooner had learned that his number was a grand prize than he buttoned up his coat and coolly walked off without uttering a word.' Everybody else, it seems, was disappointed, and the last drawing ended in gloom.

It is difficult now, after a hundred years, to judge how far those people who declared the Lottery to be a fountain of vice and misery were in the right. It is no doubt true that the Lottery brought many people to dreadful grief. But that can be said of horse-racing, and speculation on the Stock Exchange, and card playing, and setting up small general shops in poor neighbourhoods, and financing plays. Of course, there are the moral histories showing the evil effects of the

Lottery; such, for example, as the tale of Christopher Bartholomew, who began life with fine prospects and died miserably through the Lottery—or his own folly.

At one time the White Conduit House, with its tea gardens, as also the Angel Inn, in Islington, today a restaurant, were his freeholds; and he rented land to the amount of £2,000 a year in the neighbourhood of that place and Holloway. He was remarkable for having the greatest quantity of hay stacks of any grower in the neighbourhood of London. He kept his carriage and servants in livery, and was believed to have been worth £50,000. He was not only the proprietor, but the landlord, of White Conduit House, to which, 'by his taste in laying out its grounds and the manner of conducting his business, he attracted great custom.' But the Lottery mania seized upon him and devoured him. He lost all he possessed, and still persisted in his folly.

Meeting one day, in the year 1807, with an old acquaintance, he told him he had a strong presentiment that if he could purchase a particular number in the ensuing Lottery it would prove successful. His friend, after remonstrating with him on the impropriety of persevering in a practice that had been already attended with such evil consequences, was at last persuaded to advance the money to purchase a sixteenth, and go halves with him in the adventure.

The chosen number was drawn, but Bartholomew put the money back into the Lottery, and died in misery 'in a two pair of stairs room, in Angel Court, Windmill Street, Haymarket'—and I hope we may all profit by this sad example.

And then, of course, there is another sad case—that of the Dwarf in Dickens's story. This was a dwarf in a show, billed as Major Tpschof-fki, of the Imperial Bulgraderian Brigade. It was noted that his ambition was to go into Society: 'The curse of my position towards the public is, that it keeps me hout of Society.' It was also noted that Chops, as he was called, never had any money. One day a man in the crowd held up a carrier-pigeon and cried out: 'If there's any person here as has got a ticket, the Lottery's just drawed, and the number as has come up for the great prize is three seven forty-two.' Chops had won £12,000. He had spent all his earnings on buying Lottery tickets.

His end was a sad one, but that was through his misfortune in mistaking scoundrels for Society.

The Lottery Office keepers, who sold the tickets, employed literary gentlemen of the type of Mr Slum, Mrs Jarley's laureate. One of the most famous of the office keepers, a gentleman named Bish, was a great patron of these poets: here is a specimen of one of his bills:

'O dear what can the matter be?
To tell who can be at a loss?
The people are running by dozens to BISH'S
To make out their dreams, and fulfil all their wishes,
And try to come in for the loaves and the fishes,
At 4 Cornhill and 9 Charing Cross.'

The prose is of higher quality:

'By purchasing a Quarter your affairs never need be in *Crooked Lane*, nor your legs in *Fetter Lane*; you may avoid *Paper Buildings,* steer clear of the *King's Bench,* and defy the *Marshalsea;* if your heart is in *Love Lane*, you may soon get into *Sweetings Alley*, obtain your lover's consent for *Matrimony Place*, and always live in a *High* Street.'

The tickets were drawn by Bluecoat boys of Christ's Hospital, and now and then they were 'got at' by dishonest persons. For, subservient to the actual Lottery, there was a system of insuring tickets. You could insure your ticket for any amount; thus making a gamble within a gamble. So on one occasion, in 1775, a Bluecoat boy was examined with reference to a number that had been drawn out the Friday before on which an insurance had been made in almost every office in London.

'The boy confessed that he was prevailed upon to conceal the ticket, No. 21,481, by a man who gave him money for so doing; that the man copied the number; and that the next day he followed the man's instructions and put his hand into the wheel as usual, with the ticket in it, and then pretended to draw it out.'

The Lottery perished, as I say, because it had gone out of fashion. The great people had tired of it, and it had become the gamble of humble folk: servant girls, footmen, small tradesmen, even of the dwellers in Seven Dials. And when anything amusing becomes the peculiar appanage of the poor its existence is in great danger.

And I am inclined to think that there was another influence at work. In the early 'twenties the gentler sport of company promoting was highly popular. Business men were beginning to get a firm grip on England, and they felt that any loose money had much better go into companies—that is, their pockets—than into the Lottery.

So the Lottery vanished for ever, and we have to do the best we can with 'Sweeps,' 'Ballots,' and 'Certs.'

BIBLIOGRAPHICAL INFORMATION

All of these articles originally appeared in *The Graphic*:

'The Man with the Silver Staff', part I, Vol.CXI, March 28, 1925, p.482; part II, Vol.CXI, January 24, 1925, p.125, with the title of 'Mr Monaco and Mr Mackintosh.'

'The Mystery of Mr Haddock', Vol.CXI, January 31, 1925, p.157, with the title 'The Mystery of Mr Haddock: A Journalistic Puzzle of Long Ago'.

'Ceremony on the Scaffold', Vol.CXI, February 7, 1925, p.198, with the title of 'A Dissertation upon Justice.'

'Mr Lutterloh', Vol.CXI, February 14, 1925, p.242, with the title of 'Queer Things One Finds in Books.'

'A Lament for London's Lost Inns', Vol.CXI, February 21, 1925, p.280, with the title of 'A Lament for London's Lost Taverns.'

'Madame Rachel' Vol.CXI, February 28, 1925, p.312, with the title of 'A Bond St Beauty Parlour.'

'Sir Benjamin the "Baron" ', Vol.CXI, March 7, 1925, p.364.

'Our Betty's Day Out', Vol. CXI, March 21, 1925, p.445, with the title 'Our Betty's Day Out: An Eighteenth Century London Mystery'.

'How the Rich Live', Vol.CXI, April 4, 1925, p.5244.

'The Highbury Mystery', Vol.CXI, April 11, 1925, p.576, with the title of 'The Man with the Crooked Finger.'

'Deadly Nevergreen', Vol.CXI, April 18, 1925, p.618.

'Polite Correspondence', Vol.CXI, April 25, 1925, p.664, with the title of 'Different Kinds of Letters.'

'How Clubs Began', Vol.CXI, May 2, 1925, p.717.

'The Ingenious Mr Blee', Vol.CXI, May 9, 1925, p.756, with the title of 'Black Villainy of Old.'

'Old Dr Mounsey', Vol.CXI, May 16, 1925, p.803, with the title of 'The Truth About Dr Mounsey.'

'Casanova in London', Vol.CXI, May 23, 1925, p.852, with the title of 'The Greatest Scoundrel of His Time.'

' "Doubles" in Crime', Vol.CXI, May 30, 1925, p.904.
' "Characters" ', Vol.CXI, June 6, 1925, p.944, with the title of ' "Characters" in Real Life.'
'The Euston Square Mystery', Vol. CXI, June 13,1925, p.1008.
'More Inns', Vol.CXI, June 20, 1925, p.1068 with the title of 'Some Inns I Knew.'
'The Adventure of the Long-Lost Brother', Vol.CXI, June 27, 1925, p.1112, with the title of 'A Wanderer's Return.'
'The Power of Jargon', Vol. CXII, July 4, 1925, p.14.
'The Little People', Vol.CXII, July 11, 1925, p.64, with the title of 'The Little Beings of the Forest.'
'The Campden Wonder', parts I-II Vol.CXII, July 18, 1925, p.98 and July 25, 1925, p.144, with the title of 'The Man Who Came Back.'
'Morduck the Witch', Vol.CXII, August 1, 1925, p.183, with the title of 'The Man Who Ate Pins.'
'The Man from Nowhere', Vol.CXII, August 8,1925, p.216.
'Before Wembley', Vol. CXII, August 15, 1925, p.263, with the title of 'Before Wembley Days.'
'The Strange Case of Emily Weston', Vol.CXII, August 22, 1925, p.296.
'The Gay Victorians', Vol.CXII, August 29, 1925, p.396, with the title of 'The Carefree Victorian Days.'
'A Castle in Celtic Mists', Vol.CXII, September 5, 1925, p.374, with the title 'A Castle in Celtic Mists: Another Legend of the Holy Grail'.
'A Tale of a Turbot', Vol.CXII, September 12, 1925, p.424, with the title 'A Tale of a Turbot: A Story with a Moral'.
'Chivalry', Vol.CXII, September 19, 1925, p.456, with the title of 'The Truth about Romance.'
'7B Coney Court', Vol.CXII, September 26, 1925, p.502.
'Concerning Cocktails', Vol.CXII, October 3, 1925, p.549, with the title 'Concerning Cocktails: A Hundred-year-old Habit'.
'Mothers-in-Law', Vol.CXII, October 10, 1925, p.598, with the title 'Mothers-in-Law: The Woman Who Became Three Things'.
'A Pretty Parricide', Vol.CXII, October 24, 1925, p.682, with the title 'A Pretty Parricide: Mary Blandy's "Martyrdom" '.
'The Cry of a Captive', Vol.CXII, October 31,1925, p.726, with the title 'The Cry of a Captive: A Story of Napoleonic Days'.
'Our Funny Friends', Vol.CXII, November 7, 1925, p.774, with the title 'Our Funny Friends: Historic Jokes Recalled'.
'Twins', Vol.CXII, November 14, 1925, p.808.
'Hungry Weather!', Vol.CXII, November 21, 1925, p.862.

BIBLIOGRAPHICAL INFORMATION

'Medicine-Man's Magic', Vol.CXII, December 5, 1925, p.980, with the title 'Medicine-Man's Magic: Curing Toothache in Far Tibet'.

'The Best of Everything', Vol.CXII, December 12, 1925, p. 1024, with the title 'The Best of Everything and Other Curiosities of Yesteryear'.

'The Merry Widow', Vol.CXII, December 19, 1925, p.1072, with the title 'The Merry Widow: A Christmas Tragedy of 1692'.

'Knocking Legends to Smithereens', Vol.CXII, December 26, 1925, p.1120, with the title 'Knocking Legends to Smithereens: The Curses of Fyvie and Glamis Castles'.

'One Night When I Was Frightened', Vol.CXIII, January 2, 1926, p.12.

'The Wood Family', Vol.CXIII, January 9, 1926, p.48.

'Justice: A Vignette', Vol.CXIII, January 16, 1926, p.82.

'Houses', Vol.CXIII, January 23, 1926, p.194.

'The People of the Wild', Vol.CXIII, January 30,1926, p.234.

'Laugh When You Awake', Vol.CXIII, February 6, 1926, p.273, with the title 'Laugh When You Awake: The New Way to Keep Fit'.

'The Little Brown Things', Vol.CXIII, February 13, 1926, p.307.

'Shakespeare's "Bare Bones"', Vol. CXIII, February 20, 1926, p.345, with the title 'Shakespeare's "Bare Bones": Problems of the Period Play'.

'The Simplicity of Genius', Vol.CXIII, March 6, 1926, p.414.

'Books That a Queen May Read', Vol.CXIII, March 13, 1926, p.471.

'Society and the Savage', Vol.CXIII, March 20, 1926, p.503.

'Those Doctors!', Vol.CXIII, March 27, 1926, p.557, with the title 'Those Doctors! Reflections on Horses and Men'.

'The "B" in Baconian Bonnets', Vol.CXIII, April 17, 1926, p.669.

'The Scholar and the Sun-Myth', Vol.CXIII, April 24, 1926, p.716.

'Dr Johnson's Disappearing Act', Vol.CXIII, May 1, 1926, p.770.

'When the Much-Travelled Man Comes Home', Vol.CXIII, June 12, 1926, p.955, with the title 'When the Much-Travelled Man Comes Home: A Plea for the English Chop-house'.

'England's Last State Lottery', Vol.CXIV, October 16, 1926, pp. 634-635, with the title 'England's Last State Lottery: A Centenary Retrospect'.

The following articles were first collected as *Dreads and Drolls*, Martin Secker, 1926, in the following order: 'The Man With the Silver Staff', 'The Adventure of the Long-Lost Brother', '7B Coney Court', 'The Strange Case of Emily Weston', 'The Highbury Mystery', 'The Little People', 'Madame Rachel', 'Sir Benjamin the "Baron",' 'The Campden Wonder', 'The Man From Nowhere', 'Morduck the Witch', ' "Characters",' ' "Doubles" in Crime', 'How Clubs Began', 'Polite Correspondence', 'Casanova in London',

'Mr Lutterloh', 'Before Wembley', 'The Ingenious Mr Blee', 'The Gay Victorians', 'Chivalry', 'How the Rich Live', 'A Lament for London's Lost Inns', 'More Inns', 'Deadly Nevergreen', 'Ceremony on the Scaffold', 'Old Dr Mounsey', 'The Euston Square Mystery', 'The Power of Jargon'.